D0201616

THE ASSAULT ON FORT WAGNER

At that moment Wagner became a mound of fire, from which poured a stream of shot and shell. Just a brief lull, and the deafening explosions of cannon were renewed, mingled with the crash and rattle of musketry. A sheet of flame, followed by a running fire, like electric sparks, swept along the parapet . . . When this tempest of war came, before which men fell in numbers on every side, the only response the Fifty-fourth made to the deadly challenge was to change step to the double-quick, that it might the sooner close with the foe. There had been no stop, pause, or check at any period of the advance, nor was there now. As the swifter pace was taken, and officers sprang to the fore with waving swords barely seen in the darkness, the men closed the gaps, and with set jaws, panting breath, and bowed heads, charged on.

The assault on Fort Wagner, July 18, 1863
U.S. Army Military History Institute

A BRAVE BLACK REGIMENT:

HISTORY OF THE FIFTY-FOURTH REGIMENT
OF MASSACHUSETTS VOLUNTEER INFANTRY
1863–1865

* * *

Luis F. Emilio

Introduction by Gregory J. W. Urwin
General Series Editor, Paul Andrew Hutton

BANTAM BOOKS
New York • Toronto • London • Sydney • Auckland

A BRAVE BLACK REGIMENT
A Bantam Domain Book / January 1992

PRINTING HISTORY
Originally published as History of the Fifty-Fourth Regiment of
Massachusetts Volunteer Infantry, 1863–1865
The Boston Book Company edition published 1894

*General series editor: Paul Andrew Hutton
Introduction copyright © 1991 by Gregory J.W. Urwin.
Cover art copyright © 1991 by Louis Glanzman.
Designed by M 'N O Production Services, Inc.*

ISBN 0-553-29496-2

Published simultaneously in the United States and Canada

*Bantam Books are published by Bantam Books, a division of Bantam
Doubleday Dell Publishing Group, Inc. Its trademark, consisting of the
words "Bantam Books" and the portrayal of a rooster, is Registered
in U.S. Patent and Trademark Office and in other countries. Marca
Registrada. Bantam Books, 666 Fifth Avenue, New York, New York
10103.*

PRINTED IN THE UNITED STATES OF AMERICA

OPM   0   9   8   7   6   5   4   3   2   1

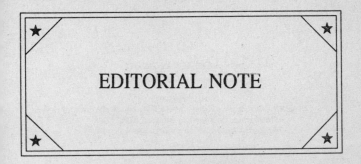

EDITORIAL NOTE

This book is a reprint of the revised, second edition of *A Brave Black Regiment*, which was published by the Boston Book Company in 1894. The regimental roster and appendix have been deleted from the Bantam Books edition.

CONTENTS

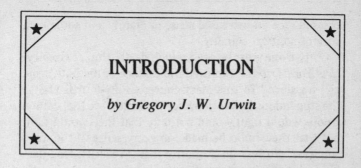

INTRODUCTION

by Gregory J. W. Urwin

OVERSHADOWED BY BREATHLESS ACCOUNTS describing the great American victory in the St. Mihiel Offensive and other news of World War I, the following paragraph appeared among the "Obituary Notes" in the September 17, 1918, issue of *The New York Times*:

> Captain LUIS FENOLLOSA EMILIO, a veteran of the civil war, died yesterday at his home, 29 West Forty-seventh Street, in this city, at the age of 74. Both his father and his grandfather were soldiers in Spain, the latter coming to this country years before the civil war.

In keeping with the racist sensibilities of Woodrow Wilson's America, the obituary omitted mention of the fact that Captain Emilio had participated in one of the most revolutionary military experiments of the Civil War. As one of the original white officers of the 54th Massachusetts Volunteer Infantry, the first black regiment raised by a Northern state east of the Mississippi, Emilio risked his life and reputation in an admirable effort to bring an op-

pressed race an increased sense of dignity and some measure of political equality.

Fifty-three years before Emilio's death, Horace Greeley's
New York Tribune captured the essence of the 54th's special mission: "To this Massachusetts Fifty-fourth was set
the stupendous task to convince the white race that colored
troops would fight,—and not only that they would fight,
but that they could be made, in every sense of the word,
soldiers." No less an authority than Frederick Douglass,
black America's most influential spokesman during the
Civil War era, declared that the regiment completely ful-
filled the purpose behind its creation. "The 54th was not
long in the field," Douglass wrote, "before it proved itself
gallant and strong, worthy to rank with the most courageous of its white companions in arms." This proud record
resulted, in large part, from the brand of leadership provided by Emilio and the regiment's other idealistic young
officers.

The story of the 54th Massachusetts deserves to be re-
told as long as Americans cherish any hope for interracial
harmony. And despite the recent interest taken by both
Hollywood and the Public Broadcasting System, no one
has ever told that story better than Emilio himself in this
touching testament to human courage and brotherhood,
A Brave Black Regiment.

Luis Fenollosa Emilio, the first child of Manuel and
Isabel Fenollosa Emilio, was born in Salem, Massachusetts,
on December 22, 1844. The boy's father, a Spanish im-
migrant, supported his family as an instructor of music,
an honored profession in a community fond of brass bands,
choral societies, and glee clubs. A friend Luis later made
in the Union army remembered him as a "city-bred youth."
The boy grew up in Salem, playing on the docks, beaches,

and crooked streets of the famous old seaport and along the banks of the Naumkeag River.

The ominous secession winter of 1860–1861 and the subsequent outbreak of civil war brought Emilio's boyhood to a premature end. In league with other militant young townsmen, he responded to the Confederate attack on Fort Sumter in April 1861 by helping to found a militia company called the Union Drill Club. Exuding the naive bravado that infected both sides in those early days of the conflict, Emilio and his new comrades decked themselves out in garish, Zouave-style uniforms—gray caps, tight gray jackets with blue facings, and dark blue trousers all trimmed with red braid. A local benefactor furnished the club with a hundred obsolete trade muskets, which enabled the men to start practicing the manual of arms. As soon as he received his soldier clothes, sixteen-year-old Luis rushed to a photographer's studio to have his portrait taken. Sporting the slightest wisp of a mustache, the scrawny teenager leaned against a pillar and struck a sheepish pose—creating an awkward image that belied his dreams of military glory.

Throughout the summer of 1861, the Union Drill Club did nothing more glorious than parade around Salem. Gradually, the make-believe warriors came to realize that they owed their embattled country greater support than attendance at home-front ceremonies. At a mass meeting on September 30, the drill club's membership voted to "enlist for the war, provided the Commander can receive authority . . . to raise a company, the nucleus of which shall be the present organization commanded by its own officers." The unit sponsored by the Union Drill Club ultimately entered federal service as Company F of the 23rd Massachusetts Volunteer Infantry.

Recruiting for Company F proceeded rapidly. When the unit entrained on October 18 for the regimental rendezvous at Lynnfield, it numbered ninety-four officers and men. Emilio belonged to the eighteen Union Drill Club alumni who enrolled in Company F. Interestingly enough, he did not sign up until October 19, the day after the company reached Lynnfield. Two years below the Union army's minimum enlistment age, Luis possibly waited to volunteer until after the company had gone too far from Salem to permit a convenient check on his birth records.

According to the 23rd's "Regimental Descriptive Book," Private Emilio stood five feet five-and-a-half inches tall. He had black hair, blue eyes, and a dark complexion. He gave his occupation as "student" and swore that he had passed his eighteenth birthday. Although they must have known Emilio was lying, Company F's officers acquiesced in his enrollment—an indication of the respect the boy already commanded from his friends and neighbors. Exhibiting a sense of history rare in one so young, Emilio procured a diary to record his experiences with the 23rd, a practice he continued for the duration of the war.

After a few weeks of awkward drilling at Lynnfield, the 23rd Massachusetts traveled south to Annapolis, Maryland, to link up with a special amphibious division drawn from the seacoast towns of New England and the Middle Atlantic states. The division commander, Major General Ambrose E. Burnside, had orders to seize Roanoke Island, North Carolina, and then lunge inland to disrupt long-distance rail movement in the eastern Confederacy. The success of Burnside's expedition would effectively cut the primary supply line of the large army the rebels were concentrating to defend Virginia.

During a two-month sojourn at Annapolis, the 23rd

Massachusetts received more intensive indoctrination in the art of soldiering. Despite his youth, Emilio took well to military life and fit in with his comrades. A high-spirited lad, he figured prominently in the games that brightened the men's off-duty hours. On one occasion, he participated in a mock court-martial, helping to conduct the defense of a Company F man accused of spilling hot tea on a tentmate and consequently "stopping the growth of a large pair of whiskers."

In early January 1862, Burnside embarked his 13,000-man "coast division" and sailed for North Carolina. Covered by Union gunboats, the division landed at Roanoke Island on February 7. The next day, the 23rd Massachusetts finally "saw the elephant," as Civil War soldiers referred to their first exposure to combat, bravely slogging through a supposedly impassable swamp to flank the Rebels out of a strong battery position. This introduction to battlefield carnage did not unnerve Private Emilio. As he entered the enemy's works he noticed corpses lying "here and there, and beneath a tree . . . an officer shot through the chest." Before moving on, the famished boy paused long enough to take "a hasty bite of hardtack."

Burnside quickly consolidated his hold on Roanoke Island and then invaded the mainland, heading for the railhead at New Berne, North Carolina's second largest port. In a fight before the town on March 14, Emilio saw Lieutenant Colonel Henry Merritt, the officer who had invited the Union Drill Club to join the 23rd Massachusetts, killed by an artillery shell. Dashing forward, Emilio positioned himself behind a clump of brush and logs in advance of his regiment's battle line and sniped at the enemy. Such conspicuous bravery did not go unrewarded. Emilio was promoted to corporal on August 23, 1862. Eight days later, he received a pair of sergeant's chevrons to sew onto the sleeves of his blue coat.

The capture of New Berne cleared the way for an advance on Goldsboro, an important junction on the Wilmington and Weldon Railroad. But before Burnside could sever the vital lifeline to Robert E. Lee's Army of Northern Virginia, he received orders to take half of his troops to Virginia and reinforce the stymied Union Army of the Potomac. The 23rd Massachusetts remained part of the force that Burnside left to garrison New Berne—a relatively passive assignment that offered the regiment few opportunities for distinction.

In December 1862, the 23rd marched with a five-regiment brigade on a raid toward Goldsboro. During an encounter at Whitehall, Sergeant Emilio volunteered to rescue some wounded men who had been left lying under enemy fire. The attempt was deemed too risky, however, and he had to be restrained from exposing himself. On the return trek to New Berne, Emilio suffered a bad case of swelling, which caused his shoes to chafe his feet. The intense pain forced him to discard his stiff military brogans. Determined to prove himself worthy of his stripes, Emilio refused to fall out of ranks or to impose on his comrades. "Each morning about the camp-fires," he recalled, "I gathered cast-off socks, drawing on three or four pairs, and in that condition marched all day. Night found me nearly barefoot at bivouac. This process I repeated daily, until our return to New Berne." The regimental historian of the 23rd Massachusetts dubbed Emilio "the hero of the socks."

While Emilio nursed his abused feet, Governor John A. Andrew of Massachusetts initiated a scheme that drastically changed the life of the plucky little sergeant and the nature of the Civil War. A confirmed abolitionist, Andrew believed that the war to destroy the Confederacy should include the annihilation of slavery. He also insisted that African-Americans should bear arms in that crusade, explaining his reasons to a black leader:

> Every race has fought for Liberty and its own progress. The colored race will create its own future by its own brains, hearts, and hands. If Southern slavery should fall by the crushing of the Rebellion, and colored men should have no hand and play no conspicuous part in the task, the result would leave the colored man a mere helot; the freedmen, a poor, despised, subordinated body of human beings, neither strangers, nor citizens, but "contrabands," who had lost their masters but not found a country.

After President Abraham Lincoln's Emancipation Proclamation went into effect on January 1, 1863, Andrew secured permission from the War Department to form "a special corps" containing "persons of African descent"— the 54th Massachusetts Volunteer Infantry. Andrew wanted his regiment to serve "as a model for all future Colored Regiments." The few black units already in existence consisted mainly of runaway slaves, uneducated "contrabands" whose years of submissive conditioning might render them unable to face white Southerners in battle. Hoping to both silence white skeptics and inspire ex-slaves, Andrew endeavored to man the 54th Massachusetts with free blacks, men who had never known the bite of the lash or the humiliation of calling someone "master." African-Americans across the North responded with enthusiasm to the Bay State's summons, filling the regiment with a thousand prime recruits by May 11, 1863.

Andrew realized that the 54th's future success would

rest on the quality of its leadership. He handed out commissions in the regiment to young gentlemen of good family who shared in his commitment to black freedom and equality. Andrew characterized his appointees as commanders "in whom the men put faith" and "who would put faith in the men." "A large number of the officers have seen service before," commented a black newspaper, "and it is noticeable that few regiments have on their roster so many names from the best families of the . . . state." Andrew begged for permission to name some black lieutenants, but the War Department insisted that all the regiment's original officers be white.

On February 12, 1863, Andrew wrote to Major General John G. Foster, commanding the XVIII Army Corps in North Carolina:

> I have appointed Sergeant *Louis Emilio* of the *23d Mass. Vol* Infantry to be a Lieutenant in the 54th Mass. Regt, now being raised here, and have requested the War Dept to order his discharge from his present reg't and to order him to report to me at Boston to assume his new command. If by any order in your power you can hasten his arrival at Boston, you will much oblige me.

The accommodating Foster had Emilio discharged by February 27. Emilio called on Andrew's Boston office on March 21, where he received instructions to report to the 54th's colonel, Robert Gould Shaw, at the regiment's camp at nearby Readville. By the month's end, Emilio possessed a second lieutenant's commission in the new unit. Shaw apparently considered the likable teenager one of his better officers, upgrading him to first lieutenant on April 14. Nearly six weeks later, Emilio became the captain of Company G. After another five days, Captain Emilio transferred to Company E, a post he held for the remainder of his military service. With typical modesty, Emilio never told the public what he did to so impress the exacting Andrew and Shaw, remarking only that "it certainly required at that time moral as well as physical courage to accept a commission in any colored organization."

In the pages that follow, Emilio provides a vivid and comprehensive account of the origins, formation, and exploits of the 54th Massachusetts. But a few points need to be made here for the edification of the modern reader.

Contrary to the events depicted in the motion picture *Glory*, Emilio and the other seasoned veterans who made up the bulk of Shaw's officers did not have to import an Irish sergeant major to supervise the training of the 54th Massachusetts. They handled that business themselves and achieved impressive results. The officers quickly prepped enough promising recruits to assist in the training as acting sergeants. A pleased Colonel Shaw wrote of his freshly minted NCOs: "They drill their squads with a great deal of snap, and I think we shall have some good soldiers. . . . It is very laughable to hear the sergeants explain the drill to the men, as they use words long enough for a Doctor of Divinity." After witnessing the 54th's first public review, a Massachusetts journalist attested to the thoroughness of the men's training:

> Here was a regiment of a thousand men, every one of them with an Enfield musket . . . and apparently with rather an uncommon amount of muscle and will to devote to the using of it. They marched well, they wheeled well, they stood well, they handled their guns well, and there was about their whole array an air of such completeness and order and *morale* such as I have not seen surpassed in any white regiment.

Gregory J.W. Urwin and students on the set of the film Glory. Civil War News

The rank and file of the 54th Massachusetts represented the cream of black Northern manhood, including two sons of the famed abolitionist and editor Frederick Douglass. The future philosopher William James, a brother of Shaw's adjutant, called the troops "a very fine set of men, finer looking than any white regiment he had seen." Reverend James Lynch, a black minister who greeted the 54th upon its arrival in South Carolina, testified, "This regiment does honor to the colored people of the North; they are all stalwart men, intelligent in appearance, and soldierly to their bearing, well armed, uniformed and drilled."

These proud soldiers expressed no uncertainties concerning the cause for which they fought. Reverend Lynch noted that they "were boiling over with joy to think they had landed on South Carolina to treat the rebels to powder and shot, and unchain their brethren in bonds." "I pray God that the sword may never be returned to its sheath," vowed First Sergeant John H. W. Collins of Company H, "nor the bayonet to its scabbard, till the last dark spot of this conflict will be at an end, and the black man acknowledged to be on the same footing as the white man." "Give me my rights," demanded another enlisted man, "the rights that this Government owes me, the same rights the white man has."

When Colonel Shaw took command of the 54th Massachusetts, he defined his mission as "to prove that a negro can be made a good soldier." Shaw's regiment carried out that awesome mandate on July 18, 1863, by leading a six-thousand-man Union column against Fort Wagner, a massive Confederate earthwork guarding one of the southern approaches to Charleston Harbor, South Carolina. Poorly conceived and poorly directed on the brigade and division levels, the assault on Fort Wagner ended in a bloody repulse with 1,515 Northern casualties.

The only bright spot Union supporters could find in the whole sorry episode was the conduct of the 54th Massachusetts. Though raked by heavy musketry and blasts of shrapnel and canister from the enemy's massed cannon, Shaw and his brave black soldiers climbed up Wagner's south wall. As he reached the top Shaw brandished his sword and cried, "Onward boys!" He fell a second later, a bullet in his heart. The 54th's surviving officers and men maintained a precarious toehold along the outer side of the wall for nearly an hour, but mounting losses and the lack of any direct support from the other regiments in the assaulting column forced a precipitate withdrawal.

The guns had hardly cooled before the Northern press started showering the 54th Massachusetts with kudos for its sacrificial courage. Brigadier General George C. Strong, Shaw's mortally wounded brigade commander, offered this widely printed deathbed tribute: "The Fifty-fourth did well and nobly; only the fall of Colonel Shaw prevented them from entering the fort. They moved up as gallantly as any troops could, and with their enthusiasm they deserved a better fate." Such reports went a long way toward winning the Northern public's support for the Lincoln administration's new policy of enlisting African-Americans as soldiers. "In that terrible battle," proclaimed Frederick Douglass, "under the wing of night, more cavils in respect to the quality of Negro manhood were set at rest than could have been during a century of ordinary life and observation." By the war's conclusion, the Union army had recruited 178,895 blacks, organizing them into 166 regiments. Without this timely infusion of African-American manpower, the North might have lacked the strength to crush the Confederacy.

The 54th Massachusetts paid a high price to put its stamp on the course of American history. Of the 21 officers and 600 enlisted men that Shaw led against Fort Wagner, 272 were killed, wounded, or captured. Emilio went into the assault as the 54th's junior captain in both age and seniority of rank. Once the slaughter subsided, he stood as the highest-ranking officer in the regiment to escape unscathed. He calmly rallied his broken regiment and functioned as its acting commander until July 24, 1863.

The horrors of war did not quench the 54th's desire to close with the enemy and vanquish the Confederacy. "I still feel more Eager for the struggle than I ever yet have," Sergeant A. S. Fisher of Company I wrote on July 31 to his wounded captain, "for I now wish to have Revenge for our galant Curnel and the spilt blood of our Captain. We Expect to Plant the Stars and Stripes on the City of Charleston next week if the Lord Spares us." When a white reporter asked the regiment's wounded if they wished they had never become soldiers, the men answered from their hospital beds: "If all our people get their freedom, we can afford to die." "Oh, never give it up till the last rebel be dead." "Oh, never give it up till the last brother breaks his chains."

Emilio served continuously with the 54th for eighteen months, not missing a single day for sickness or any other cause. On October 19, 1864, he temporarily relinquished command of Company E, heading north on a leave of absence "to visit My Home in Mass. on urgent private business." Emilio rejoined his company and resumed his duties on December 4. He did not have long to go, however, until his term of service expired. Emilio was mustered out

of the Union army effective March 27, 1865, his discharge
becoming final on April 4, five days before Lee's surrender
at Appomattox. A civilian once more, the twenty-year-old
veteran now faced the challenge of adjusting to an America
vastly changed by war.

With his release from the military, Emilio returned
home to Salem. But the venerable seaport's days of glory
had long since passed, and economic opportunities were
scarce. Emilio bade farewell to his birthplace in May 1867,
relocating to the booming city of San Francisco, California,
where he went into the real-estate business.

Emilio found love as well as prosperity on the West
Coast. A romance with Mary Elizabeth Belden of San Jose
blossomed into marriage. The two exchanged vows in a
Congregational church in San Francisco on March 29,
1876.

Mary Emilio bore her husband three children. Sadly,
none of them lived to adulthood. The first, Luis Victor
Emilio, was born in San Francisco on June 22, 1879, and
died in Seabright, New Jersey, on August 23, 1894. The
other two, Margaret Belden Emilio (January 28–July 26,
1886) and Gerald Belden Emilio (October 27, 1887–July
31, 1888), died in infancy.

In December 1881, Emilio moved his wife and little
Luis Victor to New York City, where he continued to work
in real estate. A city directory for 1892 listed the family's
address as 6 East Fifty-eighth Street. Sometime after 1892,
Emilio retired from business, devoting his time to veterans'
affairs and his historical studies. To the end of his life, he
maintained memberships in the Union League Club, the
Military Order of the Loyal Legion of the United States,
and the George Washington Post, Grand Army of the Re-

public, as well as keeping up with the survivors of his first regiment, the 23rd Massachusetts.

Emilio lost his wife on April 23, 1903, when she died during a visit to Atlantic City, New Jersey. With Mary and the children gone, Emilio faced the frightening prospect of a lonely old age. He began to spend his summers at Salem to be near his brothers and sisters. By 1907, he had also changed his New York address to 29 West Forty-seventh Street.

In July 1907, Emilio, now aged sixty-two, applied to the federal government for a veteran's pension. He began receiving monthly checks for twelve dollars in late October. As he entered his seventies, his health declined. When he applied to have his pension increased to twenty-five dollars a month in early 1915, he wrote from the confinement of a sickbed.

Following a long illness, Luis F. Emilio finally passed away on Monday, September 16, 1918. Death claimed him just three months short of his seventy-fourth birthday. Emilio's four surviving brothers and sisters had his body brought to Salem for burial.

Throughout the postwar years, Emilio never lost any of the pride that he felt in his association with the 54th Massachusetts—even though ex-officers of black regiments suffered frequent snubs in white Northern society. Long before he retired from business, Emilio began assembling materials for a history of the 54th. In addition to his own journals and papers, Emilio collected reminiscences from his black and white comrades, photographs of regimental personnel, clippings from period newspapers, copies of government records, and the records of the "Association of Officers of the Fifty-Fourth Massachusetts Volunteer Infantry." These historical treasures, contained in three bound, oversized manuscript volumes and one unbound scrapbook, now reside with the Massachusetts Historical Society in Boston.

Emilio made his first significant foray as an historian by publishing a long article on the Fort Wagner battle in a Massachusetts newspaper, the *Springfield Republican*. The piece was reprinted in pamphlet form in 1887 by the Rand Avery Company of Boston under a rather grandiose title, *The Assault on Fort Wagner, July 18, 1863: The Memorable Charge of the Fifty-Fourth Regiment of Massachusetts Volunteers*. Encouraged by this success, Emilio forged ahead with his plans to write a full-length book about the 54th Massachusetts.

The first edition of Emilio's *A Brave Black Regiment* appeared in 1891, eliciting warm approval from the author's comrades. On October 26, 1893, the 54th's association of officers asked the publisher, the Boston Book Company, to bring out a second edition. Emilio's friends also supplied him with considerable constructive criticism, which he took to heart. The 1894 version of *A Brave Black Regiment* featured a corrected text and regimental roster and a new appendix describing Confederate mistreatment of black prisoners-of-war captured from the 54th.

The recent release of *Glory* by Tri-Star Pictures has sparked a revival of interest in the 54th Massachusetts, and several new books on the regiment are in the process of being written. Nevertheless, Emilio's *A Brave Black Regiment* will remain the starting point for any reader seriously interested in the exploits of the Civil War's most famous black unit. Along with the Augustus St. Gaudens monument to Robert Gould Shaw on Boston Common, the book stands as a fitting memorial to the 1,354 black and white Americans who offered their lives to convert the nation's darkest tragedy into what Lincoln called "a new birth of freedom." The rights for which Emilio and his comrades fought were withheld from African-Americans for more than a century after Fort Wagner, but that shameful truth does not diminish the noble inspiration to be found in the history of the 54th Massachusetts.

For a brief time in the spring of 1989, I enjoyed the privilege of standing in Luis F. Emilio's shoes. I recruited, trained, and equipped thirteen of my black students from the University of Central Arkansas to portray Union infantrymen in *Glory*. As a partial reward for my efforts, I was put in charge of the movie version of Emilio's old command, Company E of the 54th Massachusetts. For an exhausting but exhilarating week, my troops and I participated in take after take of the assault on a reconstructed Fort Wagner—racing through simulated explosions on a sandy beach, plunging through the icy-cold waters of Wagner's moat, and up the fort's towering walls.

Friends and acquaintances often ask me to talk about the film's stars, but the men I remember most fondly are the hundred-odd black and white reenactors who sacrificed so much of their time and money to resurrect the 54th Massachusetts. They included professional historians, such as Allan R. Millett and Brian C. Pohanka, black college students from UCA and Ohio State University, and black professionals from Washington, D.C., Columbus, Ohio, and Little Rock, Arkansas. Like the original regiment, we came together for an idealistic purpose—to right an historical injustice by confronting the American public with a full-blown Hollywood spectacle commemorating black valor and patriotism. It was an honor to represent Luis F.

Emilio on film and I am pleased to help Bantam Books
bring his book to the attention of a wider audience.

GREGORY J. W. URWIN
Department of History
University of Central Arkansas

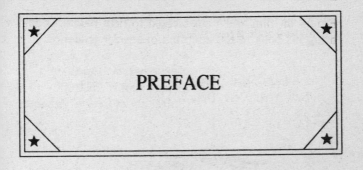

PREFACE

THIS RECORD HAS GROWN out of the researches and material gathered for the preparation of papers read before the officers of the Fifty-fourth and Fifty-fifth Massachusetts Infantry and other veteran associations at reunions in recent years, as well as newspaper articles. It is founded upon the compiler's daily record of events, his letters of the period, contemporaneous records, and the very full journal of Lieut. John Ritchie, as well as a briefer one of Capt. Lewis Reed. To both these officers grateful acknowledgments are rendered. Thanks are also due to Lieut.-Cols. H. N. Hooper and George Pope for valuable records. Sergt.-Major John H. Wilson, and Sergts. William H. Carney and Charles W. Lenox have furnished important particulars. Mention should be made of Capt. William C. Manning, Twenty-third U. S. Infantry, whose field notes were most thankfully received. Throughout the compilation Gen. A. S. Hartwell, Col. N. P. Hallowell, and Capt. Charles C.

Soule, all of the Fifty-fifth Massachusetts Infantry, have manifested unflagging interest.

L.F.E.

No. 6 EAST 58TH STREET,
  NEW YORK CITY, DEC. 22, 1890.

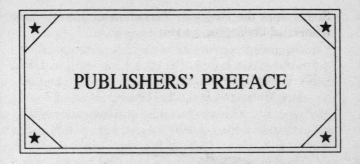

PUBLISHERS' PREFACE

It is TWENTY-SIX YEARS since our Civil War ended,—nearly the span of a generation of men. There has been almost a surfeit of war literature. Every new book issued to-day on war topics ought to be able to give good reason for its existence.

Although this volume is only a regimental history, the peculiar circumstances of the organization, character, representative position, and soldierly conduct of the regiment whose story is told, seem to give the history a sufficiently wide and permanent interest to warrant its publication, even at so late a day.

It will be sure to interest the surviving members of the regiment whose life it chronicles. To them it should be said that the author has spent many years in gradually collecting material for this record, and in arranging it methodically. What he here presents is the condensed digest of a great mass of print and manuscript carefully collated with the government records and with other regimental histories. He has not been willing to publish his material until this work of collection, arrangement, and collation could be thoroughly accomplished.

To the present generation of the race from which the Fifty-fourth Massachusetts Volunteers was recruited, the history of the regiment should have peculiar interest. The author's treatment of the subject is simple and straightforward, with hardly a word of eulogy; and yet the plain narrative of the soldierly achievements of this black regiment is better evidence of the manly qualities of the race than volumes of rhetoric and panegyric could convey.

For those veterans who served in the Department of the South, the maps of this volume, and the author's minute account of actions and operations not elsewhere fully described, will have more than transient interest and value.

For the general public,—for the surviving soldiers of other regiments, white and black, and for the younger men to whom the story of the Civil War is history,—this book should also have great significance and interest. The Fifth-fourth Massachusetts was a typical regiment—it might almost be called *the* typical regiment—of our army. It illustrated the patriotism of the period as well as any organization in the service. It required of its members even more resolution and courage at enlistment than white regiments; because at the time of its formation the chances seemed to be that black soldiers and their officers, if captured, would not be treated according to the usages of civilized war, but would be massacred as at Fort Pillow. Facing this risk at the outset, the *men of the Fifty-fourth proved their courage in so many battles and with such serious losses as to earn a place* among the three hundred fighting regiments chronicled in Fox's "Regimental Losses in the American Civil War."

But while the men of the Fifty-fourth shared the courage and patriotism which characterized all our citizen soldiery, they *also represented more conspicuously, perhaps, than any other colored regiment the political policy of emancipation into which the war forced us, and the interesting military experience embodied in the organization, from a mob of freed slaves, of a disciplined and effective army of two hundred thousand men. Though it was not absolutely the first black regiment in the field, and though there were others which saw severe service, the early distinction won in the assault on Wagner, together with the gallant death of Colonel Shaw on the ramparts, and his burial with his black soldiers where they fell, created a wider and stronger interest in the Fifty-fourth than any other colored regiment was fortunate enough to attract.*

It was also the lot of the Fifty-fourth to bear the brunt of the struggle against the bitter injustice of inferior pay to which black troops were subjected, and the further struggle to secure for the enlisted men who earned it by intelligence and bravery, the right to rise from the ranks and serve as officers.

The following editorial from the New York "Tribune," of Sept. 8, 1865, apparently from the pen of Horace Greeley, bears contemporaneous testimony to the reputation of the regiment:—

"The Fifty-fourth Regiment of Massachusetts Volunteers was welcomed back to Boston on Saturday. There was a public reception, a review by the Governor and Council at the State House, another on the Common by the mayor, an address to his officers and men by Colonel Hallowell; and then the regiment was disbanded. The demonstrations of respect were rather more than have usually been awarded to returning regiments, even in Massachusetts,

which cherishes her soldiers with an unforgetting affec-
tion. They were so honored in this case, we presume,
because the regiment is a representative one. There were
regiments from that State which had seen more fighting
than this, though none which had done any better fighting
when occasion offered; none which had a higher reputation
for discipline, patient endurance, and impetuous valor. But
the true reason why Massachusetts singled out this regiment for peculiar honor is because this was the first colored regiment organized in the North, and was that one
on whose good conduct depended for a long time the
success of the whole experiment of arming black citizens
in defence of the Republic. It is not too much to say that
if this Massachusetts Fifty-fourth had faltered when its trial
came, two hundred thousand colored troops for whom it
was a pioneer would never have been put into the field,
or would not have been put in for another year, which
would have been equivalent to protracting the war into
1866. But it did not falter. It made Fort Wagner such a
name to the colored race as Bunker Hill has been for ninety
years to the white Yankees,—albeit black men fought side
by side with white in the trenches on that 17th of June.

"To this Massachusetts Fifty-fourth was set the stupendous task to convince the white race that colored troops
would fight,—and not only that they would fight, but that
they could be made, in every sense of the word, soldiers.
It is not easy to recall at this day the state of public opinion
on that point,—the contemptuous disbelief in the courage
of an enslaved race, or rather of a race with a colored skin.
Nobody pretends now that the negro won't fight. Anglo-
Saxon prejudice takes another shape,—and says he won't
work, and don't know how to vote; but in the spring of
1863, when this regiment marched down State Street in
Boston, though it was greeted with cheers and borne on
by the hopes of the loyal city which had trusted the fame
and lives of its noblest white sons to lead their black comrades, yet that procession was the scoff of every Democratic
journal in America, and even friends feared half as much
as they hoped. Many a white regiment had shown the white

feather in its first battle; but for this black band to waver once was to fall forever, and to carry down with it, perhaps, the fortunes of the Republic. It had to wait months for an opportunity. It was sent to a department which was sinking under the prestige of almost uninterrupted defeats. The general who commanded the department, the general who commanded the division, and the general who commanded the brigade to which this regiment found itself consigned,—neither of them believed in the negro. When the hour came for it to go into action, there was probably no officer in the field outside of its own ranks who did not expect it—and there were many who desired it—to fail. When it started across that fatal beach which led to the parapet of Wagner, it started to do what had not been successfully attempted by white troops on either side during the war. It passed through such an ordeal successfully; it came out not merely with credit, but an imperishable fame.

"The ordinary chances of battle were not all which the Massachusetts Fifty-fourth had to encounter. The hesitating policy of our government permitted the Rebels to confront every black soldier with the threat of death or slavery if he were taken prisoner. If he escaped the bullet and the knife, he came back to camp to learn that the country for which he had braved that double peril intended to cheat him out of the pay on which his wife and children depended for support. We trust Mr. Secretary Stanton is by this time heartily ashamed of the dishonesty which marked his dealings with the black troops,—but we are not going into that question. We said then, and we reiterate now, that the refusal of pay to the colored soldiers was a swindle and a scandal, so utterly without excuse that it might well have seemed to them as if intended to provoke a mutiny. Few white regiments would have borne it for a month; the blacks maintained their fidelity in spite of it for a year and a half. When the Fifty-fourth was offered a compromise, the men replied with one voice: 'No. We need the money you offer; our families are starving because the government does not pay us what it promised; but we demand to be recognized as soldiers of the Republic, entitled to the same rights which white soldiers have. Until you grant that, we will not touch a dollar.' It was a sublimer heroism, a loftier sentiment of honor, than that which inspired them at Wagner. They would not mutiny because of injustice, but they would not surrender one iota of their claim to equal rights. Eventually they compelled the government to acknowledge their claim, and were paid in full by a special act of Congress.

"The name of Col. Robert G. Shaw is forever linked with that of the regiment which he first commanded, and which he inspired with so much of his own gentle and noble spirit as to make it a perpetual legacy to the men who fought under and loved him. His death at Wagner did as much perhaps for his soldiers as his life afterwards could have done. Colonel Hallowell, who succeeded him, proved the faithful and intelligent friend of the regiment. Its other officers, with no exception that we know of, were devoted and capable. They are entitled to a share of the renown which belongs to the regiment,—they would be unworthy of it if they did not esteem that their highest testimonial."

Because the Fifty-fourth Massachusetts occupied this prominent position, the publishers deem it proper that the history of its services which Captain Emilio has compiled should be put into print. They have given the volume a title the author was too modest to suggest, but which the record fully justifies,—"A Brave Black Regiment."

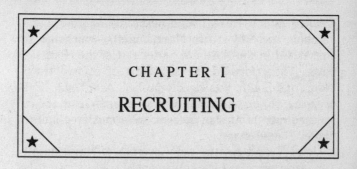

CHAPTER I

RECRUITING

AT THE CLOSE of the year 1862, the military situation was discouraging to the supporters of the Federal Government. We had been repulsed at Fredericksburg and at Vicksburg, and at tremendous cost had fought the battle of Stone River. Some sixty-five thousand troops would be discharged during the ensuing summer and fall. Volunteering was at a standstill. On the other hand, the Confederates, having filled their ranks, were never better fitted for conflict. Politically, the opposition had grown formidable, while the so-called "peace-faction" was strong, and active for mediation.

In consequence of the situation, the arming of negroes, first determined upon in October, 1862, was fully adopted as a military measure; and President Lincoln, on Jan. 1, 1863, issued the Emancipation Proclamation. In September, 1862, General Butler began organizing the Louisiana Native Guards from free negroes. General Saxton, in the Department of the South, formed the First South Carolina from contrabands in October of the same year. Col. James Williams, in the summer of 1862, recruited the First Kansas

1

Colored. After these regiments next came, in order of organization, the Fifty-fourth Massachusetts, which was the first raised in the Northern States east of the Mississippi River. Thenceforward the recruiting of colored troops, North and South, was rapidly pushed. As a result of the measure, 167 organizations of all arms, embracing 186,097 enlisted men of African descent, were mustered into the United States service.

John A. Andrew, the war Governor of Massachusetts, very early advocated the enlistment of colored men to aid in suppressing the Rebellion. The General Government having at last adopted this policy, he visited Washington in January, 1863, and as the result of a conference with Secretary Stanton, received the following order, under which the Fifty-fourth Massachusetts Volunteer Infantry was organized:—

WAR DEPARTMENT,
WASHINGTON CITY, Jan 26, 1863.

Ordered: That Governor Andrew of Massachusetts·is authorized, until further orders, to raise such number of volunteers, companies of artillery for duty in the forts of Massachusetts and elsewhere, and such corps of infantry for the volunteer military service as he may find convenient, such volunteers to be enlisted for three years, or until sooner discharged, and may include persons of African descent, organized into special corps. He will make the usual needful requisitions on the appropriate staff bureaus and officers, for the proper transportation, organization, supplies, subsistence, arms and equipments of such volunteers.

EDWIN M. STANTON,
Secretary of War.

With this document the Governor at once returned to Boston, anxious to begin recruiting under it before the

Government could reconsider the matter. One of his first steps was to transmit the following letter, outlining his plans:—

BOSTON, Jan. 30, 1863.

FRANCIS G. SHAW, Esq., Staten Island, N.Y.

DEAR SIR,—As you may have seen by the newspapers, I am about to raise a colored regiment in Massachusetts. This I cannot but regard as perhaps the most important corps to be organized during the whole war, in view of what must be the composition of our new levies; and therefore I am very anxious to organize it judiciously, in order that it may be a model for all future colored regiments. I am desirous to have for its officers—particularly for its field-officers—young men of military experience, of firm antislavery principles, ambitious, superior to a vulgar contempt for color, and having faith in the capacity of colored men for military service. Such officers must necessarily be gentlemen of the highest tone and honor; and I shall look for them in those circles of educated antislavery society which, next to the colored race itself, have the greatest interest in this experiment.

Reviewing the young men of the character I have described, now in the Massachusetts service, it occurs to me to offer the colonelcy to your son, Captain Shaw, of the Second Massachusetts Infantry, and the lieutenant-colonelcy to Captain Hallowell of the Twentieth Massachusetts Infantry, the son of Mr. Morris L. Hallowell of Philadelphia. With my deep conviction of the importance of this undertaking, in view of the fact that it will be the first colored regiment to be raised in the free States, and that its success or its failure will go far to elevate or depress the estimation in which the character of the colored Americans will be held throughout the world, the command of such a regiment seems to me to be a high object of ambition for any officer. How much your son may have reflected upon such a subject I do not know, nor have I any information of his disposition for such a task except what I have derived from his general character and reputation;

nor should I wish him to undertake it unless he could
enter upon it with a full sense of its importance, with an
earnest determination for its success, and with the assent
and sympathy and support of the opinions of his immediate
family.

I therefore enclose you the letter in which I make him
the offer of this commission; and I will be obliged to you
if you will forward it to him, accompanying it with any
expression to him of your own views, and if you will also
write to me upon the subject. My mind is drawn towards
Captain Shaw by many considerations. I am sure he would
attract the support, sympathy, and active co-operation of
many among his immediate family relatives. The more
ardent, faithful, and true Republicans and friends of liberty
would recognize in him a scion from a tree whose fruit
and leaves have always contributed to the strength and
healing of our generation. So it is with Captain Hallowell.
His father is a Quaker gentleman of Philadelphia, two of
whose sons are officers in our army, and another is a
merchant in Boston. Their house in Philadelphia is a hospital and home for Massachusetts officers; and the family
are full of good works; and he was the adviser and confidant
of our soldiery when sick or on duty in that city. I need
not add that young Captain Hallowell is a gallant and fine
fellow, true as steel to the cause of humanity, as well as
to the flag of the country.

I wish to engage the field-officers, and then get their
aid in selecting those of the line. I have offers from Oliver
T. Beard of Brooklyn, N. Y., late Lieutenant-Colonel of the
Forty-eighth New York Volunteers, who says he can already
furnish six hundred men; and from others wishing to furnish men from New York and from Connecticut; but I do
not wish to start the regiment under a stranger to Massachusetts. If in any way, by suggestion or otherwise, you
can aid the purpose which is the burden of this letter, I
shall receive your co-operation with the heartiest gratitude.

I do not wish the office to go begging; and if the offer
is refused, I would prefer it being kept reasonably private.

Hoping to hear from you immediately on receiving this letter, I am, with high regard,

Your obedient servant and friend,

JOHN A. ANDREW.

Francis G. Shaw himself took the formal proffer to his son, then in Virginia. After due deliberation, Captain Shaw, on February 6, telegraphed his acceptance.

Robert Gould Shaw was the grandson of Robert G. Shaw of Boston. His father, prominently identified with the Abolitionists, died in 1882, mourned as one of the best and noblest of men. His mother, Sarah Blake Sturgis, imparted to her only son the rare and high traits of mind and heart she possessed.

He was born Oct. 10, 1837, in Boston, was carefully educated at home and abroad in his earlier years, and admitted to Harvard College in August, 1856, but discontinued his course there in his third year. After a short business career, on April 19, 1861, he marched with his regiment, the Seventh New York National Guard, to the relief of Washington. He applied for and received a commission as second lieutenant in the Second Massachusetts Infantry; and after serving with his company and on the staff of Gen. George H. Gordon, he was promoted to a captaincy. Colonel Shaw was of medium height, with light hair and fair complexion, of pleasing aspect and composed in his manners. His bearing was graceful, as became a soldier and gentleman. His family connections were of the highest social standing, character, and influence. He married Miss Haggerty, of New York City, on May 2, 1863.

Captain Shaw arrived in Boston on February 15, and at once assumed the duties of his position. Captain Hallowell

Colonel Robert Gould Shaw
Massachusetts Commandery Military Order of the Loyal Legion and the U.S.
Army Military History Institute

was already there, daily engaged in the executive business of the new organization; and about the middle of February, his brother, Edward N. Hallowell, who had served as a lieutenant in the Twentieth Massachusetts Infantry, also reported for duty, and was made major of the Fifty-fourth before its departure for the field.

Line-officers were commissioned from persons nominated by commanders of regiments in the field, by tried friends of the movement, the field-officers, and those Governor Andrew personally desired to appoint. This freedom of selection,—unhampered by claims arising from recruits furnished or preferences of the enlisted men, so powerful in officering white regiments,—secured for this organization a corps of officers who brought exceptional character, experience, and ardor to their allotted work. Of the twenty-nine who took the field, fourteen were veteran soldiers from three-years regiments, nine from nine-months regiments, and one from the militia; six had previously been commissioned. They included representatives of well-known families; several were Harvard men; and some, descendants of officers of the Revolution and the War of 1812. Their average age was about twenty-three years.

At the time a strong prejudice existed against arming the blacks and those who dared to command them. The sentiment of the country and of the army was opposed to the measure. It was asserted that they would not fight, that their employment would prolong the war, and that white troops would refuse to serve with them. Besides the moral courage required to accept commissions in the Fifty-fourth at the time it was organizing, physical courage was also necessary, for the Confederate Congress, on May 1, 1863, passed an act, a portion of which read as follows:—

> "Section IV. That every white person being a commissioned officer, or acting as such, who, during the present war, shall command negroes or mulattoes in arms against the Confederate States, or who shall arm, train, organize, or prepare negroes or mulattoes for military service against the Confederate States, or who shall voluntarily aid negroes or mulattoes in any military enterprise, attack, or conflict in such service, shall be deemed as inciting servile insurrection, and shall, if captured, be put to death or be otherwise punished at the discretion of the Court."

The motives which influenced many of those appointed are forcibly set forth in the following extracts from a letter of William H. Simpkins, then of the Forty-fourth Massachusetts Infantry, who was killed in action when a captain in the Fifty-fourth:—

> "I have to tell you of a pretty important step that I have just taken. I have given my name to be forwarded to Massachusetts for a commission in the Fifty-fourth Negro Regiment, Colonel Shaw. This is no hasty conclusion, no blind leap of an enthusiast, but the result of much hard thinking. It will not be at first, and probably not for a long time, an agreeable position, for many reasons too evident to state. ... Then this is nothing but an experiment after all; but it is an experiment that I think it high time we should try,—an experiment which, the sooner we prove fortunate the sooner we can count upon an immense number of hardy troops that can stand the effect of a Southern climate without injury; an experiment which the sooner we prove unsuccessful, the sooner we shall establish an important truth and rid ourselves of a false hope."

From first to last the original officers exercised a controlling influence in the regiment. To them—field, staff, and line—was largely due whatever fame was gained by the Fifty-fourth as the result of efficient leadership in camp or on the battlefield.

In his "Memoirs of Governor Andrew" the Hon. Peleg W. Chandler writes:—

> "When the first colored regiment was formed, he [Governor Andrew] remarked to a friend that in regard to other regiments, he accepted men as officers who were sometimes rough and uncultivated, 'but these men,' he said, 'shall be commanded by officers who are eminently gentlemen.'"

So much for the selection of officers. When it came to filling the ranks, strenuous efforts were required outside the State, as the colored population could not furnish the number required even for one regiment.

Pending the effort in the wider field available under the plan proposed, steps were taken to begin recruiting within the State. John W. M. Appleton, of Boston, a gentleman of great energy and sanguine temperament, was the first person selected for a commission in the Fifty-fourth, which bore date of February 7. He reported to the Governor, and received orders to begin recruiting. An office was taken in Cambridge Street, corner of North Russell, upstairs, in a building now torn down. On February 16, the following call was published in the columns of the "Boston Journal":—

To Colored Men
Wanted. Good men for the Fifty-fourth Regiment of Massachusetts Volunteers of African descent, Col. Robert G. Shaw. $100 bounty at expiration of term of service. Pay $13 per month, and State aid for families All necessary

information can be obtained at the office, corner Cambridge and North Russell Streets.

LIEUT. J. W. M. APPLETON,
Recruiting Officer.

In five days twenty-five men were secured; and Lieutenant Appleton's work was vigorously prosecuted, with measurable success. It was not always an agreeable task, for the rougher element was troublesome and insulting. About fifty or sixty men were recruited at this office, which was closed about the last of March. Lieutenant Appleton then reported to the camp established and took command of Company A, made up of his recruits and others afterward obtained.

Early in February quite a number of colored men were recruited in Philadelphia, by Lieut. E. N. Hallowell, James M. Walton, who was subsequently commissioned in the Fifty-fourth, and Robert R. Corson, the Massachusetts State Agent. Recruiting there was attended with much annoyance. The gathering-place had to be kept secret, and the men sent to Massachusetts in small parties to avoid molestation or excitement. Mr. Corson was obliged to purchase railroad tickets himself, and get the recruits one at a time on the cars or under cover of darkness. The men sent and brought from Philadelphia went to form the major part of Company B.

New Bedford was also chosen as a fertile field. James W. Grace, a young business man of that place, was selected as recruiting officer, and commissioned February 10. He opened headquarters on Williams Street, near the post-office, and put out the United States flag across the street. Colored ministers of the city were informed of his plans; and Lieutenant Grace visited their churches to interest the people in his work. He arranged for William Lloyd Garrison, Wendell Phillips, Frederick Douglass, and other noted men to address meetings. Cornelius Howland, C. B. H. Fessenden, and James B. Congdon materially assisted and were good friends of the movement. While recruiting, Lieutenant Grace was often insulted by such remarks as, "There goes the captain of the Negro Company! He thinks the negroes will fight! They will turn and run at the first sight of the enemy!" His little son was scoffed at in school because his father was raising a negro company to fight the white men. Previous to departure, the New Bedford recruits and their friends gathered for a farewell meeting. William Berry presided; prayer was offered by Rev. Mr. Grimes; and remarks were made by Lieutenant-Colonel Hallowell, Lieutenant Grace, C. B. H. Fessenden, Ezra Wilson, Rev. Mr. Kelly, Wesley Furlong, and Dr. Bayne. A collation at A. Taylor and Company's followed. Temporarily the recruits took the name of "Morgan Guards," in recognition of kindnesses from S. Griffiths Morgan. At camp the New Bedford men,—some seventy-five in number,—with others from that place and elsewhere, became Company C, the representative Massachusetts company.

Only one other commissioned officer is known to the writer as having performed effective recruiting service. This is Watson W. Bridge, who had been first sergeant, Company D, Thirty-seventh Massachusetts Infantry. His headquarters were at Springfield, and he worked in Western Massachusetts and Connecticut. When ordered to camp, about April 1, he had recruited some seventy men.

Much the larger number of recruits were obtained through the organization and by the means which will now be described. About February 15, Governor Andrew appointed a committee to superintend the raising of recruits for the colored regiment, consisting of George L. Stearns, Amos A. Lawrence, John M. Forbes, William I. Bowditch, Le Baron Russell, and Richard P. Hallowell, of Boston; Mayor Howland and James B. Congdon, of New Bedford; Willard P. Phillips, of Salem; and Francis G. Shaw, of New York. Subsequently the membership was increased to one hundred, and it became known as the "Black Committee." It was mainly instrumental in procuring the men of the Fifty-fourth and fifth Massachusetts Infantry, the Fifth Massachusetts Cavalry, besides 3,967 other colored men credited to the State. All the gentlemen named were persons of prominence. Most of them had been for years in the van of those advanced thinkers and workers who had striven to help and free the slave wherever found.

The first work of this committee was to collect money; and in a very short time five thousand dollars was received, Gerrit Smith, of New York, sending his check for five hundred dollars. Altogether nearly one hundred thousand dollars was collected, which passed through the hands of Richard P. Hallowell, the treasurer, who was a brother of the Hallowells commissioned in the Fifty-fourth. A call for recruits was published in a hundred journals from east to west. Friends whose views were known were communicated with, and their aid solicited; but the response was not for a time encouraging.

With the need came the man. Excepting Governor Andrew, the highest praise for recruiting the Fifty-fourth belongs to George L. Stearns, who had been closely identified with the struggle in Kansas and John Brown's projects. He was appointed agent for the committee, and about February 23 went west on his mission. Mr. Stearns stopped at Rochester, N.Y., to ask the aid of Fred Douglass, receiving hearty co-operation, and enrolling a son of Douglass as his first recruit. His headquarters were made at Buffalo, and a line of recruiting posts from Boston to St. Louis established.

Soon such success was met with in the work that after filling the Fifty-fourth the number of recruits was sufficient to warrant forming a sister regiment. Many newspapers gave publicity to the efforts of Governor Andrew and the committee. Among the persons who aided the project by speeches or as agents were George E. Stephens, Daniel Calley, A. M. Green, Charles L. Remond, William Wells Brown, Martin R. Delany, Stephen Myers, O. S. B. Wall, Rev. William Jackson, John S. Rock, Rev. J. B. Smith, Rev. H. Garnett, George T. Downing, and Rev. J. W. Loqueer.

Recruiting stations were established, and meetings held at Nantucket, Fall River, Newport, Providence, Pittsfield, New York City, Philadelphia, Elmira, and other places throughout the country. In response the most respectable, intelligent, and courageous of the colored population everywhere gave up their avocations, headed the enlistment rolls, and persuaded others to join them.

Most memorable of all the meetings held in aid of recruiting the Fifty-fourth was that at the Joy Street Church, Boston, on the evening of February 16, which was enthusiastic and largely attended. Robert Johnson, Jr., presided; J. R. Sterling was the Vice-President, and Francis Fletcher Secretary. In opening, Mr. Johnson stated the object of the gathering. He thought that another year would show the importance of having the black man in arms, and pleaded with his hearers, by the love they bore their country, not to deter by word or deed any person from entering the service. Judge Russell said in his remarks, "You want to be line-officers yourselves." He thought they had a right to be, and said,—

"If you want commissions, go, earn, and get them. [Cheers.] Never let it be said that when the country called, this reason kept back a single man, but go cheerfully."

Edward L. Pierce was the next speaker; and he reminded them of the many equalities they had in common with the whites. He called on them to stand by those who for half a century had maintained that they would prove brave and noble and patriotic when the opportunity came. Amid great applause Wendell Phillips was introduced. The last time he had met such an audience was when he was driven from Tremont Temple by a mob. Since then the feeling toward them had much changed. Some of the men who had pursued and hunted him and them even to that very spot had given up their lives on the battlefields of Virginia. He said:—

"Now they offer you a musket and say, 'Come and help us.' The question is, will you of Massachusetts take hold? I hear there is some reluctance because you are not to have officers of your own color. This may be wrong, for I think you have as much right to the first commission in a brigade as a white man. No regiment should be without a mixture of the races. But if you cannot have a whole loaf, will you not take a slice?"

He recited reasons why it would be better to have white officers, stating among other things that they would be more likely to have justice done them and the prejudice more surely overcome than if commanded by men of their own race. He continued:—

"Your success hangs on the general success. If the Union lives, it will live with equal races. If divided, and you have done your duty, then you will stand upon the same platform with the white race. [Cheers.] Then make use of the offers Government has made you; for if you are not willing to fight your way up to office, you are not worthy of it. Put yourselves under the stars and stripes, and fight yourselves to the marquee of a general, and you shall come out with a sword. [Cheers.]"

Addresses were then made by Lieutenant-Colonel Hallowell, Robert C. Morris, and others. It was a great meeting for the colored people, and did much to aid recruiting.

Stirring appeals and addresses were written by J. M. Langston, Elizur Wright, and others. One published by Frederick Douglass in his own paper, at Rochester, N.Y., was the most eloquent and inspiring. The following is extracted:—

"We can get at the throat of treason and slavery through the State of Massachusetts. She was first in the War of Independence; first to break the chains of her slaves; first to make the black man equal before the law; first to admit colored children to her common schools. She was first to answer with her blood the alarm-cry of the nation when its capital was menaced by the Rebels. You know her patriotic Governor, and you know Charles Sumner. I need add no more. Massachusetts now welcomes you as her soldiers." ...

In consequence of the cold weather there was some suffering in the regimental camp. When this became known, a meeting was held at a private residence on March 10, and a committee of six ladies and four gentlemen was appointed to procure comforts, necessities, and

a flag. Colonel Shaw was present, and gave an account
of progress. To provide a fund, a levee was held at
Chickering Hall on the evening of March 20, when
speeches were made by Ralph Waldo Emerson, Wendell
Phillips, Rev. Dr. Neale, Rev. Father Taylor, Judge Russell, and Lieutenant-Colonel Hallowell. Later, through
the efforts of Colonel Shaw and Lieutenant-Colonel Hallowell, a special fund of five hundred dollars was contributed to purchase musical instruments and to instruct
and equip a band.

Besides subscriptions, certain sums of money were received from towns and cities of the State, for volunteers
in the Fifty-fourth credited to their quota. The members
of the committee contributed liberally to the funds required, and the following is a partial list of those who aided
the organization in various ways:—

George Putnam,
Charles G. Loring,
J. Huntington Wolcott,
Samuel G. Ward,
James M. Barnard,
William F. Weld,
J. Wiley Edmands,
William Endicott, Jr.,
Francis L. Lee,
Oakes Ames,
James L. Little,
Marshall S. Scudder,
George Higginson,
Thomas Russell,
Edward S. Philbrick,
Oliver Ellsworth,
Robert W. Hooper,
John H. Stevenson,
John H. Silsbee,

Charles Buffum,
John S. Emery,
Gerritt Smith,
Albert G. Browne, Jr.,
Mrs. S. R. Urbino,
Edward W. Kinsley,
Uriah and John Ritchie,
Pond & Duncklee,
John H. and Mary E. Cabot,
Mary P. Payson,
Manuel Emilio,
Henry W. Holland,
Miss Halliburton,
Frederick Tudor,
Samuel Johnson,
Mary E. Stearns,
Mrs. William J. Loring,
Mrs. Governor Andrew,
Mrs. Robert C. Waterston,

Manuel Fenollosa,
G. Mitchell,
John W. Brooks,
Samuel Cabot, Jr.,
John Lowell,
James T. Fields,
Henry Lee, Jr.,
George S. Hale,
William Dwight,
Richard P. Waters,
Avery Plummer, Jr.,
Alexander H. Rice,
John J. May,
John Gardner,
Mrs. Chas. W. Sumner,
Albert G. Browne,
Ralph Waldo Emerson,
William B. Rogers,

Wright & Potter,
James B. Dow,
William Cumston,
John A. Higginson,
Peter Smith,
Theodore Otis,
Avery Plummer,
James Savage,
Samuel May,
Mrs. Samuel May,
Josiah Quincy,
William Claflin,
Mrs. Harrison Gray Otis,
George Bemis,
Edward Atkinson,
Professor Agassiz,
John G. Palfrey,

besides several societies and fraternities.

Most of the papers connected with the labors of the committee were destroyed in the great Boston fire, so that it is difficult now to set forth properly in greater detail the work accomplished.

In the proclamation of outlawry issued by Jefferson Davis, Dec. 23, 1862, against Major-General Butler, was the following clause:—

"Third. That all negro slaves captured in arms be at once delivered over to the executive authorities of the respective States to which they belong, to be dealt with according to the laws of said States."

The act passed by the Confederate Congress previously referred to, contained a section which extended the same penalty to negroes or mulattoes captured, or who gave aid or comfort to the enemies of the Confederacy. Those who enlisted in the Fifty-fourth did so under these acts of outlawry bearing the penalties provided. Aware of these facts, confident in the protection the Government would and should afford, but desirous of having official assurances, George T. Downing wrote regarding the status of the Fifty-fourth men, and received the following reply:—

COMMONWEALTH OF MASSACHUSETTS, EXECUTIVE DEPARTMENT, BOSTON, March 23, 1863.

GEORGE T. DOWNING, Esq., New York.

DEAR SIR,—In reply to your inquiries made as to the position of colored men who may be enlisted into the volunteer service of the United States, I would say that their position in respect to pay, equipments, bounty, or any aid or protection when so mustered is that of any and all other volunteers.

I desire further to state to you that when I was in Washington on one occasion, in an interview with Mr. Stanton, the Secretary of War, he stated in the most emphatic manner that he would never consent that free colored men should be accepted into the service to serve as soldiers in the South, until he should be assured that the Government of the United States was prepared to guarantee and defend to the last dollar and the last man, to these men, all the rights, privileges, and immunities that are given by the laws of civilized warfare to other soldiers. Their present acceptance and muster-in as soldiers pledges the honor of the nation in the same degree and to the same rights with all. They will be soldiers of the Union, nothing less and nothing different. I believe they will earn for themselves an honorable fame, vindicating their race and redressing their future from the aspersions of the past.

I am, yours truly,

JOHN A. ANDREW.

Having recited the measures and means whereby the Fifty-fourth was organized, the history proper of the regiment will now be entered upon.

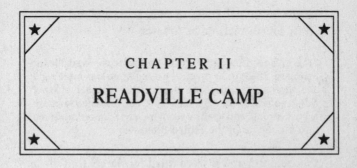

CHAPTER II

READVILLE CAMP

LIEUTENANT E. N. HALLOWELL, on Feb. 21, 1863, was ordered to Readville, Mass., where, at Camp Meigs, by direction of Brig.-Gen. R. A. Peirce, commandant of camps, he took possession with twenty-seven men of the buildings assigned to the new regiment. Readville is on the Boston and Providence Railroad, a few miles from Boston. The ground was flat, and well adapted for drilling, but in wet weather was muddy, and in the winter season bleak and cheerless. The barracks were great barn-like structures of wood with sleeping-bunks on either side. The field, staff, and company officers were quartered in smaller buildings. In other barracks near by was the larger part of the Second Massachusetts Cavalry, under Col. Charles R. Lowell, Jr., a brother-in-law of Colonel Shaw.

During the first week seventy-two recruits were received in camp, and others soon began to arrive with a steady and increasing flow; singly, in squads, and even in detachments from the several agencies established throughout the country.

Surgeon-General Dale, of Massachusetts, reported on the Fifty-fourth recruits as follows:—

"The first recruits were sent to Camp Meigs, Readville, in February, 1863; their medical examination was most rigid and thorough, nearly one third of the number offering being peremptorily rejected. As a consequence, a more robust, strong, and healthy set of men were never mustered into the service of the United States."

Companies A and B were filled by March 15; Company D was then formed; Company C came to camp from New Bedford on March 10. These four companies were mustered into the United States service on March 30. Lieutenant Partridge on March 28 was assigned to begin Company E; Lieutenant Bridge, reporting from recruiting service, was placed in command of Company F, just forming; Lieutenant Smith, on April 10, was chosen to organize Company G. As recruits came in during April at the rate of one hundred per week, these three companies were ready for muster on April 23. Companies H, I, and K were mustered May 13, completing the regiment.

With some twenty-one officers and four hundred men in camp, on April 1, the regiment was fairly under way. The material of which it was to be composed could fairly be judged from what was at hand. There were ample grounds for encouragement even to the most sceptical. It is pleasant to record that the soldier appointed to the command was early assured of the fact that he had not dared to lead in a hopeless task, for on March 25, Colonel Shaw wrote:—

"If the success of the Fifty-fourth gives you so much plea-sure, I shall have no difficulty in giving you good words of it whenever I write. Everything goes on prosperously. The intelligence of the men is a great surprise to me. They learn all the details of guard duty and camp service infinitely more readily than most of the Irish I have had under my command. There is not the least doubt that we shall leave the State with as good a regiment as any that has marched."

A considerable number of the men had prepared themselves in some measure for bearing arms, others had been officers' servants or camp followers; and as has been noted in all times and in all races of men, some were natural soldiers. Passive obedience—a race trait—characterized them. During their whole service their *esprit du corps* was admirable.

Only a small proportion had been slaves. There were a large number of comparatively light-complexioned men. In stature they reached the average of white volunteers. Compared with the material of contraband regiments, they were lighter, taller, of more regular features. There were men enough found amply qualified to more than supply all requirements for warrant officers and clerks. As a rule, those first selected held their positions throughout service. The co-operation of the non-commissioned officers helped greatly to secure the good reputation enjoyed by the Fifty-fourth; and their blood was freely shed, in undue proportion, on every battlefield. Surgeon-General Dale, in the report previously quoted from, speaks further of the Fifty-fourth as follows:—

"From the outset, the regiment showed great interest in drilling, and on guard duty it was always vigilant and active. The barracks, cook-houses, and kitchens far surpassed in cleanliness any I have ever witnessed, and were models of neatness and good order. The cooks, however, had many of them been in similar employment in other places, and had therefore brought some skill to the present responsibility.

"In camp, these soldiers presented a buoyant cheerfulness and hilarity, which impressed me with the idea that the monotony of their ordinary duties would not dampen their feeling of contentment, if they were well cared for. On parade, their appearance was marked with great neatness of personal appearance as concerned dress and the good condition in which their arms and accoutrements were kept. Their habits being imitative, it was natural that they should be punctilious in matters of military etiquette, and such observances as the well-disciplined soldier, in his subordinate position, pays to his superior. And fortunately for them, they had the teachings of those who were not only thoroughly imbued with the importance of their trusts, but were gentlemen as well as soldiers.

"It was remarked that there was less drunkenness in this regiment than in any that had ever left Massachusetts; but this may have been owing to the fact that the bounty was not paid them until a day or two previous to their departure. Nevertheless, it is my dispassionate and honest conviction that no regiments were ever more amenable to good discipline, or were more decorous and proper in their behavior than the Fifty-fourth and Fifty-fifth Massachusetts Colored Volunteers."

Owing to heavy and frequent rains in March and the early days of April, the mud was often very deep between the barracks and officers' quarters, requiring much labor to clean paths. During cold weather the quarters were kept warm by wood fires. In stormy weather squad and company drills went on in vacant barracks. Later in the season the companies under commissioned officers were taken several times each week to bathe in a pond near by to insure personal cleanliness.

Fast Day, April 2, was largely given up to rest and rec-
reation, with religious services in the afternoon. The first
dress parade took place the next day, when four companies
were in line. Every day, but especially on Sundays, large
numbers of visitors were present. Many ladies graced the
camp with their presence. People came from distant places
to witness the novel sight of colored soldiers in quarters
and on the drill ground. For the purpose of securing fa-
miliarity with drill and tactics, and to obtain uniformity
in the unwritten customs of the service, an officers' school
was begun April 20, at headquarters, and held frequent
sessions thereafter, until the regiment departed for field
service. There were a few deaths and a moderate amount
of sickness while at Readville, mainly from pneumonia and
bronchitis, as the men were first exposed in the trying
months of February and March.

Now and then the monotony of camp life was broken
by some noteworthy event. On April 21, a visit was
received from the "Ladies' Committee." Mrs. Governor
Andrew, Mrs. W. B. Rogers, Mrs. E. D. Cheney, Mrs. C. M.
Severance, Miss Abby W. May, Judge Russell, Rev. Mr.
Grimes, Charles W. Slack, and J. H. Stevenson were of
the party. Another event was the review by Governor
Andrew and Secretary Chase in the afternoon of April
30, the President's Fast Day. The line was formed with
eight hundred and fifty men; and the distinguished visitors were received with due honors. Dr. Howe, Robert
Dale Owen, Mr. Garrison, and other gentlemen were also
present.

On April 30, the regiment drew nine hundred and fifty
Enfield rifled muskets and a suitable number of non-
commissioned officers' swords. Lieutenant Jewett, appointed ordnance officer, issued the arms on the following

day. May 2, the regiment was drilled for the first time in the School of the Battalion. General Peirce, accompanied by Surgeon-General Dale and the Governor's Council, reviewed the Fifty-fourth on May 4. Brig.-Gen. Edward A. Wild, who was authorized to recruit a brigade of colored troops, visited the camp informally on the 11th. That portion of the Second Massachusetts Cavalry at Readville left for the field on May 12. At noon the Fifty-fourth formed in great haste to escort the cavalry, and marched to their camp, only to learn that the Second had already departed.

By May 11, more recruits had arrived than were required, and the Fifty-fifth Massachusetts was begun with the surplus on the succeeding day. They occupied the old cavalry camp. Of the following officers transferred to it from the Fifty-fourth, N. P. Hallowell became colonel; Alfred S. Hartwell, colonel and brevet brigadier-general; William Nutt, colonel; and Joseph Tilden, captain, during service with the Fifty-fifth. Several non-commissioned officers and privates were also transferred to the new regiment to assist in its organization. Details for guard duty at the new camp were for a time furnished from the Fifty-fourth. Rolls were made out on May 14 for the bounty of fifty dollars for each enlisted man, voted by the State.

Friends had procured flags, and it was determined to make the occasion of their presentation, on May 18, a memorable one. The day was fine and cloudless. Very early, friends of the command began to arrive in private carriages, and by the extra trains run to Readville. Many prominent persons were present, including Surgeon-General Dale, Hon. Thomas Russell, Professor Agassiz, Prof. William B. Rogers, Hon. Josiah Quincy, George S.

Hale, William Lloyd Garrison, Wendell Phillips, Samuel May, Rev. Dr. Neale, Frederick Douglass, and many others. The parade was thronged with white and colored people of both sexes, to the number of over a thousand.

Line was formed at eleven o'clock, and the regiment was broken into square by Colonel Shaw. Governor Andrew, with his military staff in full uniform, took position inside the square. Brilliant in color and of the finest texture, fluttering in the fresh breeze blowing, the flags destined for the regiment were ready for presentation. They were four in number,—a national flag, a State color, an emblematic banner of white silk with the figure of the Goddess of Liberty, and the motto, "Liberty, Loyalty, and Unity," and another with a cross upon a blue field, and the motto, *In Hoc Signo Vinces*.

By invitation, the Rev. Mr. Grimes offered an appropriate prayer. Governor Andrew then stepped forward; and the flow of eloquent words delivered with the earnestness which characterized him, heightened by the occasion, will never be forgotten by those that heard his voice. Standing in plain attire, and facing Colonel Shaw, he spoke as follows:—

> COLONEL SHAW: As the official representative of the Commonwealth, and by favor of various ladies and gentlemen, citizens of the Commonwealth, and friends of the Fifty-fourth Regiment of Massachusetts Volunteers, I have the honor and the satisfaction of being permitted to join you this morning for the purpose of presenting to your regiment the national flag, the State colors of Massachusetts, and the emblematic banners which the cordial, generous, and patriotic friendship of its patrons has seen fit to present to you. Two years of experience in all the trials and vicissitudes of war, attended with the repeated exhibition of Massachusetts regiments marching from home to the

scenes of strife, have left little to be said or suggested
which could give the interest of novelty to an occasion like
this. But, Mr. Commander, one circumstance pertaining
to the composition of the Fifty-fourth Regiment, exceptional in its character, when compared with anything we
have seen before, gives to this hour an interest and importance, solemn and yet grand, because the occasion
marks an era in the history of the war, of the Commonwealth, of the country, and of humanity. I need not dwell
upon the fact that the enlisted men constituting the rank
and file of the Fifty-fourth Massachusetts Regiment are
drawn from a race not hitherto connected with the fortunes
of the war; and yet I cannot forbear to allude to the circumstance for a brief moment, since it is uppermost in
your thoughts, and since this regiment, which for many
months has been the desire of my own heart, is present
now before this vast assembly of friendly citizens of Massachusetts, prepared to vindicate by its future,—as it has
already begun to do by its brief history of camp life here,—
to vindicate in its own person, and in the presence, I trust,
of all who belong to it, the character, the manly character,
the zeal, the manly zeal, of the colored citizens of Massachusetts, and of those other States which have cast their
lot with ours.

I owe to you, Mr. Commander, and to the officers
who, associated with you, have assisted in the formation
of this noble corps, composed of men selected from
among their fellows for fine qualities of manhood,—I
owe to you, sir, and to those of your associates who
united with me in the original organization of this body,
the heartiest and most emphatic expression of my cordial
thanks. I shall follow you, Mr. Commander, your officers,
and your men, with a friendly and personal solicitude,
to say nothing of official care, which can hardly be said
of any other corps which has marched from Massachusetts. My own personal honor, if I have any, is identified
with yours. I stand or fall, as a man and a magistrate,
with the rise or fall in the history of the Fifty-fourth
Massachusetts Regiment. I pledge not only in behalf of

myself, but of all those whom I have the honor to represent to-day, the utmost generosity, the utmost kindness, the utmost devotion of hearty love, not only for the cause, but for you that represent it. We will follow your fortunes in the camp and in the field with the anxious eyes of brethren, and the proud hearts of citizens.

To those men of Massachusetts and of surrounding States who have now made themselves citizens of Massachusetts, I have no word to utter fit to express the emotions of my heart. These men, sir, have now, in the Providence of God, given to them an opportunity which, while it is personal to themselves, is still an opportunity for a whole race of men. With arms possessed of might to strike a blow, they have found breathed into their hearts an inspiration of devoted patriotism and regard for their brethren of their own color, which has inspired them with a purpose to nerve that arm, that it may strike a blow which, while it shall help to raise aloft their country's flag—*their* country's flag, now, as well as ours—by striking down the foes which oppose it, strikes also the last shackle which binds the limbs of the bondmen in the Rebel States.

I know not, Mr. Commander, when, in all human history, to any given thousand men in arms there has been committed a work at once so proud, so precious, so full of hope and glory as the work committed to you. And may the infinite mercy of Almighty God attend you every hour of every day through all the experiences and vicissitudes of that dangerous life in which you have embarked; may the God of our fathers cover your heads in the day of battle; may He shield you with the arms of everlasting power; may He hold you always—most of all, first of all, and last of all—up to the highest and holiest conception of duty, so that if, on the field of stricken fight, your souls shall be delivered from the thraldom of the flesh, your spirits shall go home to God, bearing aloft the exulting thought of duty well performed, of glory and reward won, even at the hands of the angels who shall watch over you from above!

Mr. Commander, you, sir, and most of your officers, have been carefully selected from among the most intelligent and experienced officers who have already performed illustrious service upon the field during the two years of our national conflict. I need not say, sir, with how much confidence and with how much pride we contemplate the leadership which this regiment will receive at your hands. In yourself, sir, your staff and line officers, we are enabled to declare a confidence which knows no hesitation and no doubt. Whatever fortune may betide you, we know from the past that all will be done for the honor of the cause, for the protection of the flag, for the defence of the right, for the glory of your country, and for the safety and the honor of these men whom we commit to you, that shall lie either in the human heart, or brain, or arm.

And now, Mr. Commander, it is my most agreeable duty and high honor to hand to you, as the representative of the Fifty-fourth Regiment of Massachusetts Volunteers, the American flag, "the star-spangled banner" of the Republic. Wherever its folds shall be unfurled, it will mark the path of glory. Let its stars be the inspiration of yourself, your officers, and your men. As the gift of the young ladies of the city of Boston to their brethren in arms, they will cherish it as the lover cherishes the recollection and fondness of his mistress; and the white stripes of its field will be red with their blood before it shall be surrendered to the foe.

I have also the honor, Mr. Commander, to present to you the State colors of Massachusetts,—the State colors of the old Bay State, borne already by fifty-three regiments of Massachusetts soldiers, white men thus far, now to be borne by the Fifty-fourth Regiment of soldiers, not less of Massachusetts than the others. Whatever may be said, Mr. Commander, of any other flag which has ever kissed the sunlight or been borne on any field, I have the pride and honor to be able to declare before you, your regiment, and these witnesses, that from the beginning till now, the State colors of Massachusetts have never been surrendered to any foe. The Fifty-fourth now holds in possession this sacred charge, in the performance of their duties as citizen soldiers. You will never part with that flag so long as a splinter of the staff or a thread of its web remains within your grasp. The State colors are presented to the Fifty-fourth by the Relief Society, composed of colored ladies of Boston.

And now let me commit to you this splendid emblematic banner. It is prepared for your acceptance by a large and patriotic committee, representing many others besides themselves,—ladies and gentlemen of Boston, to whose hearty sympathy and powerful co-operation and aid much of the success which has hitherto attended the organization of this regiment is due. The Goddess of Liberty erect in beautiful guise and form; Liberty, Loyalty, and Unity,—are the emblems it bears. The Goddess of Liberty shall be the lady-love, whose fair presence shall inspire your hearts; Liberty, Loyalty, Unity, the watchwords in the fight.

And now, Mr. Commander, the sacred, holy Cross, representing passion, the highest heroism, I scarcely dare trust myself to present to you. It is the emblem of Christianity. I have parted with the emblems of the State, of the nation, —heroic, patriotic emblems they are, dear, inexpressibly dear to all our hearts; but now *In hoc signo vinces,*—the Cross which represents the passion of our Lord, I now dare to pass into your soldier hands; for we are fighting now a battle, not merely for country, not merely for humanity, not only for civilization, but for the religion of our Lord itself. When this cause shall ultimately fail, if ever failure at the last shall be possible, it will only fail when the last patriot, the last philanthropist, and the last Christian shall have tasted death, and left no descendants behind them upon the soil of Massachusetts.

This flag, Mr. Commander, has connected with its history the most touching and sacred memories. It comes to your regiment from the mother, sister, friends, family relatives, of one of the dearest and noblest boys of Mas sachusetts. I need not utter the name of Lieutenant Putnam in order to excite in every heart the tenderest emotions of fond regard, or the strongest feeling of patriotic fire. May you, sir, and these, follow not only on the field of battle, but in all the walks and ways of life, in camp and hereafter, when, on returning peace, you shall resume the more quiet and peaceful duties of citizens,—may you but follow the splendid example, the sweet devotion, mingled with manly, heroic character, of which the life and death of Lieutenant Putnam was one example! How many more there are we know not,—the record is not yet complete; but oh, how many there are of these Massachusetts sons, who, like him, have tasted death for this immortal cause! Inspired by such examples, fired by the heat and light of love and faith which illumined and warmed these heroic and noble hearts, may you, sir, and these march on to glory, to victory, and to every honor! This flag I present to you, Mr. Commander, and your regiment. *In hoc signo vinces.*

At the conclusion of the Governor's remarks, when the applause had subsided, Colonel Shaw responded as follows:—

YOUR EXCELLENCY: We accept these flags with feelings of deep gratitude. They will remind us not only of the cause we are fighting for, and of our country, but of the friends we have left behind us, who have thus far taken so much interest in this regiment, and whom we know will follow us in our career. Though the greater number of men in this regiment are not Massachusetts men, I know there is not one who will not be proud to fight and serve under our flag. May we have an opportunity to show that you have not made a mistake in intrusting the honor of the State to a colored regiment,—the first State that has sent one to the war.

I am very glad to have this opportunity to thank the officers and men of the regiment for their untiring fidelity and devotion to their work from the very beginning. They have shown that sense of the importance of the undertaking without which we should hardly have attained our end.

After the command was reviewed by the Governor, the battalion was dismissed, and officers and men devoted themselves to the entertainment of their guests.

Gen. David Hunter, commanding the Department of the South, desired the Fifty-fourth sent to South Carolina. His wishes were gratified; for on May 18 the Secretary of War telegraphed Governor Andrew to have the Fifty-fourth report to General Hunter at once. With a field of service under a commander who had shown such faith in colored soldiers, the regiment prepared to depart upon the arrival of a steamer ordered from New York.

May 28, at 6.30 A.M., the regiment formed line for the last time at Readville, and marching to the railroad station, embarked on cars, arriving at Boston about nine o'clock. As the companies filed into the street from the station, the command was received with cheers from a large gathering. One hundred policemen, under the chief, Colonel Kurtz, were present, to clear the streets. Unknown to the general public, reserves of police were held in readiness, under cover, to repress any riotous proceedings.

Preceded by Gilmore's band, the line of march was taken up through Pleasant, Boylston, Essex, Chauncy, Summer, High, Federal, Franklin, Washington, School, and Tremont streets, Pemberton Square, Somerset and Beacon streets to the State House. All along the route the sidewalks, windows, and balconies were thronged with spectators, and the appearance of the regiment caused repeated cheers and waving of flags and handkerchiefs. The national colors were displayed everywhere. Passing the house of Wendell Phillips, on Essex Street, William Lloyd Garrison was seen standing on the balcony, his hand resting on the head of a bust of John Brown. Only hearty greetings were encountered; not an insulting word was heard, or an unkind remark made. At a point on Essex Street, Colonel Shaw was presented with a bouquet by a lady.

Halting at the State House, Governor Andrew, his staff, and many distinguished gentlemen were received with due honor, and thence escorted along Beacon Street to the Common, which was entered by the Charles Street gateway. This historic parade-ground was crowded with spectators.

After a short rest, Governor Andrew, with Major-Generals Sutton and Andrews, and their respective staffs, Senator Wilson, the Executive Council, the Mayor of Boston, officers of other regiments, and other distinguished persons, took position at the reviewing stand. When all was ready, Colonel Shaw led his regiment in column over the intervening ground, and past the reviewing stand.

Again a rest; until, about noon, the regiment moved from the Common by the West Street gate, marched through Tremont, Court, State, and Commercial streets, and arrived at Battery Wharf. Entering State Street, the band played the stirring music of John Brown's hymn, while passing over ground moistened by the blood of Crispus Attucks, and over which Anthony Burns and Thomas Sims had been carried back to bondage. It is a curious fact that Sims himself witnessed the march of the Fifty-fourth. All along this street the reception accorded was most hearty; and from the steps of the Exchange, crowded with business men, the appearance of the regimental colors was the signal for repeated and rousing cheers.

Of this march the papers of the day were full of items and accounts. One journal said:—

"No regiment has collected so many thousands as the Fifty-fourth. Vast crowds lined the streets where the regiment was to pass, and the Common was crowded with an immense number of people such as only the Fourth of July or some rare event causes to assemble.... No white regiment from Massachusetts has surpassed the Fifty-fourth in excellence of drill, while in general discipline, dignity, and military bearing the regiment is acknowledged by every candid mind to be all that can be desired."

Upon arriving at Battery Wharf, the lines were maintained by the police. Many friends were allowed to remain with the officers for parting words until the vessel sailed.

It was about one o'clock in the afternoon when the regiment embarked on the steamer "De Molay," and four o'clock before the lines were cast off and the vessel slowly moved from the wharf, where friendly and loving hands waved adieus, to which those on board responded. A few friends, including Adjutant-General Schouler and Frederick Douglass, remained until the steamer was well away, when they too said their farewells, and returned to the city on a tugboat.

Soon the city, the islands, and the shores faded from view, as the "De Molay" steamed rapidly out of harbor. The Fifty-fourth was *en route* for rebellious soil.

The following roster of officers of the Fifty-fourth comprises all those who departed for the field with the regiment on May 28, and their respective rank and assignment at the time.—

Colonel, —Robert G. Shaw.
Major, —Edward N. Hallowell.
Surgeon, —Lincoln R. Stone.
Assistant-Surgeon, —Charles B. Bridgham.
Adjutant, —Garth W. James.
Quartermaster, —John Ritchie.

COMPANY A.

Capt., John W. M. Appleton.
1st Lieut., Wm. H. Homans.

COMPANY F.

Capt., Watson W. Bridge.
2d Lieut., Alexander
  Johnston.

COMPANY B.

Capt., Samuel Willard
  [Mann].
1st Lieut., James M. Walton.
2d Lieut., Thomas L.
  Appleton.

COMPANY G.

1st Lieut., Orin E. Smith.
2d Lieut., James A. Pratt.

COMPANY C.

1st Lieut., James W. Grace.
2d Lieut., Benjamin F.
  Dexter.

COMPANY H.

Capt., Cabot J. Russel.
2d Lieut., Willard Howard.

COMPANY D.

Capt., Edward L. Jones.
1st Lieut., R. H. L. Jewett.

COMPANY I.

Capt., George Pope.
1st Lieut., Francis L.
  Higginson.
2d Lieut., Charles E. Tucker.

Company E.

Capt., Luis F. Emilio.
2d Lieut., David Reid.

Company K.

Capt., William H. Simpkins.
2d Lieut., Henry W.
Littlefield.

Lewis H. Douglass, a son of Frederick Douglass, was the original sergeant-major. Arthur B. Lee, of Company A, was made commissary-sergeant; and Theodore J. Becker, hospital steward.

CHAPTER III

THE SEA ISLANDS

Many of the Fifty-fourth, born in the interior, never had seen the ocean; others had not voyaged upon it. Several of the officers, however, had been over the course, or a portion of it, before. For all it was a season of rest. The "De Molay" was a commodious, new, and excellent transport. The staterooms were comfortable, the cabin finely furnished, and the table well provided. For the men bunks were arranged between decks for sleeping, and large coppers for cooking purposes; plenty of condensed but unpalatable water was furnished. May 29, the sea was smooth all day, and the weather fine but not clear. Martha's Vineyard and Nantucket were passed in the morning. At night a fine moon rose. Foggy weather prevailed on the 30th, with an increasing ground-swell, causing some seasickness. The next day the steamer struggled against a head wind. At midnight the craft narrowly escaped grounding on Point Lookout shoals. Some one had tampered with the sounding-line. June 1, pleasant weather enabled the seasick to take some interest in life. The air was soft and balmy, as we ran down the North Carolina coast, which was dimly visible. A few porpoises and a shark or two followed the ship. Distant sails were sighted at times. When evening came, the sun sank into the sea, red and fiery, gilding the horizon. A stiff breeze blew from ahead, which freshened later. Fine weather continued throughout daylight of June 2. With the evening, however, it clouded up in the south, and a squall came up, with lightning and some rain, driving all below.

Morning dawned the next day, with the sun shining through broken clouds. At reveille, some fifteen sail of outside blockaders off Charleston were seen far away, and soon passed. The sandy shores of South Carolina were in full view, fringed here and there with low trees. A warm wind was blowing, ruffling the water beneath a clouded sky. Every one was busy with preparations for landing,— writing letters, packing knapsacks, and rolling blankets. Running below Hilton Head, a pilot came alongside in a boat rowed by contrabands, and took the vessel back into Port Royal, completing a voyage at 1 P.M., which was without accident or death to mar its recollection. Colonel Shaw, personally reporting to General Hunter, was ordered to proceed to Beaufort and disembark. On that day General Hunter wrote the following letter:—

HEADQUARTERS DEP'T OF THE SOUTH,
HILTON HEAD, PORT ROYAL, S.C., June 3, 1863.
HIS EXCELLENCY, GOVERNOR ANDREW, Massachusetts.
GOVERNOR,—I have the honor to announce that the Fifty-fourth Massachusetts (colored) troops, Colonel Shaw commanding, arrived safely in this harbor this afternoon and have been sent to Port Royal Island. The regiment had an excellent passage, and from the appearance of the men I doubt not that this command will yet win a reputation

and place in history deserving the patronage you have given them. Just as they were steaming up the bay I received from Col. James Montgomery, commanding Second South Carolina Regiment, a telegraphic despatch, of which certified copy is enclosed. Colonel Montgomery's is but the initial step of a system of operations which will rapidly compel the Rebels either to lay down their arms and sue for restoration to the Union or to withdraw their slaves into the interior, thus leaving desolate the most fertile and productive of their counties along the Atlantic seaboard.

The Fifty-fourth Regiment Massachusetts Volunteers shall soon be profitably and honorably employed; and I beg that you will send for service in this department the other colored regiment which Colonel Shaw tells me you are now organizing and have in forward preparation.

Thanking you heartily for the kindness and promptness with which you have met my views in this matter, and referring you to my letter to Mr. Jefferson Davis as a guarantee that all soldiers fighting for the flag of their country in this department will be protected, irrespective of any accident of color or birth, I have the honor to be, Governor, with the highest esteem.

Your very obedient servant,
D. HUNTER,
Major-General Commanding.

It was 4 P.M. when the "De Molay" started for Beaufort, leaving the storehouses, quarters, and long pier making up the military station of Hilton Head. The steamer crossed the grand harbor with some seventy sail moored upon its waters, including the frigates "Wabash" and "Vermont," a monitor, several gunboats, and a French steamer, and reached Beaufort before dark. Col. James Montgomery, with the Second South Carolina Colored, was just debarking from a successful foray up the Combahee River, bringing several hundred contrabands. Brig. Gen. Rufus Saxton was temporarily absent, and Col. W. W. H. Davis

was in command of the district. June 4, at 5 A.M., the
regiment landed too early in the day to attract the attention
of any but a few loiterers. Passing through the town to a
point about half a mile from the river, the command bivouacked in an old cotton-field of the Thompson plantation. Shelters from the hot sun were made from bushes
or blankets. During this first afternoon on South Carolina
soil Colonel Shaw thoughtfully sent to the officers a present of champagne.

Beaufort was our abiding-place for only four days, and
the Fifty-fourth never returned to it. Sandy streets shaded
with fine oaks crossed one another at right angles. There
were some fine old houses and gardens skirting the shell
road running along the low bluffs, with churches, public
buildings, and a spacious green. Scattered about the island
were some white and the two South Carolina colored regiments, besides some cavalry and artillery. The landward
side of Port Royal Island, fronting Rebel territory, was
strongly picketed and fortified.

While camped there, the days were intensely hot, with
cooler nights. Troublesome insects infested our camp.
Shelter tents for the men were issued and put up. Our
first taste of fatigue work in the field was on June 6, when
Companies A, D, and H were sent out on the shell road
to work on fortifications. The Second South Carolina had
departed for the Georgia coast. Late in the day orders came
to embark, Colonel Shaw having applied for active service.

Camp was struck at sunrise on the 8th, after a rainy
night, and an hour later saw the regiment in line in accordance with orders establishing the positions of the several companies for the first time. The formation was with
Company B on the right as follows:—

H F G D E K C I A B.

Having marched to the wharf, embarkation took place at once; but the start was not made until 9 A.M., when the steamer swung into the stream and ran down river, the men singing "John Brown" gayly. About a mile below town the steamer grounded, delaying arrival at Hilton Head until noon. There Colonel Shaw was instructed by General Hunter to report to Colonel Montgomery, at St. Simon's Island, Ga., and the "De Molay" steamed out of harbor at 5.30 P.M.

After a rather rough voyage of some eighty miles during the night, the "De Molay" dropped anchor at 6 A.M. in the sound off the southern point of St. Simon's Island. Colonel Shaw landed and rode across the island to report to Colonel Montgomery. At noon the steamer "Sentinel," a small craft that looked like a canal-boat with a one-story house built upon it, came alongside, and eight companies were transferred, Companies A and C under Captain Appleton remaining to get the cargo in readiness for a second trip.

The little steamer took the regiment up the winding river, along the west and inland shore of the island, past Gascoign's Bluff, where the Second South Carolina was encamped, to Pike's Bluff, some eight or ten miles, where the regiment disembarked on an old wharf. It was a pretty spot on a plantation formerly owned by a Mr. Gould. There was a large two-story house surrounded by fine trees, and situated close to the wharf, which was taken for use as headquarters. Close by it was an old barn in which the supplies were stored when they arrived. On the edge of a cleared field the men pitched shelters for the night.

Col. James Montgomery, commanding the post, was a noted man. He was born in Ohio, in 1814. In Kansas, from

1856 to 1861, he was the central figure in the Free State party. Early in the war he was for a time colonel of a Kansas regiment. By bold raids into the enemy's country in 1863, he recruited his colored regiment. He was a man of austere bearing, cool, deliberate, and of proved courage. In personal appearance he was tall, spare, rather bowed, with gentle voice and quiet manner. After his resignation in September, 1864, he returned to Kansas, and died there in December, 1871.

Colonel Montgomery, with five companies of his regiment, on June 6, had made an expedition from St. Simon's up the Turtle River to Brunswick and beyond, and destroyed a span of the railroad bridge over Buffalo Creek. Quartermaster Ritchie issued A and wall tents to the Fifty-fourth on June 10; and all were at work pitching camp and clearing the ground, when a steamer came to the wharf. Colonel Montgomery was on board, and hailing Colonel Shaw from the deck, said, "How soon can you be ready to start on an expedition?" Colonel Shaw replied, "In half an hour," and at once caused the long-roll to be sounded. Hurried preparations were at once made, and at 6 P.M. eight companies of the regiment embarked on the "Sentinel." Companies F and C were left behind as a camp guard.

Running down the river to Montgomery's camp, the armed transport "John Adams" was found with troops on board. Besides the Fifty-fourth, five companies of the Second South Carolina, and a section of Light Battery C, Third Rhode Island Artillery, under Lieut. William A. Sabin, took part in the expedition. Owing to the "Sentinel" grounding after proceeding a short distance farther, and the "Adams" also running on a shoal, there was long delay waiting for the flood-tide. Not until 1 A.M. did the "Sentinel" run up the coast, entering Doboy Sound at sunrise. There the gunboat "Paul Jones" and the "Harriet A. Weed" joined. Entering the Altamaha River, with the gunboats occasionally shelling houses and clumps of woods, the vessels proceeded until the town of Darien appeared in sight. Then the gunboats searched it with their shells and fired at a few pickets seen east of the place.

At 3 P.M. the troops landed without resistance at some of the deserted wharves. Pickets were posted, and the troops formed in the public square. Only two white women and a few negroes were found. The inhabitants were living at the "Ridge," a few miles inland. Some fifteen or twenty men of the Twentieth Georgia Cavalry, under Capt. W. A. Lane, picketed the vicinity, but had retired.

Darien, the New Inverness of early days, was a most beautiful town as Montgomery's forayers entered it that fateful June day. A broad street extended along the river, with others running into it, all shaded with mulberry and oak trees of great size and beauty. Storehouses and mills along the river-bank held quantities of rice and resin. There might have been from seventy-five to one hundred residences in the place. There were three churches, a market-house, jail, clerk's office, court-house, and an academy.

After forming line, orders came for the Fifty-fourth to make details and secure from the houses such things as would be useful in camp besides live-stock, resin, lumber, etc. Soon the plundering thus legitimized began. An officer thus describes the scene:—

> "The men began to come in by twos, threes, and dozens, loaded with every species and all sorts and quantities of furniture, stores, trinkets, etc., till one would be tired enumerating. We had sofas, tables, pianos, chairs, mirrors, carpets, beds, bedsteads, carpenter's tools, cooper's tools,

books, law-books, account-books in unlimited supply, china sets, tinware, earthen-ware, Confederate shinplasters, old letters, papers, etc. A private would come along with a slate, yard-stick, and a brace of chickens in one hand, and in the other hand a rope with a cow attached."

But the crowning act of vandalism is thus set forth in one of Colonel Shaw's letters:—

"After the town was pretty thoroughly disembowelled, he [Montgomery] said to me, 'I shall burn this town.' He speaks in a very low tone, and has quite a sweet smile when addressing you. I told him I did not want the responsibility of it, and he was only too happy to take it all on his own shoulders.... The reasons he gave me for destroying Darien were that the Southerners must be made to feel that this was a real war, and that they were to be swept away by the hand of God like the Jews of old. In theory it may seem all right to some; but when it comes to being made the instrument of the Lord's vengeance, I myself don't like it. Then he says, 'We are outlawed, and therefore not bound by the rules of regular warfare.' But that makes it none the less revolting to wreak our vengeance on the innocent and defenceless."

By Montgomery's express orders, therefore, the town was fired, only one company of the Fifty-fourth participating with the Second South Carolina, Montgomery applying the torch to the last buildings with his own hand. Fanned by a high wind, the flames eventually destroyed everything but a church, a few houses, and some lumberworks owned in the North. The schooner "Pet," with fifty-five bales of cotton for Nassau, lying in a small creek four miles above, was captured, and a flatboat with twenty-five bales near by was also secured.

Our transports had been loaded with plunder, and late

in the afternoon the troops re-embarked. Some ware-houses had been fired, and the river-bank was a sheet of flame. A few moments' delay or a change of wind might have resulted disastrously. The heat was so intense that all were driven to the farther side of our boat, and gun-barrels became so hot that the men were ordered to hold them upward. Five miles below the town the steamer an-chored. The light of the fire was seen that night at St. Simon's, fifteen miles away. Colonel Shaw wrote two of-ficial letters bearing upon this expedition. One was to Gov-ernor Andrew, giving an account of the expedition, wherein he expressed his disapprobation of Colonel Montgomery's course. The other is as follows:—

ST. SIMON'S ISLAND, GA., June 14, 1863.
LIEUTENANT-COLONEL HALPINE, A.A.G. Tenth Army Corps, and Department of the South.

DEAR SIR,—Will you allow me to ask you a private question, which of course you are at liberty to answer or not? Has Colonel Montgomery orders from General Hunter to burn and destroy all town and dwelling houses he may capture?

On the 11th inst., as you know, we took the town of Darien without opposition, the place being occupied, as far as we ascertained, by non-combatants; Colonel Mont-gomery burned it to the ground, and at leaving finally, shelled it from the river.

If he does this on his own responsibility, I shall refuse to have a share in it, and take the consequences; but, of course, if it is an order from headquarters, it is a different matter, as in that case I suppose it to have been found necessary to adopt that policy. He ordered me, if separated from him, to burn all the plantation houses I came across.

Now, I am perfectly ready to burn any place which resists, and gives some reason for such a proceeding; but it seems to me barbarous to turn women and children adrift in that way; and if I am only assisting Colonel Mont-

gomery in a private enterprise of his own, it is very dis-
tasteful to me.

I am aware that this is not a military way of getting
information; and I hope you will feel that I shall not be
hurt if you refuse to answer my question.

Believe me, very truly yours,

ROBERT G. SHAW,

*Colonel Commanding Fifty-fourth Massachusetts Regi-
ment.*

It is not known to the writer that any answer was vouch-
safed to this letter; but Colonel Shaw afterward ascertained
that Colonel Montgomery acted in accordance with General Hunter's orders.

The "Sentinel" at 3 A.M. got under way, landing the
Fifty-fourth, after a passage of twelve hours, at the camp.
Our first mail since leaving home came that afternoon.
Colonel Montgomery had gone to Hilton Head, leaving
Colonel Shaw in command of the post.

Camped on the Gould place, the Fifty-fourth quietly
remained until its departure from St. Simon's. The plunder
acquired afforded many comforts and even luxuries. Officers and men lived on army fare, supplemented with poor
fresh beef, as a few cattle had been found. Religious services
were sometimes held in the yard of a little church near
by, most beautifully situated amid a wealth of foliage which
overshadowed many old, decayed tombstones. Hardly a day
passed without more or less rain falling. It was very warm
at midday, but later came cool breezes from seaward.

Besides the usual camp guard the Fifty-fourth furnished
details for a long picket line, and a number of posts watching the river.

St. Simon's came nearer a realization of the ideal Eden
than one could hope to find the second time. There was

a subtile languor in the hum of insects, the song and flight of birds, the splash of the warm green water upon the shore. Grand old oaks, laden with moss and vines, canopied the flowers and verdure beneath. Perfume of shrubs, plants, trees, and grass filled the air, vying with the fresher and more invigorating sweetness from marsh and sea. One could almost see and hear the growth of plant and cane, as the life-giving sun warmed the sap, burst the blossom, and drew the tendril skyward. Gigantic ferns covered the shadier places, while the pools and swamps were beautiful with lilies.

There were a number of deserted plantations on the island, the most notable of which were those of T. Butler King, James E. Couper, and Pierce Butler. The latter was the husband of Fanny Kemble, and his place the one of which she wrote in her "Journal of a Residence on a Georgian Plantation, in 1838–39." All these places were neglected and abandoned, except by a few old negroes.

Historically, St. Simon's Island was noted ground. Near the camp of the Fifty-fourth were the "tabby" walls of Frederica, founded by Governor Oglethorpe in 1736, of which John Wesley was the minister. In the centre of the island was "Bloody Swamp," where the invading Spaniards were defeated July 7, 1742. It is a fact not widely known that with the Spanish force was a regiment of negroes and another of mulattoes. During the Revolution the British overran the island. On the next island to the south Lamar landed his last cargo of slaves from the "Wanderer." St. Simon's had been fortified early in the Civil War; but in February, 1862, the armament was removed, and then the few remaining inhabitants went away.

While the Fifty-fourth were enjoying the delights of St. Simon's, Brig.-Gen. Quincy A. Gillmore had relieved Gen-

eral Hunter. Admiral John A. Dahlgren was to replace
Admiral Dupont. Tidings of these changes, of Lee having
crossed the Rappahannock, the capture of Harper's Ferry,
and the investment of Port Hudson, were received by the
"Harriet A. Weed," on June 23. Orders also came for the
Fifty-fourth to report at Hilton Head.

During the afternoon and evening of June 24, the regiment was taken in detachments on the "Mayflower" to
the ocean steamer, "Ben Deford," lying off Montgomery's
camp, whence it sailed early the next day for Hilton Head.
Colonel Montgomery's regiment was also ordered away.
About noon, Colonel Shaw reported his arrival and was
ordered to St. Helena Island, across the harbor. A new
object of interest was the Confederate ironclad "Atlanta,"
captured June 17 by the monitor "Weehawken."

Rain was falling as the Fifty-fourth landed on the wharf.
Marching for a mile or so, we camped in an old cotton-
field near the water. Many regiments were on the island
preparing for active operations. The post was commanded
by Brig.-Gen. George C. Strong, a brilliant young officer
who had recently arrived. The Fifty-fourth, with the Second South Carolina camped near by, constituted the "Colored Brigade," under Colonel Montgomery.

Although it rained very frequently, the moisture was
speedily absorbed by the sandy soil. There was a terrible
thunder-storm on the 28th, accompanied with such violent
wind that many tents were blown down. One man was
killed, and several stunned, by lightning, in adjoining
camps.

Being near the water, sea-bathing was convenient and
thoroughly enjoyed. A few trees, shrubbery, and some negro houses bounded the prospect landward. There was
swampy ground in front of the camp. Beyond and back

from the shore line were many plantations and fine woods. Remains of former camps were found everywhere. Many contrabands were employed planting under Northern men.

While at this camp the condition of the regiment was excellent, and the men in high spirits, eager for service. Drills went on incessantly. A musician of the Forty-eighth New York was instructing the band. On the 30th, the Fifty-fourth was mustered for pay. It was then first rumored that the terms of enlistment would not be adhered to by the Government. The situation is best evidenced by the following letter of Colonel Shaw:—

ST. HELENA ISLAND, S.C., July 2, 1863.
HIS EXCELLENCY GOVERNOR ANDREW.

DEAR SIR,—Since I last wrote you, the Fifty-fourth has left St. Simon's Island and returned to St. Helena near Hilton Head. We are now encamped in a healthy place, close to the harbor, where we get the sea breeze.

You have probably seen the order from Washington which cuts down the pay of colored troops from $13 to $10. Of course if this affects Massachusetts regiments, it will be a great piece of injustice to them, as they were enlisted on the express understanding that they were to be on precisely the same footing as all other Massachusetts troops. In my opinion they should be mustered out of the service or receive the full pay which was promised them. The paymaster here is inclined to class us with the contraband regiments, and pay the men only $10. If he does not change his mind, I shall refuse to have the regiment paid until I hear from you on the subject. And at any rate I trust you will take the matter in hand, for every pay-day we shall have the same trouble unless there is a special order to prevent it.

Another change that has been spoken of was the arming of negro troops with pikes instead of firearms. Whoever proposed it must have been looking for a means of annihilating negro troops altogether, I should think—or have never been under a heavy musketry fire, nor observed its effects. The project is now abandoned, I believe.

My men are well and in good spirits. We have only five in hospital. We are encamped near the Second South Carolina near General Strong's brigade, and are under his immediate command. He seems anxious to do all he can for us, and if there is a fight in the Department will no doubt give the black troops a chance to show what stuff they are made of.

With many wishes for your good health and happiness, I remain,

Very sincerely and respectfully yours,
ROBERT G. SHAW.

A deserter from the Second South Carolina was brought by Lieut. George W. Brush of his regiment before Colonel Montgomery on June 28. After questioning him, the colonel ordered him to be taken away and shot, which was done at once. Montgomery was never taken to task for this illegal action. Most of the troops at St. Helena had departed for Folly Island by July 3. Fears prevailed that the colored regiments were not to take part in active operations. Colonel Shaw's disappointment found courteous expression as follows:—

ST. HELENA ISLAND, July 6, 1863.
BRIG.-GEN. GEORGE C. STRONG.

GENERAL,—I did not pay my respects to you before you left this post because I did not wish to disturb you when making your preparations for departure.

I desire, however, to express to you my regret that my regiment no longer forms a part of the force under your command. I was the more disappointed at being left behind, that I had been given to understand that we were to have our share in the work in this department. I feel convinced too that my men are capable of better service than mere guerilla warfare, and I hoped to remain permanently under your command.

It seems to me quite important that the colored soldiers should be associated as much as possible with the white troops, in order that they may have other witnesses besides their own officers to what they are capable of doing. I trust that the present arrangement is not permanent.

With many wishes for your success, believe me very sincerely and respectfully

Your obedient servant,

ROBERT G. SHAW,

Colonel Commanding Fifty-fourth Regiment Mass. Infantry.

Upon the national holiday all unnecessary duty was dispensed with. Everywhere on land and water the stars and stripes were displayed and saluted. At the camp many men were permitted to pass the lines. Several officers visited the camp of the Second South Carolina. Colonel Shaw and others attended a celebration of the day held by the freedmen in the yard of the Baptist Church, some six miles distant, where the Declaration of Independence was read, hymns sung, and addresses made. Rev. Mr. Lynch, a colored clergyman from Baltimore, held religious services for the Fifty-fourth on Sunday, the 5th. News was received of the promotion of Major Hallowell to be lieutenant-colonel in place of his brother, promoted colonel of the Fifty-fifth Massachusetts.

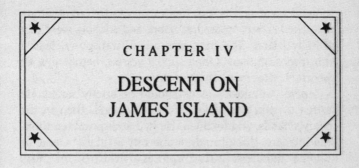

CHAPTER IV

DESCENT ON
JAMES ISLAND

ALL SUSPENSE REGARDING the employment of the Fifty-fourth ended July 8, with the receipt, about noon, of orders to move at an hour's notice, taking only blankets and rations. Three hours after, the regiment began to embark, headquarters with seven companies finding transportation on the steamer "Chasseur," the remaining ones on the steamer "Cossack," with Colonel Montgomery and staff.

Lieutenant Littlefield, with a guard of one hundred men, was detailed to remain at St. Helena in charge of the camp. Assistant-Surgeon Bridgham also remained with the sick. Captain Bridge and Lieutenant Walton were unable to go on account of illness. A start was made late in the afternoon in a thunder-storm, the "Cossack" stopping at Hilton Head to take on Captain Emilio and a detail of ninety men there. The following night was made miserable by wet clothes, a scarcity of water, and the crowded condition of the small steamers.

About 1 A.M. on the 9th, the transports arrived off Stono
Inlet; the bar was crossed at noon; and anchors were cast
off Folly Island. The inlet was full of transports, loaded
with troops, gunboats, and supply vessels, betokening an
important movement made openly.

General Gillmore's plans should be briefly stated. He
desired to gain possession of Morris Island, then in the
enemy's hands, and fortified. He had at disposal ten thousand infantry, three hundred and fifty artillerists, and six
hundred engineers; thirty-six pieces of field artillery, thirty
Parrott guns, twenty-seven siege and three Cohorn mortars, besides ample tools and material. Admiral Dahlgren
was to co-operate. On Folly Island, in our possession, batteries were constructed near Lighthouse Inlet, opposite
Morris Island, concealed by the sand hillocks and undergrowth. Gillmore's real attack was to be made from this
point by a *coup de main*, the infantry crossing the inlet
in boats covered by a bombardment from land and sea.
Brig.-Gen. Alfred H. Terry, with four thousand men, was
to make a demonstration on James Island. Col. T. W. Higginson, with part of his First South Carolina Colored and
a section of artillery, was to ascend the South Edisto River,
and cut the railroad at Jacksonboro. This latter force, however, was repulsed with the loss of two guns and the
steamer "Governor Milton."

Late in the afternoon of the 9th Terry's division moved.
The monitor "Nantucket," gunboats "Pawnee" and "Com-
modore McDonough," and mortar schooner "C. P. Williams" passed up the river, firing on James Island to the
right and John's Island to the left, followed by thirteen
transports carrying troops. Col. W. .W. H. Davis, with portions of his regiment—the One Hundred and Fourth Pennsylvania—and the Fifty-second Pennsylvania, landed on

Battery Island, advancing to a bridge leading to James Island.

Heavy cannonading was heard in the direction of Morris Island, at 5 A.M. on the 10th. Before night word came that all the ground south of Fort Wagner on Morris Island was captured with many guns and prisoners. This news was received with rousing cheers by Terry's men and the sailors. At dawn Colonel Davis's men crossed to James Island, his skirmishers driving a few cavalry. At an old house the main force halted with pickets advanced. While this movement was taking place, a portion of the other troops landed. That day a mail brought news of Vicksburg's capture and Lee's defeat at Gettysburg. Lieut. Edward B. Emerson joined the Fifty-fourth from the North.

About noon of the 11th, the regiment landed, marched about a mile, and camped in open ground on the furrows of an old field. The woods near by furnished material for brush shelters as a protection against the July sun. By that night all troops were ashore. Terry's division consisted of three brigades,—Davis's, of the Fifty-second and One Hundred and Fourth Pennsylvania and Fifty-sixth New York; Brig.-Gen. Thomas G. Stevenson's, of the Twenty-fourth Massachusetts, Tenth Connecticut, and Ninety-seventh Pennsylvania; and Montgomery's, of the Fifty-fourth Massachusetts and Second South Carolina.

James Island is separated from the mainland by Wappoo Creek. From the landing a road led onward, which soon separated into two: one running to the right through timber, across low sandy ground to Secessionville; the other to the left, over open fields across the low ground, past Dr. Thomas Grimball's house on to the Wappoo. The low ground crossed by both these roads over causeways formed the front of Terry's lines, and was commanded by our naval

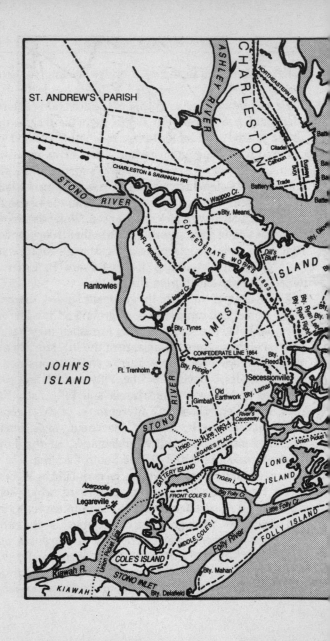

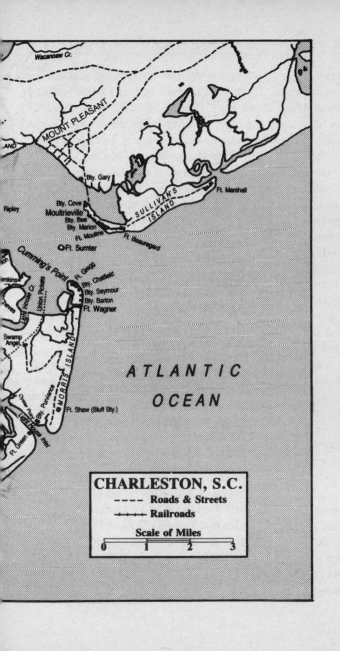

Wacanoaw Cr.

MOUNT PLEASANT

...AND

Bty. Gary

Ft. Marshall

...Ripley

Bty. Cove
Moultrieville
Bty. Bee
Bty. Marion
Ft. Moultrie

SULLIVAN'S ISLAND

Ft. Beauregard

○ Ft. Sumter

Cumming's Point

...ion

...mkins'

Light Hous Cr.

Union Plaine

Ft. Greog
Bty. Chatfield
Bty. Seymour
Bty. Barton
Ft. Wagner

MORRIS ISLAND

Swamp
Angel

...eres

Ft. Green

Oyster Point
Bty. Purviance

● Ft. Shaw (Bluff Bty.)

Light House Inlet

ATLANTIC

OCEAN

CHARLESTON, S.C.
---- Roads & Streets
+++++ Railroads

Scale of Miles

0   1   2   3

vessels. Fort Pemberton, on the Stono, constituted the enemy's right. Thence the line was retired partially behind James Island Creek, consisting of detached light works for field-guns and infantry. Their left was the fortified camp of Secessionville, where, before Battery Lamar, General Benham was repulsed in the spring of 1862.

General Beauregard, the Confederate Department commander, considered an attack on Charleston by way of James Island as the most dangerous to its safety. He posted his forces accordingly, and on July 10 had 2,926 effectives there, with 927 on Morris Island, 1,158 on Sullivan's Island, and 850 in the city. Few troops from other points were spared when Morris Island was attacked on the 10th; therefore Terry's diversion had been effective. Had Beauregard's weakness been known, Terry's demonstration in superior force might have been converted into a real attack, and James Island fallen before it, when Charleston must have surrendered or been destroyed.

Captain Willard, on the 11th, with Company B, was sent to John's Island at Legareville to prevent a repetition of firing upon our vessels by artillery such as had occurred that morning.

In the afternoon the Tenth Connecticut and Ninety-seventh Pennsylvania, covered by the "Pawnee's" fire, advanced the picket line. Word was received of an unsuccessful assault on Fort Wagner, with considerable loss to us. Abraham F. Brown of Company E accidentally shot himself to death with a small pistol he was cleaning. Late that afternoon Lieutenant-Colonel Hallowell, with Companies D, F, I, and K, went out on picket in front of our right, remaining throughout a dark and stormy night. During the night of the 13th, Captain Emilio, with Company E, picketed about Legareville. Capt. A. P. Rockwell's

First Connecticut Battery arrived from Beaufort on the 14th.

Between the 10th and 16th there had arrived for the enemy from Georgia and North Carolina two four-gun batteries and six regiments of infantry. Beauregard also reduced his force on Morris Island and concentrated on James, under command of Brig.-Gen. Johnson Hagood. Gillmore still kept Terry there, inviting attack, although the purpose of the diversion had been accomplished. On the 15th the enemy demonstrated in front of the Tenth Connecticut pickets. It was rumored that two scouts had been seen about our lines.

Some thought had been given to securing a line of retreat; for the engineers were reconstructing the broken bridge leading from James Island, and repairing causeways, dikes, and foot-bridges across the marshes along the old road to Cole's Island, formerly used by the Confederates.

Companies B, H, and K, of the Fifty-fourth, under command of Captain Willard, were detailed for picket on the 15th, and about 6 P.M. relieved men of Davis's brigade. Captain Russel and Lieutenant Howard, with Company H, held the right from near a creek, over rolling ground and rather open country covered with high grass and thistles. Captain Simpkins and Lieut. R. H. L. Jewett held the left of the Fifty-fourth line with Company K and a portion of Company B. It was over lower ground, running obliquely through a growth of small timber and brush. There was a broken bridge in the front. A reserve, consisting of the remainder of Company B, under Lieut. Thomas L. Appleton, was held at a stone house. Captain Willard's force was five officers and about two hundred men. From Simpkins's left to the Stono the picket line was continued by men of the Tenth Connecticut, holding a dangerous position, as it had a swamp in rear. Frequent showers of rain fell that evening. All night following, the enemy was uneasy. Lurking men were seen, and occasional shots rang out. Captain Willard, mounting the roof of the house, could see great activity among the signal corps of the enemy. He sent word to his officers to be vigilant, and prepared for attack in the morning.

About midnight the men were placed in skirmishing order, and so remained. Sergeant Stephens of Company B relates that George Brown of his company, a "dare-devil fellow," crawled out on his hands and knees and fired at the enemy's pickets.

An attack was indeed impending, arranged on the following plan: Brig.-Gen. A. H. Colquitt, with the Twenty-fifth South Carolina, Sixth and Nineteenth Georgia, and four companies Thirty-second Georgia, about fourteen hundred men, supported by the Marion Artillery, was to cross the marsh at the causeway nearest Secessionville, "drive the enemy as far as the lower causeway [nearest Stono] rapidly recross the marsh at that point by a flank movement, and cut off and capture the force encamped at Grimball's." Col. C. H. Way, Fifty-fourth Georgia, with eight hundred men, was to follow and co-operate. A reserve of one company of cavalry, one of infantry, and a section of artillery, was at Rivers's house. Two Napoleon guns each, of the Chatham Artillery, and Blake's Battery, and four twelve-pounders of the Siege Train, supported by four hundred infantry, were to attack the gunboats "Pawnee" and "Marblehead" in the Stono River.

In the gray of early dawn of July 16, the troops in bivouac on James Island were awakened by dropping shots, and then heavy firing on the picket line to the right. Clambering to the top of a pile of cracker-boxes, an officer of the Fifty-fourth, looking in the direction of the firing, saw the flashes of musketry along the outposts. In a few moments came the sharp metallic explosions from field-guns to the left by the river-bank. Wilkie James, the adjutant, rode in post-haste along the line, with cheery voice but unusually excited manner, ordering company commanders to form. "Fall in! fall in!" resounded on all sides, while drums of the several regiments were beating the long-roll. But a few moments sufficed for the Fifty-fourth to form, when Colonel Shaw marched it to the right and some little distance to the rear, where it halted, faced to the front, and stood in line of battle at right angles to the Secessionville road.

Rapid work was going on at the outposts. Before dawn the pickets of the Fifty-fourth had heard hoarse commands and the sound of marching men coming from the bank of darkness before them. Soon a line of men in open order came sweeping toward them from the gloom into the nearer and clearer light.

Colquitt, with six companies of the Eutaw Regiment (Twenty-fifth South Carolina), skirmishing before his infantry column, crossing Rivers's causeway, was rapidly advancing on the black pickets.

Simpkins's right was the first point of contact; and the men, thus suddenly attacked by a heavy force, discharged their pieces, and sullenly contested the way, firing as they went, over rough and difficult ground, which obstructed the enemy's advance as well as their own retirement.

Soon the enemy gained the road at a point in rear of Russel's right. Some of the men there, hardly aware of their extremity, were still holding their positions against those of the enemy who appeared in the immediate front. It seemed to Sergt. Peter Vogelsang of Company H, who had his post at a palmetto-tree, that in a moment one hundred Rebels were swarming about him. He led his comrades to join men on his left, where they advanced, firing. With effect too, for they came to the body of a dead Rebel, from whom Vogelsang took a musket.

Russel's right posts, thus cut off, were followed by a company of the Nineteenth Georgia, and after the desultory fighting were driven, to escape capture, into the creek on the right of the line, where some were drowned. Those most courageous refused to fall back, and were killed or taken as prisoners. Sergt. James D. Wilson of Company H was one of the former. He was an expert in the use of the musket, having been employed with the famous Ellsworth Zouaves of Chicago. Many times he had declared to his comrades that he would never retreat or surrender to the enemy. On that morning, when attacked, he called to his men to stand fast. Assailed by five men, he is said to have disabled three of them. Some cavalrymen coming up, he charged them with a shout as they circled about him, keeping them all at bay for a time with the bayonet of his discharged musket, until the brave fellow sank in death with three mortal besides other wounds.

Captain Russel, finding that the enemy had turned his flank before he could face back, had to retire with such men as were not cut off, at double-quick, finding the foe about the reserve house when he reached it. A mounted officer charged up to Russel, and cut twice at his head with his sword. Preston Williams of Company H caught the second sweep upon his bayonet and shot the Confederate through the neck, thus saving his captain's life. From the reserve house Russel and his men retired, fighting as they could.

Captain Simpkins's right, as has been told, first bore

the force of the attack. By strenuous efforts and great personal exposure that cool and gallant officer collected some men in line. With them he contested the way back step by step, halting now and then to face about and fire, thus gaining time, the loss of which thwarted the enemy's plan. Of his men, Corp. Henry A. Field of Company K especially distinguished himself.

Captain Willard at the reserve house at once sent back word, by a mounted orderly, of the situation. To the support of his right he sent Lieutenant Appleton with some men, and to the left First Sergeant Simmons of Company B with a small force, and then looked for aid from our main body. He endeavored to form a line of skirmishers, when the men began coming back from the front, but with little success. The men could not be kept in view because of the underbrush nearly as high as a man. As the expected succor did not come, the officers and the remaining men made their way back to the division.

It will be remembered that with the first musket-shots came the sound of field-guns from the Stono. The enemy's four Napoleons had galloped into battery within four hundred yards of the gunboats, and fired some ten rounds before they were replied to; their shots crashed through the "Pawnee" again and again, with some loss. It was impossible for the gunboats to turn in the narrow stream, and their guns did not bear properly. To drop down was dangerous, but it was done; when out of close range, the "Marblehead," "Pawnee," and "Huron" soon drove their tormentors away from the river-bank.

To capture the Tenth Connecticut, the enemy, after dealing with the Fifty-fourth, sent a portion of his force; but the resistance made by Captain Simpkins had allowed time for the Tenth Connecticut to abandon its dangerous position at the double-quick. None too soon, however, for five minutes' delay would have been fatal. A correspondent of "The Reflector," writing from Morris Island a few days later, said:—

> "The boys of the Tenth Connecticut could not help loving the men who saved them from destruction. I have been deeply affected at hearing this feeling expressed by officers and men of the Connecticut regiment; and probably a thousand homes from Windham to Fairfield have in letters been told the story how the dark-skinned heroes fought the good fight and covered with their own brave hearts the retreat of brothers, sons, and fathers of Connecticut."

The valuable time gained by the resistance of the Fifty-fourth pickets had also permitted the formation of Terry's division in line of battle. Hardly had the Fifty-fourth taken its position before men from the front came straggling in, all bearing evidence of struggles with bush and brier, some of the wounded limping along unassisted, others helped by comrades. One poor fellow, with his right arm shattered, still carried his musket in his left hand.

Captain Russel appeared in sight, assisting a sergeant, badly wounded. Bringing up the rear came Captains Willard and Simpkins, the latter with his trousers and rubber coat pierced with bullets. As the pickets and their officers reached the regiment, they took their places in line.

A few minutes after these events, the enemy, having advanced to a position within about six hundred yards of the Federal line, opened fire with guns of the Marion Artillery, making good line shots, but fortunately too high.

It was a supreme moment for the Fifty-fourth, then under fire as a regiment for the first time. The sight of wounded comrades had been a trial; and the screaming shot and shell flying overhead, cutting the branches of trees to the right, had a deadly sound. But the dark line stood stanch, holding the front at the most vital point. Not a man was out of place, as the officers could see while they stood in rear of the lines, observing their men.

In reply to the enemy's guns the Connecticut battery fired percussion-shells, and for some time this artillery duel continued. To those who were anticipating an attack by infantry, and looking for the support of the gunboats, their silence was ominous. Every ear was strained to catch the welcome sound, and at last it came in great booms from Parrott guns. Very opportunely, too, on the night before, the armed transports "John Adams" and "Mayflower" had run up the creek on our right flank, and their guns were fired twelve or fifteen times with good effect before the enemy retired.

The expected attack on Terry's line by infantry did not take place, for after about an hour the enemy retired in some confusion. By General Terry's order, the Fifty-fourth was at once directed to reoccupy the old picket line. Captain Jones with two companies advanced, skirmishing; and the main body followed, encountering arms and equipments of the enemy strewn over a broad trail. At the reserve house the regiment halted in support of a strong picket line thrown out. Parties were sent to scour the ground, finding several wounded men lying in the brush or in the marsh across the creek. They also brought in the body of a Confederate, almost a child, with soft skin and long fair hair, red with his own blood. This youthful victim of the fight was tenderly buried soon after.

Some of our dead at first appeared to be mutilated; but closer inspection revealed the fact that the fiddler-crabs, and not the enemy, did the work. It was told by some of those who lay concealed, that where Confederate officers were, the colored soldiers had been protected; but that in other cases short shrift was given, and three men had been shot and others bayonetted.

Colonel Shaw had despatched Adjutant James to report that the old line was re-established. He returned with the following message from General Terry: "Tell your colonel that I am exceedingly pleased with the conduct of your regiment. They have done all they could do."

During the afternoon a mail was received. After reading their letters Colonel Shaw and Lieutenant-Colonel Hallowell conversed. The colonel asked the major if he believed in presentiments, and added that he felt he would be killed in the first action. Asked to try to shake off the feeling, he quietly said, "I will try."

General Beauregard reported his loss as three killed, twelve wounded, and three missing, which is believed to be an under-estimate. We found two dead Confederates, and captured six prisoners representing four regiments. The Adjutant-General of Massachusetts gives the Fifty-fourth loss as fourteen killed, eighteen wounded, and thirteen missing. Outside our regiment the casualties were very light.

General Terry in his official report says:—

"I desire to express my obligations to Captain Balch, United States Navy, commanding the naval forces in the river, for the very great assistance rendered to me, and to report to the commanding general the good services of Captain Rockwell and his battery, and the steadiness and soldierly conduct of the Fifty-fourth Massachusetts Regiment who were on duty at the outposts on the right and met the brunt of attack."

General Terry was ordered to evacuate James Island that night. At about five o'clock P.M., the Fifty-fourth was relieved by the Fifty-second Pennsylvania, and returned to the bivouac. While awaiting the marching orders, several officers and men of the Tenth Connecticut came to express their appreciation of the service rendered by the Fifty-fourth companies attacked in the morning, by which they were enabled to effect a safe retreat. Afterward, upon Morris Island the colonel of that regiment made similar expressions.

Col. W. W. H. Davis, with his own and Montgomery's brigades, and the Tenth Connecticut, was to retire by the land route. Brigadier-General Stevenson's Twenty-fourth Massachusetts and Ninety-seventh Pennsylvania were ordered to take transports from James Island.

By Colonel Davis's order the Fifty-fourth Massachusetts was given the advance, moving at 9.30 o'clock that night, followed by the other regiments, the route being pointed out by guides from the engineers, who accompanied the head of column.

All stores, ammunition, and horses of the Fifty-fourth were put on board the steamer "Boston" by Quartermaster Ritchie, who, with his men, worked all night in the mud and rain. Surgeon Lincoln R. Stone of the Fifty-fourth and Surgeon Samuel A. Green of the Twenty-fourth Massachusetts saw that all the wounded were properly cared for, and also embarked.

It was a stormy night, with frequent flashes of lightning, and pouring rain. Colonel Davis, at the proper time, saw to the withdrawal of the Fifty-second Pennsylvania, which held the front lines. So silently was the operation accomplished that the enemy did not discover our evacuation until daylight. When the Fifty-sixth New York, the rear-guard, had crossed the bridge leading from James Island, at 1 A.M., on the 17th, it was effectually destroyed, thus rendering pursuit difficult.

That night's march was a memorable one, for the difficulties of the way were exceptional, and only to be encountered upon the Sea Islands. After passing the bridge, the road led along narrow causeways and paths only wide enough for two men to pass abreast; over swamps, and streams bridged for long distances by structures of frail piling, supporting one or two planks with no hand-rail. A driving rain poured down nearly the whole time, and the darkness was intense. Blinding flashes of lightning momentarily illumined the way, then fading but to render the blackness deeper.

Throughout most of the march the men were obliged to move in single file, groping their way and grasping their leader as they progressed, that they might not separate or go astray. Along the foot-bridges the planks became slippery with mire from muddy feet, rendering the footing insecure, and occasioning frequent falls, which delayed progress. Through the woods, wet branches overhanging the path, displaced by the leaders, swept back with bitter force into the faces of those following. Great clods of clay gathered on the feet of the men.

Two hours were consumed in passing over the dikes and foot-bridges alone. In distance the route was but a few miles, yet it was daybreak when the leading companies reached firmer ground. Then the men flung themselves on the wet ground, and in a moment were in deep sleep, while the column closed up. Reunited solidly again, the march was resumed, and Cole's Island soon reached. The regiments following the Fifty-fourth had the benefit of daylight most of the way.

Footsore, weary, hungry, and thirsty, the regiment was halted near the beach opposite Folly Island about 5 A.M., on the 17th. Sleep was had until the burning sun awakened the greater number. Regiments had been arriving and departing all the morning. Rations were not procurable, and they were fortunate who could find a few crumbs or morsels of meat in their haversacks. Even water was hard to obtain, for crowds of soldiers collected about the few sources of supply. By noon the heat and glare from the white sand were almost intolerable.

In the evening a moist cool breeze came; and at eight o'clock the regiment moved up the shore to a creek in readiness to embark on the "General Hunter," lying in the stream. It was found that the only means of boarding the steamer was by a leaky long-boat which would hold about thirty men. Definite orders came to report the regiment to General Strong at Morris Island without delay, and at 10 P.M. the embarkation began. By the light of a single lantern the men were stowed in the boat.

Rain was pouring down in torrents, for a thunderstorm was raging. Throughout that interminable night the longboat was kept plying from shore to vessel and back, while those on land stood or crouched about in dripping clothes, awaiting their turn for ferriage to the steamer, whose dim light showed feebly in the gloom. The boat journey was made with difficulty, for the current was strong, and the crowded soldiers obstructed the rowers in their task. It was an all night's work. Colonel Shaw saw personally to the embarkation; and as daylight was breaking he stepped in with the last boat-load, and himself guided the craft to the "Hunter." Thus with rare self-sacrifice and fine example, he shared the exposure of every man, when the comfortable cabin of the steamer was at his disposal from the evening before.

CHAPTER V

THE GREATER ASSAULT
ON WAGNER

O N THE "GENERAL HUNTER" the officers procured breakfast; but the men were still without rations. Refreshed, the officers were all together for the last time socially; before another day three were dead, and three wounded who never returned. Captain Simpkins, whose manly appearance and clear-cut features were so pleasing to look upon, was, as always, quiet and dignified; Captain Russel was voluble and active as ever, despite all fatigue. Neither appeared to have any premonition of their fate. It was different with Colonel Shaw, who again expressed to Lieutenant-Colonel Hallowell his apprehension of speedy death.

Running up Folly River, the steamer arrived at Pawnee Landing, where, at 9 A.M., the Fifty-fourth disembarked. Crossing the island through woods, the camps of several regiments were passed, from which soldiers ran out, shouting, "Well done! we heard your guns!" Others cried, "Hurrah, boys! you saved the Tenth Connecticut!" Leaving the timber, the Fifty-fourth came to the sea beach, where marching was easier. Stretching away to the horizon, on the right, was the Atlantic; to the left, sand hillocks, with pine woods farther inland. Occasional squalls of rain came, bringing rubber blankets and coats into use. At one point on the beach, a box of water-soaked hard bread was discovered, and the contents speedily divided among the hungry men. Firing at the front had been heard from early morning, which toward noon was observed to have risen into a heavy cannonade.

After a march of some six miles, we arrived at Lighthouse Inlet and rested, awaiting transportation. Tuneful voices about the colors started the song, "When this Cruel War is Over," and the pathetic words of the chorus were taken up by others. It was the last song of many; but few then thought it a requiem. By ascending the sand-hills, we could see the distant vessels engaging Wagner. When all was prepared, the Fifty-fourth boarded a small steamer, landed on Morris Island, about 5 P.M., and remained near the shore for further orders.

General Gillmore, on the 13th, began constructing four batteries, mounting forty-two guns and mortars, to damage the slopes and guns of Wagner, which were completed under the enemy's fire, and in spite of a sortie at night, on the 14th. He expected to open with them on the 16th; but heavy rains so delayed progress that all was not prepared until the 18th. Beyond this siege line, which was 1,350 yards south of Wagner, stretched a narrow strip of land between the sea and Vincent's Creek, with its marshes. At low tide, the beach sand afforded a good pathway to the enemy's position; but at high tide, it was through deep, loose sand, and over low sand hillocks. This stretch of sand was unobstructed, until at a point two hundred yards in front of Wagner, the enemy had made a line of rifle trenches. Some fifty yards nearer Wagner, an easterly bend of the marsh extended to within twenty-five yards of the sea at high tide, forming a defile, through which an assaulting column must pass.

Nearly covered by this sweep of the marsh, and commanding it as well as the stretch of sand beyond to the Federal line, was "Battery Wagner," so named by the Confederates, in memory of Lieut.-Col. Thomas M. Wagner, First South Carolina Artillery, killed at Fort Sumter. This field work was constructed of quartz sand, with turf and palmetto log revetment, and occupied the whole width of the island there,—some six hundred and thirty feet. Its southern and principal front was double-bastioned. Next the sea was a heavy traverse and curtain covering a sally-port. Then came the southeast bastion, prolonged westerly by a curtain connected with the southwest bastion. At the western end was another sally-port. An infantry parapet closed the rear or north face. It had large bombproofs, magazines, and heavy traverses.

Wagner's armament was reported to its commander, July 15, as follows: on sea face, one ten-inch Columbiad, and two smooth-bore thirty-two-pounders; on southeast bastion, operating on land and sea, one rifled thirty-two-pounder; on south point of bastion operating on land, one forty-two-pounder carronade; in the curtain, with direct fire on land approach to embrasure, two eight-inch naval shell-guns, one eight-inch sea-coast howitzer, and one thirty-two-pounder smooth-bore; on the flank defences of the curtain, two thirty-two-pounder carronades in embrasures; on the southerly face, one thirty-two-pounder carronades in embrasure; in southwest angle, one ten-inch sea-coast mortar; on bastion gorge, one thirty-two-

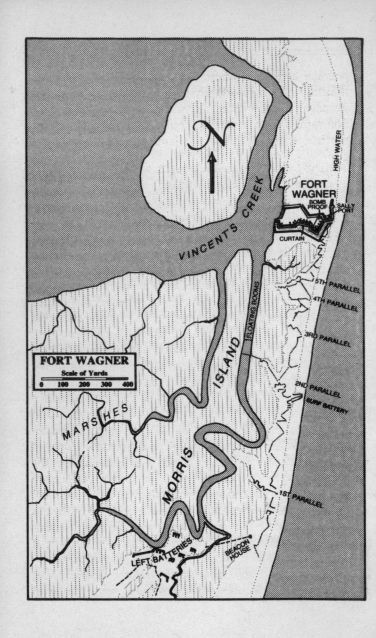

FORT WAGNER

Scale of Yards
0   100   200   300   400

N

HIGH WATER

VINCENTS CREEK

MORRIS ISLAND

FLOATING BOOMS

FORT WAGNER

BOMB PROOF

SALLY PORT

CURTAIN

5TH PARALLEL

4TH PARALLEL

3RD PARALLEL

2ND PARALLEL

SURF BATTERY

1ST PARALLEL

MARSHES

LEFT BATTERIES

BEACON HOUSE

pounder carronade. There were also four twelve-pounder howitzers. All the northerly portion of Morris Island was in range of Fort Sumter, the eastern James Island and the Sullivan's Island batteries, besides Fort Gregg, on the northerly extremity of Morris Island, which mounted three guns.

Brig.-Gen. William B. Taliaferro, an able officer, who had served with distinction under "Stonewall" Jackson, was in command of Morris Island, for the Confederates. Wagner's garrison, on the 18th, consisted of the Thirty-first and Fifty-first North Carolina, the Charleston Battalion, two companies Sixty-third Georgia Heavy Artillery, and two companies First South Carolina Infantry, acting as artillery, and two guns each of the Palmetto and Blake's Artillery,—a total force of seventeen hundred men. Such was the position, armament, and garrison of the strongest single earthwork known in the history of warfare.

About 10 A.M., on the 18th, five wooden gunboats joined the land batteries in shelling Wagner, lying out of the enemy's range. At about 12.30 P.M., five monitors and the "New Ironsides" opened, and the land batteries increased their fire. A deluge of shot was now poured into the work, driving the main portion of its garrison into the bomb-proofs, and throwing showers of sand from the slopes of Wagner into the air but to fall back in place again. The enemy's flag was twice shot away, and, until replaced, a battle-flag was planted with great gallantry by daring men. From Gregg, Sumter, and the James Island and Sullivan's Island batteries, the enemy returned the iron compliments; while for a time Wagner's cannoneers ran out at intervals, and served a part of the guns, at great risk.

A fresh breeze blew that day; at times the sky was clear; the atmosphere, lightened by recent rains, resounded with the thunders of an almost incessant cannonade. Smoke-clouds hung over the naval vessels, our batteries, and those of the enemy. During this terrible bombardment, the two infantry regiments and the artillery companies, except gun detachments, kept in the bombproofs. But the Charleston Battalion lay all day under the parapets of Wagner,—a terrible ordeal, which was borne without demoralization. In spite of the tremendous fire, the enemy's loss was only eight men killed and twenty wounded, before the assault.

General Taliaferro foresaw that this bombardment was preliminary to an assault, and had instructed his force to take certain assigned positions when the proper time came. To three companies of the Charleston Battalion was given the Confederate right along the parapet; the Fifty-first North Carolina, along the curtain; and the Thirty-first North Carolina, the left, including the southeast bastion. Two companies of the Charleston Battalion were placed outside the work, covering the gorge. A small reserve was assigned to the body of the fort. Two field-pieces were to fire from the traverse flanking the beach face and approach. For the protection of the eight-inch shell-guns in the curtain and the field-pieces, they were covered with sandbags, until desired for service. Thoroughly conversant with the ground, the Confederate commander rightly calculated that the defile would break up the formation of his assailants at a critical moment, when at close range.

General Gillmore, at noon, ascended the lookout on a hill within his lines, and examined the ground in front. Throughout the day this high point was the gathering-place of observers. The tide turned to flow at 4 P.M., and about the same time firing from Wagner ceased, and not a man was to be seen there. During the afternoon the troops were moving from their camps toward the front.

Late in the day the belief was general that the enemy had been driven from his shelter, and the armament of Wagner rendered harmless. General Gillmore, after calling his chief officers together for conference, decided to attack that evening, and the admiral was so notified. Firing from land and sea was still kept up with decreased rapidity, while the troops were preparing.

Upon arriving at Morris Island, Colonel Shaw and Adjutant James walked toward the front to report to General Strong, whom they at last found, and who announced that Fort Wagner was to be stormed that evening. Knowing Colonel Shaw's desire to place his men beside white troops, he said, "You may lead the column, if you say 'yes.' Your men, I know, are worn out, but do as you choose." Shaw's face brightened, and before replying, he requested Adjutant James to return and have Lieutenant-Colonel Hallowell bring up the Fifty-fourth. Adjutant James, who relates this interview, then departed on his mission. Receiving this order, the regiment marched on to General Strong's headquarters, where a halt of five minutes was made about 6 o'clock P.M. Noticing the worn look of the men, who had passed two days without an issue of rations, and no food since morning, when the weary march began, the general expressed his sympathy and his great desire that they might have food and stimulant. It could not be, however, for it was necessary that the regiment should move on to the position assigned.

Detaining Colonel Shaw to take supper with him, General Strong sent the Fifty-fourth forward under the lieutenant-colonel toward the front, moving by the middle road west of the sand-hills. Gaining a point where these elevations gave place to low ground, the long blue line of the regiment advancing by the flank attracted the attention of the enemy's gunners on James Island. Several solid shot were fired at the column, without doing any damage, but they ricochetted ahead or over the line in dangerous proximity. Realizing that the national colors and the white flag of the State especially attracted the enemy's fire, the bearers began to roll them up on the staves. At the same moment, Captain Simpkins, commanding the color company (K) turned to observe his men. His quick eye noted the half-furled flags, and his gallant spirit took fire in a moment at the sight. Pointing to the flags with uplifted sword, he commanded in imperative tones, "Unfurl those colors!" It was done, and the fluttering silks again waved, untrammelled, in the air.

Colonel Shaw, at about 6.30 P.M., mounted and accompanied General Strong toward the front. After proceeding a short distance, he turned back, and gave to Mr. Edward L. Pierce, a personal friend, who had been General Strong's guest for several days, his letters and some papers, with a request to forward them to his family if anything occurred to him requiring such service. That sudden purpose accomplished, he galloped away, overtook the regiment, and informed Lieutenant-Colonel Hallowell of what the Fifty-fourth was expected to do. The direction was changed to the right, advancing east toward the sea. By orders, Lieutenant-Colonel Hallowell broke the column at the sixth company, and led the companies of the left wing to the rear of those of the right wing. When the sea beach was reached, the regiment halted and came to rest, awaiting the coming up of the supporting regiments.

General Gillmore had assigned to General Seymour the command of the assaulting column, charging him with its organization, formation, and all the details of the attack. His force was formed into three brigades of infantry: the

first under General Strong, composed of the Fifty-fourth
Massachusetts, Sixth Connecticut, Forty-eighth New York,
Third New Hampshire, Ninth Maine, and Seventy-sixth
Pennsylvania; the second, under Col. Haldimand S. Putnam, of his own regiment,—the Seventh New Hampshire,—One Hundredth New York, Sixty-second and
Sixty-seventh Ohio; the third, or reserve brigade, under
Brig.-Gen. Thomas G. Stevenson, of the Twenty-fourth
Massachusetts, Tenth Connecticut, Ninety-seventh Pennsylvania, and Second South Carolina. Four companies
of the Seventh Connecticut, and some regular and volunteer artillery-men manned and served the guns of the
siege line.

Formed in column of wings, with the right resting near
the sea, at a short distance in advance of the works, the
men of the Fifty-fourth were ordered to lie down, their
muskets loaded but not capped, and bayonets fixed. There
the regiment remained for half an hour, while the formation of the storming column and reserve was perfected.
To the Fifty-fourth had been given the post of honor,
not by chance, but by deliberate selection. General Seymour has stated the reasons why this honorable but dangerous duty was assigned the regiment in the following
words:—

> "It was believed that the Fifty-fourth was in every re-
> spect as efficient as any other body of men; and as it was
> one of the strongest and best officered, there seemed to
> be no good reason why it should not be selected for the
> advance. This point was decided by General Strong and
> myself."

In numbers the Fifty-fourth had present but six hundred
men, for besides the large camp guard and the sick left at

St. Helena Island, and the losses sustained on James Island, on the 16th, a fatigue detail of eighty men under Lieut. Francis L. Higginson, did not participate in the attack.

The formation of the regiment for the assault was, as shown in the diagram below, with Companies B and E on the right of the respective wings.

RIGHT WING:	K	C	I	A	B
LEFT WING:	H	F	G	D	E

Colonel Shaw, Lieutenant-Colonel Hallowell, Adjutant James, seven captains, and twelve lieutenants,—a total of twenty-two officers,—advanced to the assault.

Surgeon Stone and Quartermaster Ritchie were present on the field. Both field officers were dismounted; the band and musicians acted as stretcher-bearers.

To many a gallant man these scenes upon the sands were the last of earth; to the survivors they will be ever present. Away over the sea to the eastward the heavy sea-fog was gathering, the western sky bright with the reflected light, for the sun had set. Far away thunder mingled with the occasional boom of cannon. The gathering host all about, the silent lines stretching away to the rear, the passing of a horseman now and then carrying orders,— all was ominous of the impending onslaught. Far and indistinct in front was the now silent earthwork, seamed, scarred, and ploughed with shot, its flag still waving in defiance.

Among the dark soldiers who were to lead veteran regiments which were equal in drill and discipline to any in the country, there was a lack of their usual lightheartedness, for they realized, partially at least, the dangers they were to encounter. But there was little nervousness and no depression observable. It took but a touch to bring out their irrepressible spirit and humor in the old way. When a cannon-shot from the enemy came toward the line and passed over, a man or two moved nervously, calling out a sharp reproof from Lieutenant-Colonel Hallowell, whom the men still spoke of as "the major." Thereupon one soldier quietly remarked to his comrades, "I guess the major forgets what kind of balls them is!" Another added, thinking of the foe, "I guess they kind of 'spec's we're coming!"

Naturally the officers' thoughts were largely regarding their men. Soon they would know whether the lessons they had taught of soldierly duty would bear good fruit. Would they have cause for exultation or be compelled to sheathe their swords, rather than lead cowards? Unknown to them, the whole question of employing three hundred thousand colored soldiers hung in the balance. But few, however, doubted the result. Wherever a white officer led that night, even to the gun-muzzles and bayonet-points, there, by his side, were black men as brave and steadfast as himself.

At last the formation of the column was nearly perfected. The Sixth Connecticut had taken position in column of companies just in rear of the Fifty-fourth. About this time, Colonel Shaw walked back to Lieutenant-Colonel Hallowell, and said, "I shall go in advance with the National flag. You will keep the State flag with you; it will give the men something to rally round. We shall take the fort or die there! Good-by!"

Presently, General Strong, mounted upon a spirited gray horse, in full uniform, with a yellow handkerchief bound around his neck, rode in front of the Fifty-fourth, accompanied by two aids and two orderlies. He addressed the men; and his words, as given by an officer of the regiment, were: "Boys, I am a Massachusetts man, and I know you will fight for the honor of the State. I am sorry you must go into the fight tired and hungry, but the men in the fort are tired too. There are but three hundred behind those walls, and they have been fighting all day. Don't fire a musket on the way up, but go in and bayonet them at their guns." Calling out the colorbearer, he said, "If this man should fall, who will lift the flag and carry it on?" Colonel Shaw, standing near, took a cigar from between his lips, and said quietly, "I will." The men loudly responded to Colonel Shaw's pledge, while General Strong rode away to give the signal for advancing.

Colonel Shaw calmly walked up and down the line of his regiment. He was clad in a close-fitting staff-officer's jacket, with a silver eagle denoting his rank on each shoulder. His trousers were light blue; a fine narrow silk sash was wound round his waist beneath the jacket. Upon his head was a high felt army hat with cord. Depending from his sword-belt was a field-officer's sword of English manufacture, with the initials of his name worked into the ornamentation of the guard. On his hand was an antique gem set in a ring. In his pocket was a gold watch, marked with his name, attacked to a gold chain. Although he had given certain papers and letters to his friend, Mr. Pierce, he retained his pocket-book, which doubtless contained papers which would establish his identity. His manner, generally reserved before his men, seemed to unbend to them, for he spoke as he had never done before. He said,

"Now I want you to prove yourselves men," and reminded them that the eyes of thousands would look upon the night's work. His bearing was composed and graceful; his cheek had somewhat paled; and the slight twitching of the corners of his mouth plainly showed that the whole cost was counted, and his expressed determination to take the fort or die was to be carried out.

Meanwhile the twilight deepened, as the minutes, drawn out by waiting, passed, before the signal was given. Officers had silently grasped one another's hands, brought their revolvers round to the front, and tightened their sword-belts. The men whispered last injunctions to comrades, and listened for the word of command.

The preparations usual in an assault were not made. There was no provision for cutting away obstructions, filling the ditch, or spiking the guns. No special instructions were given the stormers; no line of skirmishers or covering party was thrown out; no engineers or guides accompanied the column; no artillery-men to serve captured guns; no plan of the work was shown company officers. It was understood that the fort would be assaulted with the bayonet, and that the Fifty-fourth would be closely supported.

While on the sands a few cannon-shots had reached the regiment, one passing between the wings, another over to the right. When the inaction had become almost unendurable, the signal to advance came. Colonel Shaw walked along the front to the centre, and giving the command, "Attention!" the men sprang to their feet. Then came the admonition, "Move in quick time until within a hundred yards of the fort; then double quick, and charge!" A slight pause, followed by the sharp command, "Forward!" and the Fifty-fourth advanced to the storming.

There had been a partial resumption of the bombardment during the formation, but now only an occasional shot was heard. The enemy in Wagner had seen the preparations, knew what was coming, and were awaiting the blow. With Colonel Shaw leading, sword in hand, the long advance over three quarters of a mile of sand had begun, with wings closed up and company officers admonishing their men to preserve the alignment. Guns from Sumter, Sullivan's Island, and James Island, began to play upon the regiment. It was about 7.45 P.M., with darkness coming on rapidly, when the Fifty-fourth moved. With barely room for the formation from the first, the narrowing way between the sand hillocks and the sea soon caused a strong pressure to the right, so that Captains Willard and Emilio on the right of the right companies of their wings were with some of their men forced to march in water up to their knees, at each incoming of the sea.

Moving at quick time, and preserving its formation as well as the difficult ground and narrowing way permitted, the Fifty-fourth was approaching the defile made by the easterly sweep of the marsh. Darkness was rapidly coming on, and each moment became deeper. Soon men on the flanks were compelled to fall behind, for want of room to continue in line. The centre only had a free path, and with eyes strained upon the colonel and the flag, they pressed on toward the work, now only two hundred yards away.

At that moment Wagner became a mound of fire, from which poured a stream of shot and shell. Just a brief lull, and the deafening explosions of cannon were renewed, mingled with the crash and rattle of musketry. A sheet of flame, followed by a running fire, like electric sparks, swept along the parapet, as the Fifty-first North Carolina gave a direct, and the Charleston Battalion a left-oblique, fire on the Fifty-fourth. Their Thirty-first North Carolina had lost heart, and failed to take position in the southeast bastion,—fortunately, too, for had its musketry fire been added to that delivered, it is doubtful whether any Federal troops could have passed the defile.

When this tempest of war came, before which men fell in numbers on every side, the only response the Fifty-fourth made to the deadly challenge was to change step to the double-quick, that it might the sooner close with the foe. There had been no stop, pause, or check at any period of the advance, nor was there now. As the swifter pace was taken, and officers sprang to the fore with waving swords barely seen in the darkness, the men closed the gaps, and with set jaws, panting breath, and bowed heads, charged on.

Wagner's wall, momentarily lit up by cannon-flashes, was still the goal toward which the survivors rushed in sadly diminished numbers. It was now dark, the gloom made more intense by the blinding explosions in the front. This terrible fire which the regiment had just faced, probably caused the greatest number of casualties sustained by the Fifty-fourth in the assault; for nearer the work the men were somewhat sheltered by the high parapet. Every flash showed the ground dotted with men of the regiment, killed or wounded. Great holes, made by the huge shells of the navy or the land batteries, were pitfalls into which the men stumbled or fell.

Colonel Shaw led the regiment to the left toward the curtain of the work, thus passing the southeast bastion, and leaving it to the right hand. From that salient no musketry fire came; and some Fifty-fourth men first entered it, not following the main body by reason of the darkness. As the survivors drew near the work, they encountered the flanking fire delivered from guns in the southwest salient, and the howitzers outside the fort, which swept the trench, where further severe losses were sustained. Nothing but the ditch now separated the stormers and the foe. Down into this they went, through the two or three feet of water therein, and mounted the slope beyond in the teeth of the enemy, some of whom, standing on the crest, fired down on them with depressed pieces. Both flags were planted on the parapet, the national flag carried there and gallantly maintained by the brave Sergt. William H. Carney of Company C.

In the pathway from the defile to the fort many brave men had fallen. Lieutenant-Colonel Hallowell was severely wounded in the groin, Captain Willard in the leg, Adjutant James in the ankle and side, Lieutenant Homans in the shoulder. Lieutenants Smith and Pratt were also wounded. Colonel Shaw had led his regiment from first to last. Gaining the rampart, he stood there for a moment with uplifted sword, shouting, "Forward, Fifty-fourth!" and then fell dead, shot through the heart, besides other wounds.

Not a shot had been fired by the regiment up to this time. As the crest was gained, the crack of revolver-shots was heard, for the officers fired into the surging mass of upturned faces confronting them, lit up redly but a moment by the powder-flashes. Musket-butts and bayonets were freely used on the parapet, where the stormers were gallantly met. The garrison fought with muskets, handspikes, and gun-rammers, the officers striking with their swords, so close were the combatants. Numbers, however, soon told against the Fifty-fourth, for it was tens against hundreds. Outlined against the sky, they were a fair mark for the foe. Men fell every moment during the brief struggle. Some of the wounded crawled down the slope to shelter; others fell headlong into the ditch below.

It was seen from the volume of musketry fire, even before the walls were gained, that the garrison was stronger than had been supposed, and brave in defending the work. The first rush had failed, for those of the Fifty-fourth who reached the parapet were too few in numbers to overcome the garrison, and the supports were not at hand to take full advantage of their first fierce attack.

Repulsed from the crest after the short hand-to-hand struggle, the assailants fell back upon the exterior slope of the rampart. There the men were encouraged to remain by their officers, for by sweeping the top of the parapet with musketry, and firing at those trying to serve the guns, they would greatly aid an advancing force. For a time this was done, but at the cost of more lives. The enemy's fire became more effective as the numbers of the Fifty-fourth diminished. Hand grenades or lighted shells were rolled down the slope, or thrown over into the ditch.

All this time the remaining officers and men of the Fifty-fourth were firing at the hostile figures about the guns, or that they saw spring upon the parapet, fire, and jump away. One brave fellow, with his broken arm lying across his breast, was piling cartridges upon it for Lieutenant Emerson, who, like other officers, was using a musket he had picked up. Another soldier, tired of the enforced combat, climbed the slope to his fate; for in a moment his dead body rolled down again. A particularly severe fire came from the southwest bastion. There a Confederate was observed, who, stripped to the waist, with daring exposure for some time dealt out fatal shots; but at last three eager marksmen fired together, and he fell back into the fort, to appear no more. Capt. J. W. M. Appleton distinguished himself before the curtain. He crawled into an embrasure, and with his pistol prevented the artillery-men from serving the gun. Private George Wilson of Company A had been shot through both shoulders, but refused to go back until he had his captain's permission. While occupied with this faithful soldier, who came to him as he lay in the embrasure, Captain Appleton's attention was distracted, and the gun was fired.

In the fighting upon the slopes of Wagner, Captains Russel and Simpkins were killed or mortally wounded. Captain Pope there received a severe wound in the shoulder.

All these events had taken place in a short period of time. The charge of the Fifty-fourth had been made and repulsed before the arrival of any other troops. Those who had clung to the bloody slopes or were lying in the ditch, hearing fighting going on at their right, realized at last that the expected succor would not reach them where they were. To retire through the enveloping fire was as dangerous and deadly as to advance. Some that night preferred capture to the attempt at escaping; but the larger portion managed to fall back, singly or in squads, beyond the musketry fire of the garrison.

Captain Emilio, the junior of that rank, succeeded to the command of the Fifty-fourth on the field by casualties. After retiring from Wagner to a point where men were encountered singly or in small squads, he determined to rally as many as possible. With the assistance of Lieutenants Grace and Dexter, a large portion of the Fifty-fourth survivors were collected and formed in line, together with a considerable number of white soldiers of various regiments. While thus engaged, the national flag of the Fifty-fourth was brought to Captain Emilio; but as it was useless as a rallying-point in the darkness, it was sent to the rear for safety. Sergeant Carney had bravely brought this flag from Wagner's parapet, at the cost of two grievous wounds. The State color was torn from the staff, the silk was found by the enemy in the moat, while the staff remained with us.

Finding a line of rifle trench unoccupied and no indication that dispositions were being made for holding it, believing that the enemy would attempt a sortie, which was indeed contemplated but not attempted, Captain Emilio there stationed his men, disposed to defend the line. Other men were collected as they appeared. Lieutenant Tucker, slightly wounded, who was among the last to leave the sand hills near the fort, joined this force.

Desultory firing was still going on, and after a time, being informed that some troops were in the open ground, the force, numbering some two hundred, was formed by its commander, and advanced from the rifle trench. It is believed this was the only organized body of rallied men ready and able to support Stevenson's brigade, which alone was prepared after the repulse of the others to resist attack. Presently the Twenty-fourth Massachusetts was encountered; but upon reporting, it was found that support was not required. Marching back to the still deserted trench, that line was again occupied. By midnight firing entirely ceased. About 1 A.M., on the 19th, a mounted officer rode up, inquired what force held the trench, and asked for the commanding officer. Captain Emilio responded, and recognized General Stevenson, who thanked him for the support given the reserve brigade, and his dispositions for holding the line. He was also informed that a regiment would be sent to relieve his men, and shortly after, the Tenth Connecticut arrived for that purpose. When this was done, the white soldiers were formed into detachments by regiments, and sent to find their colors.

The Fifty-fourth men were then marched to the rear, and after proceeding a short distance down the beach, encountered Lieutenants Jewett, Emerson, and Appleton, with some of the men. There the Fifty-fourth bivouacked for the night, under the shelter of the sand-bluffs.

Although the storming column and supports did not move forward with a close formation and promptness in support of the Fifty-fourth, which might have won Wagner that night, their attacks when made were delivered with a gallantry and persistence that made their severe losses the more deplorable and fruitless, by reason of such faulty generalship.

When Strong's brigade advanced, it met the same devastating fire at the defile; but a considerable number of the survivors, mainly of the Sixth Connecticut and Forty-eighth New York, pushed on to the southeast bastion, feebly defended by the Thirty-first North Carolina, and entered, securing a portion of the salient. Farther they could not penetrate against superior numbers. General Strong accompanied his column, and, as always, exhibited the utmost bravery.

General Seymour, learning the failure of Strong's brigade to carry the work, ordered Colonel Putnam to advance his regiments. That officer gallantly led forward his brigade, meeting the same severe fire as he neared the fort. With survivors of the Seventh New Hampshire, he entered the disputed salient, followed by portions of the Sixty-second and Sixty-seventh Ohio. His One Hundredth New York advanced to a point near the work, in the confusion and darkness poured a volley into our own men in the salient, and then retired. It must be understood, however, that all these regiments suffered severe losses; but losses that night do not necessarily indicate effective regimental action. The greatest number of men in the salient at any time hardly equalled a regiment, and were of different organizations. They were fighting in a place unknown to them, holding their ground and repelling attacks, but were incapable of aggressive action. Fighting over traverses and sand-bags, hemmed in by a fire poured across their rear, as well as from the front and flanks, the struggle went on pitilessly for nearly two hours. Vainly were precious lives freely offered up, in heroic attempts to encourage a charge on the flanking guns. The enveloping darkness covered all; and the valiant, seeing how impotent were their efforts, felt like crying with Ajax, "Give us but light, O Jove! and in the light, if thou seest fit, destroy us!"

Every field-officer in the bastion was at last struck down except Major Lewis Butler, Sixty-seventh Ohio. Colonel Putnam had been shot through the head. When all hope of expected support was gone, Major Butler sent out the regimental colors, and gave orders to leave the bastion. There were, according to his account, about one hundred men each of the Sixty-second and Sixty-seventh Ohio, about fifty of the Forty-eighth New York, and some small detachments of other regiments, some with and some without officers. When this force had departed, and the enemy had been re-enforced by the arrival of the Thirty-second Georgia, the wounded, those who feared to encounter the enclosing fire, and those who failed to hear or obey the order for abandonment, were soon surrounded and captured. General Stevenson's brigade had advanced toward the fort, but it was too late, and the men were withdrawn.

Upon the beach in front of the siege line, drunken soldiers of the regular artillery, with swords and pistol-shots, barred the passage of all to the rear. They would listen to no protestations that the regiments were driven back or broken up, and even brutally ordered wounded men to the front. After a time, their muddled senses came to them on seeing the host of arrivals, while the vigorous actions of a few determined officers who were prepared to enforce a free passage, made further opposition perilous.

Thus ended the great assault on Fort Wagner. It was the second and last attempted. The Confederate loss was 181 killed and wounded, including Lieut.-Col. J. C. Simkins, Captains W. H. Ryan, W. T. Tatom, and P. H. Waring, and Lieut. G. W. Thompson, killed. Our loss was 1,515, including 111 officers, and embracing General Seymour wounded, General Strong mortally wounded, and Colonel Putnam (acting brigadier) killed. Of the ten regimental commanders, Colonel Shaw was killed, Col. J. L. Chatfield, Sixth Connecticut, mortally wounded, and five others wounded. Such severe casualties stamp the sanguinary character of the fighting, and mark the assault as one of the fiercest struggles of the war, considering the numbers engaged. This is further evidenced by the fact that the losses exceeded those sustained by our forces in many much better-known actions during the Rebellion,— notably Wilson's Creek, Pea Ridge, Cedar Mountain, Chantilly, Prairie Grove, Pleasant Hills, Sailor's Creek, Jonesborough, Bentonville, and High Bridge, in most of which a much larger Federal force was engaged.

The following is the official report of the part borne by the Fifty-fourth in the assault:—

HEADQUARTERS FIFTY-FOURTH MASS. VOLS.,
MORRIS ISLAND, S.C., Nov. 7, 1863.
BRIG.-GEN. T. SEYMOUR, Commanding U.S. Forces, Morris Island, S.C.

GENERAL,—In answer to your request that I furnish you

with a report of the part taken by the Fifty-fourth Massachusetts Volunteers in the late assault upon Fort Wagner, I have to state:—

During the afternoon of the 18th of July last, the Fifty-fourth Massachusetts Volunteers, Col. R. G. Shaw commanding, landed upon Morris Island and reported at about six o'clock P.M. to Brig.-Gen. G. C. Strong. Colonel Shaw's command present consisted of a lieutenant-colonel of the field, a surgeon, adjutant, and quartermaster of the staff, eight captains and eleven subaltern officers of the line and six hundred enlisted men. General Strong presented himself to the regiment, and informed the men of the contemplated assault upon Fort Wagner, and asked if they would lead it. They answered in the affirmative. The regiment was then formed in column by wing, at a point upon the beach a short distance in the advance of the Beacon house. Col. R. G. Shaw commanded the right wing, and Lieut.-Col. E. N. Hallowell the left.

In this formation, as the dusk of evening came on, the regiment advanced at quick time, leading the column. The enemy opened on us a brisk fire, our pace now gradually increasing till it became a run. Soon canister and musketry began to tell on us. With Colonel Shaw leading, the assault was commenced. Exposed to the direct fire of canister and musketry, and, as the ramparts were mounted, to a like fire on our flanks, the havoc made in our ranks was very great.

Upon leaving the ditch for the parapet, they obstinately contested with the bayonet our advance. Notwithstanding these difficulties, the men succeeded in driving the enemy from most of their guns, many following the enemy into the fort. It was here upon the crest of the parapet that Colonel Shaw fell; here fell Captains Russel and Simpkins; here were also most of the officers wounded. The colors of the regiment reached the crest, and were there fought for by the enemy; the State flag there torn from its staff, but the staff remains with us. Hand grenades were now added to the missiles directed against the men.

The fight raged here for about an hour, when, com

pelled to abandon the fort, the men formed a line about seven hundred yards from the fort, under the command of Capt. Luis F. Emilio,—the ninth captain in the line; the other captains were either killed or wounded. The regiment then held the front until relieved by the Tenth Connecticut at about two o'clock A.M. of the 19th.

The assault was made upon the south face of the fort. So many of the officers behaved with marked coolness and bravery, I cannot mention any above the others. It is due, however, to the following-named enlisted men that they be recorded above their fellows for especial merit:—

Sergt. Robt. J. Simmons...................... Co. B.
  "   William H. Carney.....................   "   C.
Corp. Henry F. Peal..........................   "   F.
Pvt. Geo. Wilson.............................   "   A.

The following is the list of casualties:—

Officers.

Col. R. G. Shaw................................ killed
Lieut.-Col. E. N. Hallowell.................. wounded
Adjt. G. W. James............................   "
Capt. S. Willard.............................   "
  "   C. J. Russel, missing, supposed to be killed
  "   W. H. Simpkins   "   "   "   "   "
  "   Geo. Pope .... wounded
  "   E. L. Jones...........................   "
  "   J. W. M. Appleton ....   "
  "   O. E. Smith..........................   "
1st Lieut. R. H. L. Jewett ....   "
  "   Wm. H. Homans ....   "
2d Lieut. C. E. Tucker......................   "
  "   J. A. Pratt ....   "

Enlisted Men.

Killed 9
Wounded 147

Missing.. <u>100</u>

Total.. 256

I have the honor to be, very respectfully,
Your obedient servant,
E. N. HALLOWELL,
Colonel Commanding Fifty-fourth Massachusetts Volunteers.

Lieutenant Howard, in falling back from the fort, with a few men he had gathered, retired directly down the beach, not encountering the larger part of the regiment. Lieut. T. L. Appleton retired first but a short distance, where, in the sand-hills, he found General Strong with some detachments which he was urging to advance. Lieutenant Appleton moved forward again a short distance, but finding there was no concerted advance, went rearward. Sergeant Swails of Company F was with Captains Simpkins and Russel under the left bastion. They climbed the parapet, and were at once fired upon. Captain Russel fell wounded, and Simpkins asked him if he would be carried off. When he declined, and asked to lie straightened out, Simpkins directed Swails to help him do this, and while kneeling over his friend's head, facing the enemy, was himself hit. Putting his hand to his breast, he fell across Russel, and never spoke or moved again. Swails, who relates this, says he was soon asked by Russel to change his position, that he (Swails) might not draw the Rebel fire on the wounded, and did so. Frank Myers, of Company K, whose arm was shattered, states that he stood under the uplifted arm of Colonel Shaw, while that officer was on the parapet, waving his sword, and crying, "Forward, Fifty-fourth!" He saw the colonel suddenly fall, and was struck himself a moment after. Thomas Burgess, of Company I, makes a similar statement.

Capt. J. W. M. Appleton, at the curtain, hearing firing at last on the right, climbed with Captain Jones and Lieutenant Emerson into the southeast bastion, and joined in the desperate fighting there. Captain Appleton was finally badly wounded, and made his way out with great difficulty, to report the situation in the bastion. Captain Jones was also severely wounded. He fell into the moat, where he remained until assisted rearward by George Remsley of Company C. Lieutenant Emerson in the bastion used the musket he had picked up before the curtain. To protect the wounded lying near he pulled out sand-bags. When a volunteer was wanted to report their situation to some general officer, he offered himself, saying, "I will go, but if I am killed, just tell them I did not run away!" As he was still able to fight, Captain Appleton, who was disabled, went instead. Lieutenant Homans was wounded near the fort, and thought himself mortally hurt, as he was spitting blood, but staggered along until he was met by Lieutenant Dexter, who assisted him to the rear.

Sergt. George E. Stephens of Company B, in a letter to the writer, says,—

"I remember distinctly that when our column had charged the fort, passed the half-filled moat, and mounted to the parapet, many of our men clambered over, and some entered by the large embrasure in which one of the big guns was mounted, the firing substantially ceased there by the beach, and the Rebel musketry fire steadily grew hotter on our left. An officer of our regiment called out, 'Spike that gun!'... Just at the very hottest moment of the struggle, a battalion or regiment charged up to the moat, halted, and did not attempt to cross it and join us, but from their position commenced to fire upon us. I was one of the men who shouted from where I stood, 'Don't fire on us! We are the Fifty-fourth.' I have heard it was a Maine regiment.

... Many of our men will join me in saying that in the early stages of the fight we had possession of the sea end of Battery Wagner. . . . When we reached the Gatling battery drawn up to repel a counter-attack, I remember you were the only commissioned officer present, and you placed us indiscriminately,—that is, without any regard to companies in line,—and proposed to renew the charge. The commanding officer, whom I do not know, ordered us to the flanking rifle-pits, and we then awaited the expected counter-charge the enemy did not make."

Lieutenant Smith, severely wounded, remained on the field until the next day, when he was brought in. Lieutenant Pratt, wounded in two places, concealed himself in the marsh. There he remained many hours, until at last, braving the fire of Rebel pickets, he escaped into our lines. First Sergeant Simmons of Company B was the finest-looking soldier in the Fifty-fourth,—a brave man and of good education. He was wounded and captured. Taken to Charleston, his bearing impressed even his captors. After suffering amputation of the arm, he died there.

Contemporaneous testimony is complete as to the gallant part taken by the Fifty-fourth in the assault. Samuel W. Mason, correspondent of the New York "Herald," on Morris Island, wrote under date of July 19, 1863, of the regiment:—

"I saw them fight at Wagner as none but splendid soldiers, splendidly officered, could fight, dashing through shot and shell, grape, canister, and shrapnel, and showers of bullets, and when they got close enough, fighting with clubbed muskets, and retreating when they did retreat, by command and with choice white troops for company."

Edward L. Pierce, the correspondent of the New York "Tribune," in a letter to Governor Andrew, dated July 22, 1863, wrote,—

"I asked General Strong if he had any testimony in relation to the regiment to be communicated to you. These are his precise words, and I give them to you as I noted them at the time: 'The Fifty-fourth did well and nobly; only the fall of Colonel Shaw prevented them from entering the fort. They moved up as gallantly as any troops could, and with their enthusiasm they deserved a better fate.'"

To the correspondent of the New York "Evening Post" General Strong said that the Fifty-fourth "had no sleep for three nights, no food since morning, and had marched several miles. . . . Under cover of darkness they had stormed the fort, faced a stream of fire, faltered not till the ranks were broken by shot and shell; and in all these severe tests, which would have tried even veteran troops, they fully met my expectations, for many were killed, wounded, or captured on the walls of the fort."

The Confederate commander of Wagner has written,—

"One of the assaulting regiments was composed of negroes (the Fifty-fourth Massachusetts), and to it was assigned the honor of leading the white columns to the charge. It was a dearly purchased compliment. Their colonel (Shaw) was killed upon the parapet, and the regiment almost annihilated, although the Confederates in the darkness could not tell the color of their assailants."

Official reports show, and the same Confederate officer has stated as his impression, that "the greater part of our loss was sustained at the beginning of the assault, and in front of the curtain, although we suffered some additional loss from the troops who gained the bastion," which loss must necessarily have been inflicted by the Fifty-fourth, as it was the leading regiment, and attacked the curtain.

Further Confederate testimony is furnished in a letter of Lieut. Iredell Jones, who writes,—

> "I visited the battery [Fort Wagner] yesterday. The dead and wounded were piled up in a ditch together sometimes fifty in a heap, and they were strewn all over the plain for a distance of three fourths of a mile. They had two [only one, the Fifty-fourth?] negro regiments, and they were slaughtered in every direction. One pile of negroes numbered thirty. Numbers of both white and black were killed on top of our breastworks as well as inside. The negroes fought gallantly, and were headed by as brave a colonel as ever lived. He mounted the breastworks waving his sword, and at the head of his regiment, and he and a negro orderly sergeant fell dead over the inner crest of the works. The negroes were as fine-looking a set as I ever saw,—large, strong, muscular fellows."

Of those reported missing belonging to the Fifty-fourth, some sixty were captured, about twenty of whom were wounded. The remainder were killed. Their capture occasioned one of a number of new and important questions raised for governmental consideration, which it was the fortune of the regiment to present and have decided for the benefit of all other colored soldiers. Before the actions of July 16 and 18, no considerable number of black soldiers had been captured. Under the acts of the Confederate Congress they were outlaws, to be delivered to the State authorities when captured, for trial; and the penalty of servile insurrection was death.

The fate of Captains Russel and Simpkins was also unknown. It was thought possible that they too were captured. Governor Andrew and the friends of the regiment therefore exerted themselves to have the Government throw out its protecting hand over its colored soldiers and their officers in the enemy's hands.

Two sections were at once added to General Orders No. 100 of the War Department, relating to such prisoners, a copy of which was transmitted to the Confederate commissioner, Robert Ould. The first set forth that once a soldier no man was responsible individually for warlike acts; the second, that the law of nations recognized no distinctions of color, and that if the enemy enslaved or sold the captured soldier, as the United States could not enslave, death would be the penalty in retaliation. The President also met the case in point involving the Fifty-fourth prisoners, by issuing the following proclamation:

EXECUTIVE MANSION, WASHINGTON, July 30, 1863.
It is the duty of every government to give protection to its citizens of whatever class, color, or condition, and especially to those who are duly organized as soldiers in the public service. The law of nations and the usages and customs of war, as carried on by civilized powers, permit no distinction as to color in the treatment of prisoners of war as public enemies. To sell or enslave any captured person on account of his color, and for no offence against the laws of war, is a relapse into barbarism and a crime against the civilization of the age. The Government of the United States will give the same protection to all its soldiers; and if the enemy shall sell or enslave any one because of his color, the offence shall be punished by retaliation upon the enemy's prisoners in our hands.

It is therefore ordered that for every soldier of the United States killed in violation of the laws of war, a Rebel soldier shall be executed, and for every one enslaved by the enemy or sold into slavery, a Rebel soldier shall be placed at hard labor on the public works, and continue at such labor until the other shall be released and receive the treatment due a prisoner of war.

ABRAHAM LINCOLN.

By order of the Secretary of War,
E. D. TOWNSEND, *Assistant Adjutant-General.*

Such prompt and vigorous enunciations had a salutary effect; and the enemy did not proceed to extremities. But the Fifty-fourth men were demanded by Governor Bonham, of South Carolina, from the military authorities. A test case was made; and Sergt. Walter A. Jeffries of Company H, and Corp. Charles Hardy of Company B, were actually tried for their lives. They were successfully defended by the ablest efforts of one of the most brilliant of Southern advocates, the Union-loving and noble Nelson Mitchell, of Charleston, who, with a courage rarely equalled, fearlessly assumed the self-imposed task. Thenceforth never noticed, this devoted man died a few months after in Charleston, neglected and in want, because of this and other loyal acts. For months no list could be obtained of the Fifty-fourth prisoners, the enemy absolutely refusing information. After long imprisonment in Charleston jail, they were taken to Florence stockade, and were finally released in the spring of 1865. The best attainable information shows that the survivors then numbered some twenty-seven, some of whom rejoined the regiment, while others were discharged from parole camps or hospitals.

Colonel Shaw's fate was soon ascertained from those who saw him fall, and in a day or two it was learned from the enemy that his body had been found, identified, and, on July 19, buried with a number of his colored soldiers. The most circumstantial account relating thereto is contained in a letter to the writer from Capt. H. W. Hendricks, a Confederate officer who was present at the time, dated

from Charleston, S.C., June 29, 1882; and the following
extracts are made therefrom:—

> "... Colonel Shaw fell on the left of our flagstaff about ten
> yards towards the river, near the bombproof immediately
> on our works, with a number of his officers and men. He
> was instantly killed, and fell outside of our works. The
> morning following the battle his body was carried through
> our lines; and I noticed that he was stripped of all his
> clothing save under-vest and drawers. This desecration of
> the dead we endeavored to provide against; but at that
> time—the incipiency of the Rebellion—our men were so
> frenzied that it was next to impossible to guard against it;
> this desecration, however, was almost exclusively partic-
> ipated in by the more desperate and lower class of our
> troops. Colonel Shaw's body was brought in from the sally-
> port on the Confederate right, and conveyed across the
> parade-ground into the bombproof by four of our men of
> the burial party. Soon after, his body was carried out *via*
> the sally-port on the left river-front, and conveyed across
> the front of our works, and there buried.... His watch and
> chain were robbed from his body by a private in my com-
> pany, by name Charles Blake. I think he had other personal
> property of Colonel Shaw.... Blake, with other members
> of my company, jumped our works at night after hostilities
> had ceased, and robbed the dead.... Colonel Shaw was the
> only officer buried with the colored troops...."

Such disposal of the remains of an officer of Colonel Shaw's
rank, when his friends were almost within call, was so
unusual and cruel that there seemed good ground for the
belief that the disposition made was so specially directed,
as a premeditated indignity for having dared to lead colored
troops. When known throughout the North, it excited general indignation, and fostered bitterness. Though recognizing the fitness of his resting-place, where in death he
was not separated from the men he was in life not ashamed

to lead, the act was universally condemned. It was even specifically stated in a letter which appeared in the "Army and Navy Journal," of New York City, written by Asst.-Surg. John T. Luck, U.S.N., who was captured while engaged in assisting our wounded during the morning of July 19, that Gen. Johnson Hagood, who had succeeded General Taliaferro in command of Battery Wagner that morning, was responsible for the deed. The following is extracted from that letter:—

"... While being conducted into the fort, I saw Colonel Shaw of the Fifty-four Massachusetts (colored) Regiment lying dead upon the ground just outside the parapet. A stalwart negro man had fallen near him. The Rebels said the negro was a color sergeant. The colonel had been killed by a rifle-shot through the chest, though he had received other wounds. Brigadier-General Hagood, commanding the Rebel forces, said to me: 'I knew Colonel Shaw before the war, and then esteemed him. Had he been in command of white troops, I should have given him an honorable burial; as it is, I shall bury him in the common trench with the negroes that fell with him.' The burial party were then at work; and no doubt Colonel Shaw was buried just beyond the ditch of the fort in the trench where I saw our dead indiscriminately thrown. Two days afterwards a Rebel surgeon (Dr. Dawson, of Charleston, S.C., I think) told me that Hagood had carried out his threat."

Assistant-Surgeon Luck's statement is, however, contradicted by General Hagood; for having requested information upon the matter, the writer, in December, 1885, received from Gen. Samuel Jones, of Washington, a copy of a letter written by Gen. Johnson Hagood to Col. T. W. Higginson, of Cambridge, Mass., dated Sept. 21, 1881. General Hagood quotes from Colonel Higginson's letter of inquiry relative to Colonel Shaw's burial, the conversation which Assistant-Surgeon Luck alleges to have had with him at Battery Wagner about the disposition of Colonel Shaw's body, as set forth in the extract given from Assistant-Surgeon Luck's letter, and then gives his (General Hagood's) account of the meeting with Assistant-Surgeon Luck as follows, the italics being those of the general:—

"On the day after the night assault and while the burial parties of both sides were at work on the field, a chain of sentinels dividing them, a person was brought to me where I was engaged within the battery in repairing damages done to the work. The guard said he had been found wandering within our lines, engaged apparently in nothing except making observations. The man claimed to be a naval surgeon belonging to gunboat 'Pawnee;' and after asking him some questions about the damages sustained by that vessel a few days before in the Stono River from an encounter with a field battery on its banks, I informed him that he would be sent up to Charleston for such disposition as General Beauregard deemed proper. I do not recall the name of this person, and have not heard of him since, but he must be the Dr. Leech [Luck?] of whom you speak. *I have no recollection of other conversation with him than that given above*. He has, however, certainly reported me incorrectly in one particular. *I never saw or heard of Colonel Shaw until his body was pointed out to me that morning, and his name and rank mentioned*.... I simply give my recollection in reply to his statement. As he has confounded what he probably heard from others within the battery of their previous knowledge of Colonel Shaw, he may at the distance of time at which he spoke have had his recollection of his interview with me confounded in other respects.

"You further ask if a request from General Terry for Colonel Shaw's body was refused the day after the battle. I answer distinctly, No. At the written request of General Gillmore, I, as commander of the battery, met General Vogdes (not Terry), on a flag of truce on the 22d. Upon this flag an exchange of wounded prisoners was arranged, and Colonel Putnam's body was asked for and delivered. Colonel Shaw's body was not asked for then or at any other time to my knowledge.... *No special order was ever issued by me, verbally or otherwise, in regard to the burial of Colonel Shaw or any other officer or man at Wagner.* The only order was a verbal one to bury all the dead in trenches as speedily as possible, on account of the heat; and as far as I knew then, or have reason to believe now, each officer was buried where he fell, with the men who surrounded him. It thus occurred that Colonel Shaw, commanding negroes, was buried with negroes."

These extracts from the letters of Assistant-Surgeon Luck and General Hagood are submitted to the reader with the single suggestion that what is said about Colonel Shaw's body being brought into Fort Wagner, contained in Captain Hendricks's letter, should be borne in mind while reading the latter portion of the extracts from General Hagood's letter.

But how far General Hagood may be held responsible for the lack of generous and Christian offices to the remains of Colonel Shaw, his family and comrades, is another matter. And the writer submits that these faults of omission are grave; that the acknowledged bravery of Colonel Shaw in life, and his appearance even in death, when, as General Hagood acknowledges, "his body was pointed out to me that morning," should have secured him a fitting sepulture, or the tender of his body to his friends. This burial of Colonel Shaw, premeditated and exceptional, was without question intended as an ignominy. It served to crown the sacrifices of that young life, so short and eventful, and to place his name high on the roll of martyrs and leaders of the Civil War.

Colonel Shaw's sword was found during the war in a

house in Virginia, and restored to his family. His silk sash was purchased in Battery Wagner from a private soldier, by A. W. Muckenfuss, a Confederate officer, who, many years after, generously sent it North to Mr. S. D. Gilbert, of Boston, for restoration to the Shaw family. Only these two articles have been recovered, so far as known.

No effort was made to find Colonel Shaw's grave when our forces occupied the ground. This was in compliance with the request contained in the following letter:—

NEW YORK, Aug. 24, 1863.

BRIGADIER-GENERAL GILLMORE, Commanding Department of the South.

SIR,—I take the liberty to address you because I am informed that efforts are to be made to recover the body of my son, Colonel Shaw of the Fifty-fourth Massachusetts Regiment, which was buried at Fort Wagner. My object in writing is to say that such efforts are not authorized by me or any of my family, and that they are not approved by us. We hold that a soldier's most appropriate burial-place is on the field where he has fallen. I shall therefore be much obliged, General, if in case the matter is brought to your cognizance, you will forbid the desecration of my son's grave, and prevent the disturbance of his remains or those buried with him. With most earnest wishes for your success, I am, sir, with respect and esteem,

Your obedient servant,

FRANCIS GEORGE SHAW.

Captains Russel and Simpkins were doubtless interred with other white soldiers, after their bodies had been robbed of all evidences of their rank during the hours of darkness.

After all firing had ceased, about midnight, Brig.-Gen. Thomas G. Stevenson, commanding the front lines, ordered two companies of the Ninety-seventh Pennsylvania, under Lieutenant-Colonel Duer, to advance from the abatis as skirmishers toward Wagner, followed by four companies of the Ninety-seventh, without arms, under Captain Price, to rescue the wounded. General Stevenson saw to this service personally, and gave special instructions to rescue as many as possible of the Fifty-fourth, saying, "You know how much harder they will fare at the hands of the enemy than white men." The rescuing party, with great gallantry and enterprise, pushed the search clear up to the slopes of Wagner, crawling along the ground, and listening for the moans that indicated the subjects of their mission. When found, the wounded were quietly dragged to points where they could be taken back on stretchers in safety. This work was continued until daylight, and many men gathered in by the Ninety-seventh; among them was Lieutenant Smith of the Fifty-fourth. It was a noble work fearlessly done.

Throughout the assault and succeeding night, Quartermaster Ritchie was active and efficient in rendering help to the wounded of the regiment and endeavoring to ascertain the fate of Colonel Shaw and other officers. Surgeon Stone skilfully aided all requiring his services, sending the severely wounded men and officers from temporary hospitals to the steamer "Alice Price."

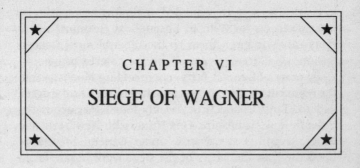

CHAPTER VI

SIEGE OF WAGNER

EARLY ON THE MORNING of July 19, the men of the Fifty-fourth were aroused, and the regiment marched down the beach, making camp near the southern front of the island at a point where the higher hills give way to a low stretch of sand bordering the inlet. On this spot the regiment remained during its first term of service, at Morris Island.

That day was the saddest in the history of the Fifty-fourth, for the depleted ranks bore silent witness to the severe losses of the previous day. Men who had wandered to other points during the night continued to join their comrades until some four hundred men were present. A number were without arms, which had either been destroyed or damaged in their hands by shot and shell, or were thrown away in the effort to save life. The officers present for duty were Captain Emilio, commanding, Surgeon Stone, Quartermaster Ritchie, and Lieutenants T. W. Appleton, Grace, Dexter, Jewett, Emerson, Reid, Tucker, Johnston, Howard, and Higginson.

Some fifty men, slightly wounded, were being treated

111

in camp. The severely wounded, including seven officers, were taken on the 19th to hospitals at Beaufort, where every care was given them by the medical men, General Saxton, his officers, civilians, and the colored people.

By order of General Terry, commanding Morris Island, the regiment on the 19th was attached to the Third Brigade with the Tenth Connecticut, Twenty-fourth Massachusetts, Seventh New Hampshire, One Hundredth New York, and Ninety-seventh Pennsylvania, under General Stevenson. Upon the 20th the labors of the siege work began, for in the morning the first detail was furnished. Late in the afternoon the commanding officer received orders to take the Fifty-fourth to the front for grand-guard duty. He reported with all the men in camp—some three hundred— and was placed at the Beacon house, supporting the Third New Hampshire and Ninety-seventh Pennsylvania. There was no firing of consequence that night. In the morning the Fifty-fourth was moved forward into the trenches.

Capt. D. A. Partridge, left sick in Massachusetts, joined July 21, and, as senior officer, assumed command.

Preparations were made for a bombardment of Sumter as well as for the siege of Wagner. Work began on the artillery line of July 18, that night, for the first parallel, 1,350 yards from Wagner. When completed, it mounted eight siege and field guns, ten mortars, and three Requa rifle batteries. July 23, the second parallel was established some four hundred yards in front of the first. Vincent's Creek on its left was obstructed with floating booms. On its right was the "Surf Battery," armed with field-pieces. This parallel was made strong for defence for the purpose of constructing in its rear the "Left Batteries" against Sumter. It mounted twenty-one light pieces for defence and three thirty-pounder Parrotts and one Wiard rifle. The two parallels were connected by zigzag approaches to protect passing troops. In the construction of these works and the transportation of siege material, ordnance, and quartermaster's stores, the Fifty-fourth was engaged, in common with all the troops on the island, furnishing large details. So many men were called for that but a small camp guard could be maintained, and at times noncommissioned officers volunteered to stand on post.

Col. M. S. Littlefield, Fourth South Carolina Colored, on July 24, was temporarily assigned to command the Fifty-fourth. The colonel's own regiment numbered but a few score of men, and this appointment seemed as if given to secure him command commensurate with the rank he held. It gave rise to much criticism in Massachusetts as well as in the regiment, for it was made contrary to custom and without the knowledge of Governor Andrew. Though silently dissatisfied, the officers rendered him cheerful service.

Anticipating a bombardment of Sumter, the enemy were busy strengthening the gorge or south wall with both cotton-bales and sand-bags. A partial disarmament of the fort was being effected. Wagner was kept in repair by constant labor at night. To strengthen their circle of batteries the enemy were busy upon new works on James Island. About 10 A.M., on the 24th, the Confederate steamer "Alice" ran down and was met by the "Cosmopolitan," when thirty-eight Confederates were given up, and we received one hundred and five wounded, including three officers. There was complaint by our men that the Confederates had neglected their wounds, of the unskillful surgical treatment received, and that unnecessary amputations were suffered. From Col. Edward C. Anderson it was ascertained that the Fifty-fourth's prisoners would not be given up, and Colonel Shaw's death was confirmed.

Battery Simkins on James Island opened against our trenches for the first time on the 25th. For the first time also sharpshooters of the enemy fired on our working parties with long-range rifles. Orders came on the 26th that, owing to the few officers and lack of arms, the Fifty-fourth should only furnish fatigue details.

Quartermaster Ritchie, who was sent to Hilton Head, returned on the 29th with the officers, men, and camp equipage from St. Helena, and tents were put up the succeeding day. Some six hundred men were then present with the colors, including the sick. The number of sick in camp was very large, owing to the severe work and terrible heat. About nineteen hundred were reported on August 1 in the whole command. The sight of so many pale, enfeebled men about the hospitals and company streets was dispiriting. As an offset, some of those who had recovered from wounds returned, and Brig.-Gen. Edward A. Wild's brigade of the First North Carolina and Fifty-fifth Massachusetts, both colored, arrived and camped on Folly Island.

Mr. De Mortie, the regimental sutler, about this time brought a supply of goods. After August 2 the details were somewhat smaller, as the colored brigade on Folly Island began to send over working parties. But calls were filled from the regiment daily for work about the landing and the front. Two men from each company reported as sharpshooters in conjunction with those from other regiments.

The famous battery known as the "Swamp Angel" was begun August 4, and built under direction of Col. E. W. Serrell, First New York Engineers, and was situated in the marsh between Morris and James Islands. It was constructed upon a foundation of timber, with sand-bags filled upon Morris Island and taken out in boats. A two-hundred-pounder Parrott gun was lightered out to the work at night with great difficulty. Its fire reached Charleston, a distance of 8,800 yards. This gun burst after the first few discharges. Later, two mortars were mounted in the work in place of the gun. Capt. Lewis S. Payne, One Hundredth New York, the most daring scout of our forces, at night, August 3, while at Payne's dock, was captured with a few men.

August 5 the men were informed that the Government was ready to pay them $10 per month, less $3 deducted for clothing. The offer was refused, although many had suffering families. About this time a number of men were detached, or detailed, as clerks, butchers, and as hands on the steamers "Escort" and "Planter." Work was begun on the third parallel within four hundred yards of Wagner on the night of the 9th. When completed, it was one hundred yards in length, as the island narrowed. Water was struck at a slight depth. The weather was excessively hot, and flies and sand-fleas tormenting. Only sea-bathing and cooler nights made living endurable. The Fifty-fourth was excused from turning out at reveille in consequence of excessive work, for we were daily furnishing parties reporting to Lieut. P. S. Michie, United States Engineers, at the Left Batteries, and to Colonel Serrell at the "Lookout."

Fancied security of the Fifty-fourth camp so far from the front was rudely dispelled at dark on August 13 by a shell from James Island bursting near Surgeon Stone's tent. These unpleasant visits were not frequent, seemingly being efforts of the enemy to try the extreme range of their guns. Reinforcements, consisting of Gen. George H. Gordon's division from the Eleventh Corps, arrived on the 13th and landed on the 15th upon Folly Island. No rain fell from July 18 until August 13, which was favorable for the siege work, as the sand handled was dry and light. This dryness, however, rendered it easily displaced by the wind, requiring constant labor in re-covering magazines, bomb-proofs, and the slopes. The air too was full of the gritty particles, blinding the men and covering everything in camp.

By this date twelve batteries were nearly ready for action, mounting in all twenty-eight heavy rifles, from thirty to three hundred pounders, besides twelve ten-inch mortars. Those for breaching Sumter were at an average distance of 3,900 yards. Detachments from the First United States Artillery, Third Rhode Island Artillery, One Hundredth New York, Seventh Connecticut, Eleventh Maine, and the fleet, served the guns. These works had been completed under fire from Sumter, Gregg, Wagner, and the James Island batteries, as well as the missiles of sharp-shooters. Most of the work had been done at night. Day and night heavy guard details lay in the trenches to repel attack. The labor of transporting the heavy guns to the front was very great, as the sinking of the sling-carts deep into the sand made progress slow. Tons of powder, shot, and shell had been brought up, and stored in the service-magazines. It was hoped by General Gillmore that the demolition of Sumter would necessitate the abandonment of Morris Island, for that accomplished, the enemy could be prevented from further relief of the Morris Island garrison. Sumter was then commanded by Col. Alfred Rhett, First South Carolina Artillery; and the garrison was of his regiment. In all this work preparatory to breaching Sumter the Fifty-fourth had borne more than its share of labor, for it was exclusively employed on fatigue duty, which was not the case with the white troops. There had been no time for drill or discipline. Every moment in camp was needed to rest the exhausted men and officers. The faces and forms of all showed plainly at what cost this labor was done. Clothes were in rags, shoes worn out, and haversacks full of holes. On the 16th the medical staff was increased by the arrival of Asst.-Surg. G. M. Pease. Lieut. Charles Silva, Fourth South Carolina (colored), was detached to the Fifty-fourth on the 21st, doing duty until November 6.

Shortly after daybreak, August 17, the first bombardment of Sumter began from the land batteries, the navy soon joining in action. The fire of certain guns was directed against Wagner and Gregg. Capt. J. M. Wampler, the engineer officer at Wagner, and Capt. George W. Rodgers and Paymaster Woodbury of the monitor "Catskill" were killed. Sumter was pierced time and again until the walls looked like a honeycomb. All the guns on the northwest face were disabled, besides seven others. A heavy gale came on the 18th, causing a sand-storm on the island and seriously interfering with gun practice. Wagner and Gregg replied slowly. Lieut. Henry Holbrook, Third Rhode Island Heavy Artillery, was mortally wounded by a shell.

By premature explosion of one of our shells, Lieut. A. F. Webb, Fortieth Massachusetts, was killed and several men wounded at night on the 19th. The water stood in some of the trenches a foot and a half deep. Our sap was run from the left of the third parallel that morning. The One Hundredth New York, Eighty-fifth Pennsylvania, and Third New Hampshire were detailed as the guard of the advance trenches. An event of the 20th was the firing for the first time of the great three-hundred-pounder Parrott. It broke down three sling-carts, and required a total of 2,500 days' labor before it was mounted. While in transit it was only moved at night, and covered with a tarpaulin and grass during the daytime. The enemy fired one hundred and sixteen shots at the Swamp Angel from James Island, but only one struck. Sumter's flag was shot away twice on the 20th. All the guns on the south face were disabled. Heavy fire from land and sea continued on the 21st, and Sumter suffered terribly.

A letter from Gillmore to Beauregard was sent on the 21st, demanding the surrender of Morris Island and Sumter, under penalty, if not complied with, of the city being shelled. The latter replied, threatening retaliation. Our fourth parallel was opened that night 350 yards from Wagner, and the One Hundredth New York unsuccessfully attempted to drive the enemy's pickets from a small ridge two hundred yards in front of Wagner. The Swamp Angel opened on Charleston at 1:30 A.M. on the 22d. By one shell a small fire was started there. Many non-combatants left the city. Wagner now daily gave a sharp fire on our advanced works to delay progress. The "New Ironsides" as often engaged that work with great effect. Late on the 22d a truce boat came from Charleston, causing firing to be temporarily suspended.

Although almost daily the Fifty-fourth had more or less men at the front, it had suffered no casualties. The men were employed at this period in throwing up parapets, enlarging the trenches, covering the slopes, turfing the batteries, filling sand-bags, and other labors incident to the operations. In the daytime two men were stationed on higher points to watch the enemy's batteries. Whenever a puff of smoke was seen these "lookouts" called loudly, "Cover!" adding the name by which that particular battery was known. Instantly the workers dropped shovels and tools, jumped into the trench, and, close-covered, waited the coming of the shot or shell, which having exploded, passed, or struck, the work was again resumed. Some of the newer batteries of the enemy were known by peculiar or characteristic names, as "Bull in the Woods," "Mud Digger," and "Peanut Battery." At night the men worked better, for the shells could be seen by reason of the burning fuses, and their direction taken; unless coming in the direction of the toilers, the work went on. Becoming accustomed to their exposure, in a short time this "dodging shells" was reduced almost to a scientific calculation by the men. Most of all they dreaded mortar-shells, which, describing a curved course in the sky, poised for a moment apparently, then, bursting, dropped their fragments from directly overhead. Bomb or splinter proofs alone protected the men from such missiles, but most of the work was in open trenches. Occasionally solid shot were thrown, which at times could be distinctly seen bounding over the sand-hills, or burying themselves in the parapets.

Our batteries and the navy were still beating down the walls of Sumter on the 23d, their shots sweeping through it. That day Colonel Rhett, the commander, and four other officers were there wounded. With Sumter in ruins, the breaching fire ceased that evening, and General Gillmore reported that he "considered the fort no longer a fit work from which to use artillery." He then deemed his part of the work against Charleston accomplished, and expected that the navy would run past the batteries into the harbor. Admiral Dahlgren and the Navy Department thought otherwise, declining to risk the vessels in the attempt.

Captain Partridge about August 23 applied for sick leave and shortly went north. In consequence Captain Emilio again became the senior officer and was at times in charge of the regiment until the middle of October. On the 23d

Rare photograph of Sergeant William H.
Carney with the flag he saved at Fort Wagner, July 18, 1863.
(U.S. Army Military History Institute)

the brigade was reviewed on the beach by General Gillmore, accompanied by General Terry. The latter compli-
mented the Fifty-fourth on its appearance. That evening
Captain Emilio and Lieutenant Higginson took one
hundred and fifty men for grand guard, reporting to Col.
Jos. R. Hawley, Seventh Connecticut, field-officer of the
trenches. This was the first detail other than fatigue since
July 21. The detachment relieved troops in the second
parallel. During the night it was very stormy, the rain
standing in pools in the trenches. But few shots were fired.
Charleston's bells could be heard when all was still. At
midnight the Swamp Angel again opened on the city. About
10 A.M., on the 24th, Wagner and Johnson both opened
on us, the former with grape and canister sweeping the
advanced works. In the camp, by reason of rain and high
tides, the water was several inches deep in the tents on
lowest ground. A new brigade—the Fourth—was formed
on the 24th, composed of the Second South Carolina, Fifty-
fourth Massachusetts, and Third United States Colored
Troops (the latter a new regiment from the north), under
Colonel Montgomery.

About dark on the 25th a force was again advanced
against the enemy's picket, but was repulsed. It was found
that a determined effort must be made to carry the sand
ridge crowned by the enemy's rifle-pits. Just before dark
the next day, therefore, a concentrated fire was maintained
against this position for some time. Col. F. A. Osborn,
Twenty-fourth Massachusetts, with his regiment, supported by the Third New Hampshire, Capt. Jas. F. Randlett,
then advanced and gallantly took the line in an instant,
the enemy only having time to deliver one volley. They
captured sixty-seven men of the Sixty-first North Carolina.
Cover was soon made, a task in which the prisoners assisted

to insure their own safety. The Twenty-fourth lost Lieut. Jas. A. Perkins and two enlisted men killed, and five wounded. Upon this ridge, two hundred yards from Wagner, the fifth parallel was immediately opened. Beyond it the works, when constructed, were a succession of short zigzags because of the narrow breadth of the island and the flanking and near fire of the Confederates. Our fire was being more directed at Wagner, which forced its garrison to close their embrasures in the daytime. It had also become more difficult to send their customary relieving force every third day to Morris Island. Fire upon us from the James Island batteries on the left became very troublesome, occasioning numerous casualties. Our own mortar-shells, on the 27th, in the evening killed seven men, and wounded two of the Eighty-fifth Pennsylvania.

That night there was a severe thunder-storm drenching everything in camp and leaving pools of water in the tents. A warm drying sun came out on the 28th. In the evening there was some disturbance, soon suppressed, in consequence of ill feeling toward the regimental sutler. In the approaches work was slow by reason of the high tides and rain. Moonlight nights interfered also, disclosing our working parties to the enemy. Colonel Montgomery, commanding the brigade, on the 29th established his headquarters near the right of our camp. It was learned that a list of prisoners recently received from the enemy contained no names of Fifty-fourth men. On the 30th Lieut.-Col. Henry A. Purviance, Eighty-fifth Pennsylvania, was killed by the premature explosion of one of our own shells. The enemy's steamer "Sumter," returning from Morris Island early on the 31st with six hundred officers and men, was fired into by Fort Moultrie, and four men were killed or drowned.

With our capture of the ridge on the 26th the last natural cover was attained. Beyond for two hundred yards stretched a strip of sand over which the besiegers must advance. It seemed impossible to progress far, as each attempt to do so resulted in severe losses. Every detail at the front maintained its position only at the cost of life. So numerous were the dead at this period of the siege that at almost any hour throughout the day the sound of funeral music could be heard in the camps. Such was the depressing effect upon the men that finally orders were issued to dispense with music at burials. The troops were dispirited by such losses without adequate results. That the strain was great was manifested by an enormous sick list. It was the opinion of experienced officers that the losses by casualties and sickness were greater than might be expected from another assault.

Success or defeat seemed to hang in the balance. Under no greater difficulties and losses many a siege had been raised. General Gillmore, however, was equal to the emergency. He ordered the fifth parallel enlarged and strengthened, the cover increased, and a line of rifle trench run in front of it. New positions were constructed for the sharpshooters. All his light mortars were moved to the front, and his guns trained on Wagner. A powerful calcium light was arranged to illumine the enemy's work, that our fire might be continuous and effective. Changes were also made in the regiments furnishing permanent details in the trenches and advanced works, and an important part, requiring courage and constancy, was now assigned to our regiment. It is indicated in the following order:—

HEADQUARTERS U.S. FORCES,
MORRIS ISLAND, S.C., Aug. 31, 1863.
Special Orders No. 131.

II. The Fifty-fourth Massachusetts Volunteers, Col.
M. S. Littlefield, Fourth South Carolina Volunteers, commanding, are hereby detailed for special duty in the
trenches under the direction of Maj. T. B. Brooks, A.D.C.
and Assistant Engineer. The whole of the available force
of the regiment will be divided into four equal reliefs,
which will relieve each other at intervals of eight hours
each. The first relief will report to Major Brooks at the
second parallel at 8 A.M. this day. No other details will be
made from the regiment until further orders.

By order of
BRIG.-GEN. A. H. TERRY.

ADRIAN TERRY,
Captain, and Assistant Adjutant-General.

Major Brooks, in his journal of the siege under date of
August 31, thus writes,—

"The Third United States Colored Troops, who have been
on fatigue duty in the advance trenches since the 20th
inst., were relieved to-day by the Fifty-fourth Massachusetts Volunteers (colored), it being desirable to have older
troops for the important and hazardous duty required at
this period."

Throughout the whole siege the First New York Engineers held the post of honor. Their sapping brigades took
the lead in the advance trench opening the ground, followed by fatigue details which widened the cut and threw
up the enlarged cover. These workers were without arms,
but were supported by the guard of the trenches. Upon
this fatigue work with the engineers, the Fifty-fourth at
once engaged. During the night of the 31st work went on
rapidly, as the enemy fired but little. Out of a detail of

forty men from the One Hundred and Fourth Pennsylvania, one was killed and six were wounded. One of the guard was killed by a torpedo. A man of Company K, of our regiment, was mortally wounded that night.

Early on September 1 our land batteries opened on Sumter, and the monitors on Wagner. Four arches in the north face of Sumter with platforms and guns were carried away. Lieut. P. S. Michie, United States Engineers, was temporarily in charge of the advance works on the right. Much work was done in strengthening the parapets and revetting the slopes. Our Fifty fourth detail went out under Lieutenant Higginson that morning, and had one man wounded. Rev. Samuel Harrison, of Pittsfield, Mass., commissioned chaplain of the regiment, arrived that day.

September 2 the land batteries were throwing some few shots at Sumter and more at Wagner. Capt. Jos. Walker, First New York Engineers, started the sap at 7 P.M. in a new direction under heavy fire. Considering that the trench was but eighty yards from Wagner, good progress was made. The sap-roller could not be used, because of torpedoes planted thereabout. Our fire was concentrated upon Wagner on the 3d, to protect sapping. But little success resulted, for the enemy's sharpshooters on the left enfiladed our trench at from one hundred to three hundred yards. At this time the narrowest development in the whole approach was encountered,—but twenty-five yards; and the least depth of sand,—but two feet. Everywhere torpedoes were found planted, arranged with delicate explosive mechanism. Arrangements were made to use a calcium light at night. From August 19 to this date, when the three regiments serving as guards of the trenches were relieved by fresher troops, their loss aggregated ten per cent of their whole force, mainly from artillery fire.

On the night of the 3d, Wagner fired steadily, and the James Island batteries now and then. Our detail at the front had George Vanderpool killed and Alexander Hunter of the same company—H—wounded. Throughout the 4th we fired at Wagner, and in the afternoon received its last shot in daylight. Captain Walker ran the sap twenty-five feet in the morning before he was compelled to cease.

When the south end of Morris Island was captured, Maj. O. S. Sanford, Seventh Connecticut, was placed in charge of two hundred men to act as "boat infantry." From their camp on the creek, near the Left Batteries, details from this force were sent out in boats carrying six oarsmen and six armed men each. They scoured and patrolled the waters about Morris Island. Throughout the whole siege of Charleston this boat infantry was kept up, under various commanders. It was thought that could Gregg be first taken, Wagner's garrison might be captured entire; and an attempt to do so was arranged for the night of September 4. Details for the enterprise, which was to be a surprise, were made from four regiments under command of Major Sanford. The admiral was to send boats with howitzers as support. When all was ready, the boats started toward Gregg. Nearing that work, several musketshots were heard. A navy-boat had fired into and captured a barge of the enemy with Maj. F. F. Warley, a surgeon, and ten men. This firing aroused Gregg's garrison; our boats were discovered and fired upon. Thus the surprise was a failure, and the attack given up.

Wagner was now *in extremis,* and the garrison enduring indescribable misery. A pen picture of the state of things there is given by a Southerner as follows:—

"Each day, often from early dawn, the 'New Ironsides' or
the monitors, sometimes all together, steamed up and
delivered their terrific fire, shaking the fort to its centre.
The noiseless Cohorn shells, falling vertically, searched
out the secret recesses, almost invariably claiming victims.
The burning sun of a Southern summer, its heat intensified
by the reflection of the white sand, scorched and blistered
the unprotected garrison, or the more welcome rain and
storm wet them to the skin. An intolerable stench from
the unearthed dead of the previous conflict, the carcasses
of cavalry horses lying where they fell in the rear, and
barrels of putrid meat thrown out on the beach sickened
the defenders. A large and brilliantly colored fly, attracted
by the feast and unseen before, inflicted wounds more
painful though less dangerous than the shot of the enemy.
Water was scarcer than whiskey. The food, however good
when it started for its destination, by exposure, first, on
the wharf in Charleston, then on the beach at Cumming's
Point, being often forty-eight hours *in transitu,* was unfit
to eat. The unventilated bombproofs, filled with smoke of
lamps and smell of blood, were intolerable, so that one
endured the risk of shot and shell rather than seek their
shelter. The incessant din of its own artillery, as well as
the bursting shell of the foe, prevented sleep...."

General Beauregard on September 4 ordered Sumter's
garrison reduced to one company of artillery and two of
infantry under Maj. Stephen Elliott. Early on the 5th the
land batteries, "Ironsides," and two monitors opened a
terrific bombardment on Wagner which lasted forty-two
hours. Under its protection our sap progressed in safety.
Wagner dared not show a man, while the approaches were
so close that the more distant batteries of the enemy feared
to injure their own men. Our working parties moved about
freely. Captain Walker ran some one hundred and fifty
yards of sap; and by noon the flag, planted at the head of

the trench to apprise the naval vessels of our position, was within one hundred yards of the fort. The Fifty-fourth detail at work there on this day had Corp. Aaron Spencer of Company A mortally wounded by one of our own shells, and Private Chas. Van Allen of the same company killed. Gregg's capture was again attempted that night by Major Sanford's command. When the boats approached near, some musket-shots were exchanged; and as the defenders were alert, we again retired with slight loss.

Daylight dawned upon the last day of Wagner's memorable siege on September 6. The work was swept by our searching fire from land and water, before which its traverses were hurled down in avalanches covering the entrances to magazines and bombproofs. Gregg was also heavily bombarded. As on the previous day our sappers worked rapidly and exposed themselves with impunity. The greatest danger was from our own shells, by which one man was wounded. Lieutenant McGuire, U.S.A., was in charge a part of the day. He caused the trenches to be prepared for holding a large number of troops, with means for easy egress to the front. Late that evening General Gillmore issued orders for an assault at nine o'clock the next morning, the hour of low tide, by three storming columns under General Terry, with proper reserves. Artillery fire was to be kept up until the stormers mounted the parapet. At night the gallant Captain Walker, who was assisted by Captain Pratt, Fifty-fifth Massachusetts, observed that the enemy's sharpshooters fired but scatteringly, and that but one mortar-shell was thrown from Wagner. About 10 P.M. he passed into the ditch and examined it thoroughly. He found a *fraise* of spears and stakes, of which he pulled up some two hundred. Returning, a flying sap was run along the crest of the *glacis*, throwing the earth level, to enable assailants to pass over readily.

From early morning Col. L. M. Keitt, the Confederate commander of Morris Island, had been signalling that his force was terribly reduced, the enemy about to assault, and that to save the garrison there should be transportation ready by nightfall of the 6th. He reported his casualties on the 5th as one hundred out of nine hundred; that a repetition of that day's bombardment would leave the work a ruin. He had but four hundred effectives, exclusive of artillerymen. His negro laborers could not be made to work; and thirty or forty soldiers had been wounded that day in attempting to repair damages. General Beauregard, who had been, since the 4th at least, jeopardizing the safety of the brave garrison, then gave the necessary order for evacuation.

A picket detail of one hundred men went out from the Fifty-fourth camp at 5 P.M. on the 6th. Our usual detail was at work in the front under the engineers. It was not until two o'clock on the morning of September 7 that the officers and men of the regiment remaining in camp were aroused, fell into line, and with the colored brigade marched up over the beach line to a point just south of the Beacon house, where these regiments rested, constituting the reserve of infantry in the anticipated assault. Many of the regiments were arriving or in position, and the advance trenches were full of troops. Soon came the gray of early morning, and with it rumors that Wagner was evacuated. By and by the rumors were confirmed, and the glad tidings spread from regiment to regiment. Up and down through the trenches and the parallels rolled repeated cheers and shouts of victory. It was a joyous time; our men threw up their hats, dancing in their gladness.

Officers shook hands enthusiastically. Wagner was ours at last.

In accordance with instructions, at dark on the 6th the Confederate ironclads took position near Sumter. Some transport vessels were run close in, and forty barges under Lieutenant Ward, C.S.N., were at Cumming's Point. A courier reported to Colonel Keitt that everything was prepared, whereupon his troops were gradually withdrawn, and embarked after suffering a few casualties in the movement. By midnight Wagner was deserted by all but Capt. T. A. Huguenin, a few officers, and thirty-five men. The guns were partially spiked, and fuses prepared to explode the powder-magazine and burst the guns. At Gregg the heavy guns and three howitzers were spiked, and the magazine was to be blown up. The evacuation was complete at 1.30 A.M. on the 7th. At a signal the fuses were lighted in both forts; but the expected explosion did not occur in either work, probably on account of defective matches.

Just after midnight one of the enemy, a young Irishman, deserted from Wagner and gained our lines. Taken before Lieut.-Col. O. L. Mann, Thirty-ninth Illinois, general officer of the trenches, he reported the work abandoned and the enemy retired to Gregg. Half an hour later all the guns were turned upon Wagner for twenty minutes, after which Sergeant Vermillion, a corporal, and four privates of the Thirty-ninth Illinois, all volunteers, went out. In a short time they returned, reporting no one in Wagner and only a few men in a boat rowing toward Gregg. On the receipt of this news the flag of the sappers and the regimental color of the Thirty-ninth Illinois were both planted on the earthwork. A hasty examination was made of Wagner, in the course of which a line of fuse connecting with two magazines was cut. Every precaution was taken, and guards posted at all dangerous points.

A few moments after our troops first entered Wagner two companies of the Third New Hampshire under Captain Randlett were pushed toward Gregg. Capt. C. R. Brayton, Third Rhode Island Heavy Artillery, and some Fifty-fourth men started for the same point. Amid the sand-hills the Third New Hampshire men stopped to take charge of some prisoners, while Captain Brayton kept on, and was the first to enter Gregg, closely followed by the Fifty-fourth men. In Wagner eighteen pieces of ordnance were found, and in Gregg, seven pieces. All about the former work muskets, boarding-pikes, spears, and boards filled with spikes were found arranged to repel assaults. Inside and all around, the stench was nauseating from the buried and unburied bodies of men and animals. The bombproof was indescribably filthy. One terribly wounded man was found who lived to tell of his sufferings, but died on the way to hospital. Everywhere were evidences of the terrific bombardment beyond the power of pen to describe.

About half a dozen stragglers from the retiring enemy were taken on the island. Our boats captured two of the enemy's barges containing a surgeon and fifty-five men, and a boat of the ram "Chicora" with an officer and seven sailors.

Wagner's siege lasted fifty-eight days. During that period 8,395 soldiers' day's work of six hours each had been done on the approaches; eighteen bomb or splinter proof service-magazines made, as well as eighty-nine emplacements for guns,—a total of 23,500 days' work. In addition, forty-six thousand sand-bags had been filled, hundreds of gabions and fascines made, and wharves and landings constructed. Of the nineteen thousand days' work performed by infantry, the colored troops had done one half, though numerically they were to white troops as one to ten. Three quarters of all the work was at night, and nine tenths under artillery and sharpshooters' fire or both combined.

Regarding colored troops, Major Brooks, Assistant Engineer, in his report, says,—

> "It is probable that in no military operations of the war have negro troops done so large a proportion, and so important and hazardous fatigue duty, as in the siege operations on the island."

The colored regiments participating were the Fifty-fourth and Fifty-fifth Massachusetts, First North Carolina, Second South Carolina, and Third United States Colored Troops. Officers serving in charge of the approaches, when called upon by Major Brooks to report specifically upon the comparative value of white and colored details under their charge for fatigue duty during the period under consideration, gave testimony that for perseverance, docility, steadiness, endurance, and amount of work performed, the blacks more than equalled their white brothers. Their average of sick was but 13.97, while that of the whites was 20.10. The percentage of duty performed by the blacks as compared with the whites was as fifty-six to forty-one.

Major Brooks further says,—

> "Of the numerous infantry regiments which furnished fatigue parties, the Fourth New Hampshire did the most and best work, next follow the blacks,—the Fifty-fourth Massachusetts and Third United States Colored Troops."

General Beauregard reports his loss during the siege as a total of 296, exclusive of his captured. But the official

"War Records" show that from July 18 to September 7 the Confederate loss was a total of 690. The Federal loss during the same period by the same authority was but 358.

Despite the exposure of the Fifty-fourth details day and night with more or less officers and men at the front, the casualties in the regiment during the siege as given by the Adjutant-General of Massachusetts were but four killed and four wounded.

Shortly after the fall of Wagner the following order was issued to the troops.

DEPARTMENT OF THE SOUTH,
  MORRIS ISLANDS, S.C., Sept. 15, 1863.

It is with no ordinary feelings of gratification and pride that the brigadier-general commanding is enabled to congratulate this army upon the signal success which has crowded the enterprise in which it has been engaged. Fort Sumter is destroyed. The scene where our country's flag suffered its first dishonor you have made the theatre of one of its proudest triumphs.

The fort has been in the possession of the enemy for more than two years, has been his pride and boast, has been strengthened by every appliance known to military science, and has defied the assaults of the most powerful fleet the world ever saw. But it has yielded to your courage and patient labor. Its walls are now crumbled to ruins, its formidable batteries are silenced, and though a hostile flag still floats over it, the fort is a harmless and helpless wreck.

Forts Wagner and Gregg, works rendered memorable by their protracted resistance and the sacrifice of life they have cost, have also been wrested from the enemy by your persevering courage and skill, and the graves of your fallen comrades rescued from desecration and contumely.

You now hold in undisputed possession the whole of Morris Island; and the city and harbor of Charleston lie at the mercy of your artillery from the very spot where the first shot was fired at your country's flag and the Rebellion itself was inaugurated.

To you, the officers and soldiers of this command, and to the gallant navy which has co-operated with you are due the thanks of your commander and your country. You were called upon to encounter untold privations and dangers, to undergo unremitting and exhausting labors, to sustain severe and disheartening reverses. How nobly your patriotism and zeal have responded to the call the results of the campaign will show and your commanding general gratefully bears witness.

Q. A. GILLMORE,
Brigadier-General Commanding.

CHAPTER VII

BOMBARDMENT OF CHARLESTON

Morris Island was ours; but no sooner had the enemy evacuated than Wagner, Gregg, and the intervening ground were daily subjected to a fire from the James and Sullivan's Island batteries. A heavy action on land and water occurred on the morning of September 8, occasioned by the grounding of the monitor "Weehawken;" and in the course of the day a magazine blew up in Moultrie, and the village of Moultrieville was set on fire by our shells.

Admiral Dahlgren having demanded the surrender of Sumter, which was refused, a night assault was determined upon jointly by the army and navy; but differences arose regarding the command. When the time came, Gillmore's force was detained in shallow waters by the tide. Commander T. H. Stevens, with eighteen officers and some four hundred sailors and marines, embarked in thirty boats for the enterprise. The leaders landed at Sumter after midnight on the 9th. Major Elliott was prepared for and received the assault with musketry and fragments of the epaulment. In a few minutes all was over, for the brave leaders, finding it impossible to scale the walls, were made prisoners. Our loss was ten officers and one hundred and four men captured and three men killed.

As Forts Wagner and Gregg were ordered to be turned for offensive purposes, a covered way between these two works begun, and new batteries ordered to be constructed, there were heavy demands for fatigue. Besides its details at Cumming's Point, the Fifty-fourth soon began to send working parties for the "Bluff Battery" in the southerly sand-hills near the beach-front. To retard our progress with the works at the front, the enemy maintained a constant cannonade. Batteries Simkins and Cheves were most active against us. On the 15th the enemy's magazine in the latter work was accidentally blown up with 1,200 pounds of powder, causing some casualties. The force of this explosion was felt all over Morris Island. Black Island, between Morris and James Islands, where we had a battery, was also frequently shelled.

First Sergeant Gray of Company C had received a Masonic character and organized a lodge on Morris Island. The meeting-place was a dry spot in the marsh near our camp, where boards were set up to shelter the members. Furloughs for thirty days having been granted a certain proportion of the troops, the Fifty-fourth men selected departed, overjoyed at the prospect of seeing home and friends. The equinoctial storm set in about the middle of September, accompanied by high tides and wind. The dike protecting our camp was broken, and the parade overflowed, necessitating considerable labor to repair damages. With the cessation of this severe storm cooler weather came,—a most welcome relief.

In recognition of the capture of Morris Island and the demolition of Sumter, General Gillmore was promoted major-general of volunteers. To do him honor, a review of the First Division, Tenth Army Corps, took place on Morris Island September 24. Partial relief from excessive labors had permitted the troops to refit. Line was formed on the beach at low tide, the division extending a distance of some two miles. The pageant was unsurpassed in the history of the department. Our colored brigade presented a fine appearance, and many compliments for the Fifty-fourth were received by Captain Emilio, commanding.

Paymaster Usher arrived in camp September 27, ready to pay the men $10 per month from enlistment, less $3 per month deducted for clothing. Upon the non-commissioned officers being assembled, they with great unanimity declined the reduced payment for themselves and their comrades. The paymaster again came on the 30th to renew his offer. It was on this date that Colonel Montgomery appeared and made the men a remarkable and characteristic address, which Sergeant Stephens of Company B has given in substance as follows:—

"Men: the paymaster is here to pay you. You must remember you have not proved yourselves soldiers. You must take notice that the Government has virtually paid you a thousand dollars apiece for setting you free. Nor should you expect to be placed on the same footing with white men. Any one listening to your shouting and singing can see how grotesquely ignorant you are. I am your friend and the friend of the negro. I was the first person in the country to employ nigger soldiers in the United States Army. I was out in Kansas. I was short of men. I had a lot of niggers and a lot of mules; and you know a nigger and a mule go very well together. I therefore enlisted the niggers, and made teamsters of them. In refusing to take the pay offered you, and what you are only legally entitled to, you are guilty of insubordination and mutiny, and can be tried and shot by court-martial."

Montgomery besides made some gross and invidious insinuations and reflections because the Fifty-fourth men were so light-colored, which it would be improper to repeat. The colonel seemed to be unaware that his remarks were insulting, and most of the men he addressed born free.

Sergt. Henry Stewart, of Company E, a faithful soldier who had actively engaged in recruiting the regiment, died of disease September 27, and was buried with proper honors. His and other deaths, with an increased sick list, called for sanitary measures about this time. No radical change of camp was possible, as the ground available for such purposes was limited; but tents were struck so that the air and sun could reach the ground beneath, and a daily inspection of streets, sinks, and the cooked food instituted.

The Sanitary Commission furnished ice, raspberry vinegar, pickles, and other needed supplies; but there was a lack of fresh vegetables. Early in October, however, Mr. Reuben Tomlinson brought a large supply for the Fifty-fourth,—a present from the contrabands about Beaufort; and similar welcome gifts followed from the same source from time to time. Tobacco, dried apples, lime-juice, writing-paper, brushes, etc., were purchased with the company funds, as the men had no money.

To replace the State color lost on July 18, Governor Andrew caused a new one to be forwarded to the Fifty-fourth. Its receipt on October 2 was attended with great enthusiasm, the rousing cheers of the men being heard for a mile around.

It was noticeable about the 1st of October that our fire was stronger than for several weeks upon Sumter, Johnson, and Moultrie. Two monitors were doing picket duty near the island.

The monotony of daily events was broken at 10 A.M., October 5, by the sound of the long-roll. Shots had been heard among the naval vessels. Our regiment took position in the old Confederate rifle trenches near Oyster Point on the inlet. This alarm was caused by the attempt of Lieut. William T. Glassell, C.S.N., to blow up the "Ironsides." With a small boat—the "David"—he exploded a spar torpedo near our iron-clad without serious damage to that vessel; but the "David" was swamped. Glassell and one of his men were captured. The other two men righted their craft and returned to the city by midnight. This enterprise was one of the boldest undertakings of the war, and nearly successful.

Henry N. Hooper, formerly captain, Thirty-second Massachusetts Infantry, commissioned major of the Fifty-fourth, arrived October 16, and relieved Captain Emilio of the command. It was his fortune to lead the regiment for a longer period and in more actions than any other officer, owing to the assignment of Colonel Hallowell to higher command. On all occasions he proved an able and courageous soldier. Colonel Hallowell, promoted during his absence, returned the day after Major Hooper's arrival, and was waited upon by the officers, who expressed their pleasure at his recovery and return. A stanch friend of the Fifty-fourth was a visitor in camp about this time, in the person of Albert G. Browne, Esq., the special agent of the Treasury Department, whose headquarters were at Beaufort. His son, Col. Albert G. Browne, Jr., was the military secretary of Governor Andrew, and also one of the regiment's early and tried friends.

There had been several promotions in consequence of the action of July 18. Lieutenant Smith was made captain of Company G, but was still North; Lieutenant Walton, captain of Company B, *vice* Willard, resigned. Second Lieutenants T. L. Appleton, Tucker, Howard, Pratt, and Littlefield were made first lieutenants. These officers were all present except Lieutenant Pratt, who never re-joined. Captain Bridge and Lieutenant Emerson had returned from sick leave. Lieutenants E. G. Tomlinson and Charles G. Chipman, appointed to the regiment, had joined. A number of the wounded had returned from hospital, and the first lot of furloughed men came back, and with them Capt. J. W. M. Appleton. By these accessions the Fifty-fourth had more officers and men present toward the last of October than at any time after it left St. Helena Island.

Our new and old works being in readiness at Cumming's Point, what General Gillmore calls the "second bombardment of Sumter" was begun October 26. Its purpose was to prevent guns being mounted there, and to cut down the southeast face, that the casemates of the channel face be taken in reverse. General Seymour had returned and assumed command of the island on the 18th. Under his direction our batteries opened from seven heavy rifles (including a three-hundred-pounder) in Wagner, and four in Gregg and from two mortars. Some fire was directed against Fort Johnson also, the enemy replying briskly. The next day the cannonade was renewed with one gun in Gregg turned upon the city. Our range against Sumter being less than was the case during Wagner's siege, rendered the force of our shot much greater. Sharpshooters in Sumter armed with the long-range Whitworth rifles were trying to disable our gunners in Gregg, without success.

After four days' bombardment, a breach was disclosed in the southeast face of Sumter, extending half its length, on which our land and sea fire was concentrated. For about a week longer our bombardment was kept up with great vigor, during which time the enemy suffered many casualties, and Sumter was pounded into a mound of debris covering the lower casemates, in which the garrison found safe refuge. Through the centre of the Morris Island face of Sumter the *terre-plein* could be seen. Major Elliott apprehended another assault and prepared for it.

In honor of some of the officers who had fallen during the operations, Gregg was renamed Fort Putnam; Wagner, Fort Strong; the Bluff Battery, Fort Shaw; the new work near Gregg, Battery Chatfield; a work on Lighthouse Inlet, Battery Purviance; and another opposite the last, on Folly Island, Fort Green. By the same order General Gillmore announced that medals of honor, his personal gift, would be furnished to three per cent of the enlisted men who had borne part in the engagements and siege. This medal, however, was not received for some months. In the case of the Fifty-fourth it was awarded to the four men specially mentioned in Colonel Hallowell's report of the assault of July 18, previously printed herein. There arrived for the regiment a present from Mrs. Colonel Shaw of one thousand small copies of the Gospels, neatly bound in morocco of various colors, which were distributed.

Fine weather continued to prevail, although the month of October was drawing to a close. Early each morning a dense fog swept in from the eastward, covering land and sea until dispelled by the rising sun. Then came warm fall days, followed by cooler night hours.

Our gunners at the front were firing from Chatfield and Gregg with mortars and the heavy rifles mainly at night, besides using field-pieces in Gregg for accurate practice against the enemy's sharpshooters lodged in the ruins. Their shots caused small daily casualties in Sumter, swelling out to nineteen in number October 31, when a falling wall killed many, and fifteen on November 6, when a mortar-shell exploded in front of a bombproof. Capt. T. C. Ferris, Independent New York Battalion (Les Enfans Perdus), made a daring reconnoissance of the fort at night, November 2. He landed, and with one man scaled the wall until discovered and fired upon. Then they retired safely to their comrade in the boat, bringing some bricks away as trophies.

There was a gala day in Charleston on November 2 when Jefferson Davis arrived on his return from a visit to General Bragg at Dalton. General Beauregard extended to him all official courtesy; but their private relations were strained. Davis found the troops and works in good condition. Beauregard was apprehensive of attack at some point on his long lines at this period, and thought an attack on Sullivan's Island or another assault on Sumter not improbable.

Colonel Hallowell on his return used every means to have the many detached and detailed men returned to the colors, as heavy working parties of from one hundred to two hundred men were still called for to labor on the new works. Our first instalment of furloughed men having returned, the second left for Hilton Head on November 12. Lieutenant Howard relieved Lieutenant Littlefield as acting adjutant. Sergeant Swails of Company F was made acting sergeant-major and Sergeant Vogelsang of Company H quartermaster-sergeant.

News was received the last of November that the matter of pay had come up in a new form. Governor Andrew in his message recommended the provisions of an Act which passed the Massachusetts Legislature November 16 in words as follows: "An Act to make up the Deficiencies in the Monthly Pay of the Fifty-fourth and Fifty-fifth Regiments," etc., and Section I. of this Act read as follows:—

"There shall be paid out of the Treasury of the Commonwealth to the non-commissioned officers, musicians, and privates of the Fifty-fourth and Fifty-fifth regiments of Massachusetts Volunteer Infantry, to those who have been honorably discharged from the service, and to the legal representatives of those who have died in the service, such sums of money as, added to the amounts paid them by the United States, shall render their monthly pay and allowances from the time of their being mustered into the service of the United States equal to that of the other non-commissioned officers, musicians, and privates in the volunteer or regular military service of the United States."

Upon the receipt of a copy of the Governor's address and the Act, Colonel Hallowell, on November 23, wrote to Governor Andrew, that notwithstanding the generous action of the State authorities, the men of the Fifty-fourth had enlisted as other soldiers from Massachusetts, and that they would serve without pay until mustered out, rather than accept from the United States less than the amount paid other soldiers. Enlisted men were not less prompt to write to their friends expressing their disapprobation. Theodore Tilton, in a communication to the Boston "Journal," dated New York, Dec. 12, 1863, quotes from a letter received by him "from a Massachusetts soldier in the Fifty-fourth":—

"A strange misapprehension exists as to the matter of pay, and it pains us deeply. We came forward at the call of Governor Andrew, in which call he distinctly told us that we were to be subsisted, clothed, paid, and treated in all respects the same as other Massachusetts soldiers. Again, on the presentation of flags to the regiment at Camp Meigs, the Governor reiterated this promise, on the strength of which we marched through Boston, holding our heads high as men and as soldiers. Nor did we grumble because we were not paid the portion of United States bounty paid to other volunteer regiments in advance. Now that we have gained some reputation, we claim the right to be heard.

"Three times have we been mustered in for pay. Twice have we swallowed the insult offered us by the United States paymaster, contenting ourselves with a simple refusal to acknowledge ourselves different from other Massachusetts soldiers. Once, in the face of insult and intimidation such as no body of men and soldiers were ever subjected to before, we quietly refused and continued to do our duty. For four months we have been steadily working night and day under fire. And such work! Up to our knees in mud half the time, causing the tearing and wearing out of more than the volunteer's yearly allowance of clothing, denied time to repair and wash (what we might by that means have saved), denied time to drill and perfect ourselves in soldierly qualities, denied the privilege of burying our dead decently. All this we've borne patiently, waiting for justice.

"Imagine our surprise and disappointment on the receipt by the last mail of the Governor's address to the General Court, to find him making a proposition to them to pay this regiment the difference between what the United States Government offers us and what they are legally bound to pay us, which, in effect, advertises us to the world as holding out for *money* and not from *principle*,—that we sink our manhood in consideration of a few more dollars. How has this come about? What false friend has been misrepresenting us to the Governor, to make him think that our necessities outweigh our self-respect? I am sure no representation of *ours* ever impelled him to that action."

To the letter Theodore Tilton added some forcible sentences. Among other things he wrote,—

"They are not willing that the Federal Government should throw mud upon them, even though Massachusetts stands ready to wipe it off. And perhaps it is not unsoldierly in a soldier, white or black, to object to being insulted by a government which he heroically serves. The regiment whose bayonets pricked the name of Colonel Shaw into the roll of immortal honor can afford to be cheated out of their money, but not out of their manhood."

Our brigade number was changed from "Fourth" to "Third" on November 23. Its colored regiments were still required to perform an undue proportion of fatigue work, and but few details for grand guards came for them. After this discrimination had long been borne, General Gillmore in an order said,—

"Colored troops will not be required to perform any labor which is not shared by the white troops, but will receive in all respects the same treatment, and be allowed the same opportunities for drill and instruction."

During the third week of November several events of interest occurred. On the 15th the Moultrie House on Sullivan's Island, which had long flown a hospital flag, was torn down, disclosing a powerful battery, which opened a terrible fire on us in unison with two other works. This, occurring at 10 P.M., it was thought might cover a boat attack, so our troops were called into line, where they remained until firing ceased. Meanwhile from Gregg and the "Ironsides" our calcium lights swept the waters about the harbor to discover any force approaching. Our monitor "Lehigh" grounded the next morning. Under a fierce cannonade a hawser was carried from the "Nahant," and by it and the rising tide she was floated at 11 A.M.

From Gregg and Chatfield our guns, mounted for the purpose, began to fire on the city at 10 A.M. on the 17th, throwing twenty-one shells. We could see the smoke from the explosions as the shells struck about the wharves, in the "burnt district," or well up among the houses. This bombardment of Charleston was from this time maintained with more or less vigor each day and night. Against Sumter, from November 1 to the 20th, we fired an average of five hundred shots daily. Our new work nearest Gregg was named Battery Seymour, and was armed with ten-inch mortars; another still farther south was called Battery Barton.

Major Conyngham, Fifty-second Pennsylvania, with two hundred and fifty men from his regiment, the One Hundred and Fourth Pennsylvania, and the Third New Hampshire, made a boat reconnoissance of Sumter at night, November 19. Our expedition approached to within three hundred yards of the fort, was discovered, and after an engagement of fifteen minutes withdrew with three men wounded. In this affair a portion of Sumter's garrison acted badly, and three officers were censured. Capt. F. H. Harleston, First South Carolina Artillery, a most gallant and able officer, while examining the defences of the fort on November 24 was struck by a Parrott-shell, and died in a few hours.

Thanksgiving Day, November 26, by general orders, was observed by the suspension of all unnecessary labor. At 1.30 P.M. the Fifty-fourth formed with side-arms only, and marched to the beach in front of the Third Brigade head-quarters. There, with all the other troops on the island, they joined in religious services. It was a glorious day, well fitted for the thorough enjoyment of the feast and sports which followed. In response to a call of the "Black" Committee the friends of the regiment had contributed for Thanksgiving dinner many luxuries. From this source, the company funds, and the efforts of the officers and company cooks, a most abundant and unusual feast was provided. In the afternoon there was much amusement and sport indulged in by the men. A greased pole some twenty feet high was erected, and at the top was suspended a pair of trousers the pockets of which contained $13. After four hours of ludicrously unsuccessful trials on the part of a number of men, Butler of Company K secured the "full pay" and the trousers. Wheelbarrow and sack races closed the games.

December came in, cold and rainy, for the winter weather had set in. The day, however, was a happy and memorable one, for news was received of General Grant's great victory at Missionary Ridge, and every fort fired a salute, causing spiteful replies from the enemy. A high wind prevailed on the 6th, and those who were upon the bluff or beach witnessed a terrible disaster to the fleet. At 2 P.M. the monitor "Weehawken," off the island, foundered, carrying to their death, imprisoned below, four officers and twenty-seven men.

There was much heavy weather about the first ten days of December. After it subsided, the beach of Morris Island was strewn with logs some thirty feet long and eighteen inches through, a number of which were bolted together with iron. Others were found floating with the tide. A wooden affair, some fifty by thirty feet, double planked, looking like a floating battery, was washed ashore on Folly Island about the same time. The enemy had been loosing a part of the harbor obstructions.

We were now firing an average of twenty shells each day into Charleston. The time of firing was purposely varied throughout the day and night, that the Confederates might not be prepared to reply. From "Mother Johnson," Simkins, and Moultrie we received an average of two hundred shots per day, most of which failed to strike our works. But few casualties were sustained, the warning cry of the lookouts sending all to cover.

Against Sumter our firing was light after November. But on December 11 some two hundred and twenty shots were hurled at that work. While we were firing slowly at 9.30 A.M., the southwest magazine there exploded. Timbers, bricks, and debris, as well as the flag, were shot up into the air, while below arose a black cloud of smoke which streamed out over the harbor. A fire broke out later. The garrison lost on this day eleven men killed and forty-one wounded.

By reference to his official correspondence, it is found that about the middle of December General Gillmore entertained the project of attacking Savannah, and then, with a portion of his force, operating in Florida. He thought that to move with the fleet against Charleston's inner defences, now bristling with guns, either by way of the Stono or Bull's Bay, he should be reinforced with ten thousand or twelve thousand men. He urged that the War Department adopt measures which would enable him to go to work at once.

Calls for fatigue were now lighter and better borne, for seventy-three conscripts arrived for the Fifty-fourth on November 28, and twenty-two recruits on December 4.

Battalion and brigade drills were resumed. We were furnishing heavier details for grand guard, composed usually of several officers and two hundred and fifty men. They went out every third or fourth day during our further stay on the island. For the diversion of the officers the "Christy Minstrels" gave their first performance December 5 in Dr. Bridgham's hospital tent, enlarged by a wall tent on one side. Songs were sung and jokes cracked in genuine minstrel style.

To carry out the provisions of the Act for the relief of the Fifty-fourth and Fifty-fifth Massachusetts Infantry, Maj. James Sturgis, accompanied by Mr. E. W. Kinsley, a public-spirited citizen, arrived at our camp December 12. They had previously visited the Fifty-fifth Massachusetts, when Colonel Hartwell informed Major Sturgis that neither regiment would receive the relief. Upon meeting Colonel Hallowell the same information was given. At Major Sturgis's request the officers and first sergeants were then assembled, when the matter was freely discussed. Both gentlemen explained fully the purpose of the Governor and the legislation securing it. Some of the officers and non-commissioned officers replied by a recital of the reasons for refusal hereinbefore set forth. Finally the non-commissioned officers on behalf of the men positively refused the State aid. At their conclusion cheers were given for Governor Andrew, to whom they were grateful for the proffered help. The result of his unsuccessful mission was reported in writing by Major Sturgis to the Governor under date of December 13. In his report he says,—

"I deem it proper to say here, that among the many regiments that I saw at Hilton Head, St. Helena Island, Beaufort, Folly, and Morris Island, white and colored, there are none, to my inexperienced eye, that equalled the Fifty-fourth and Fifty-fifth, unless it was the Fortieth Massachusetts, while none surpassed them in any respect."

Late in the afternoon of December 17 the Fifty-fourth with all the troops was formed to see a deserter shot. The unfortunate man was Joseph Lane, a drafted soldier of the Third New Hampshire. On November 28 he started from Morris Island toward James. At last, despairing of crossing the water ways, he turned back to our lines, representing himself as a Rebel deserter. Taken to the post guard-house, he was recognized by some of his own company, whereupon he was tried and sentenced to death. General Stevenson commanded the division, by reason of General Terry's illness. After forming, the column moved slowly up the beach followed by a wagon, in which, seated upon his coffin, rode Lane. When the troops halted, the wagon passed along the line to the lower beach. There the coffin was unloaded, the deserter knelt upon it, and at a signal, in full view of all the troops, the blindfolded man received the musket-shots of the firing party, falling forward on his face a quivering corpse.

Christmas day was cold and windy. The only noteworthy event in camp was the arrival of a mail. Besides fatigue parties a detail for grand guard of two hundred and fifty men went out under Captain Pope. Our rifles had sounded their fearful Christmas chimes by throwing shells into the city for three hours after one o'clock that morning. About 3 A.M. a fire broke out in Charleston which illumined the whole sky and destroyed twelve buildings before it was subdued, the falling walls injuring many firemen. Chatfield joined Gregg in the bombardment directed upon the fire. The enemy opened rapidly for a time and then gradually ceased, but our guns continued to fire with more or less vigor all day. On their part the Confederates prepared a Christmas surprise for the gunboat "Marblehead" lying in the Stono near Legareville. At 6 A.M. some pieces on John's Island, brought there at night, opened on the gunboat, but were soon driven away with loss of men and guns.

New Year's Day being the first anniversary of the Emancipation Proclamation, the non-commissioned officers arranged for a celebration. The men formed and proceeded to the parade-ground, where a dry-goods box covered with a rubber blanket was placed, to serve as a speaker's stand. Chaplain Harrison offered a prayer and then introduced the orator of the day, Sergeant Barquet of Company H. Barquet was in high spirits, and began with the quotation, "What means this sea of upturned faces," etc. The speaker had hardly warmed up to his work, when in the midst of a most impassioned harangue the dry-goods box caved in, carrying him down. Barquet, in no way disconcerted, from the wreck shouted out the appropriate but well-worn gag: "Gentlemen, I admire your principles, but damn your platform!" After the hilarity resulting from the discomfiture of the chief speaker had subsided, others addressed the meeting with more or less effect. In the evening the non-commissioned officers had a supper in the large tent used to cover quartermaster's stores. Among the good things provided were baked beans and Indian pudding.

From November 1 to January 8 the following changes took place among the officers,—Major Hooper was promoted lieutenant-colonel, and Capt. J. W. M. Appleton, major; Lieutenant Grace, captain of Company A; Lieut. R. H. L. Jewett, captain of Company K; and Lieutenant Higginson, captain of Company H; Second Lieutenants David Reid, Emerson, and Tomlinson became first lieu-

tenants; Lieutenants A. W. Leonard, Lewis Reed, Alfred H.
Knowles, Robert R. Newell, and Chas. M. Duren, newly
appointed, reported. Captains Jones and Pope and Assistant-Surgeon Pease re-joined. Surgeon Stone went North,
and was then appointed surgeon, United States Volunteers.
Lieutenant Higginson was promoted while absent sick, and
was afterward transferred to the Fifth Massachusetts Cavalry as captain. Lieutenant Johnston was discharged. A
change in the line formation was necessary after these
promotions, which was ordered as follows, Company D
being on the left:—

D B A E H F K C G I

Greek fire was used from our "city guns" experimentally
in twenty shells on January 3. Previous firings with this
compound had not been satisfactory in result. The charges
on this day seemed more effective, apparently causing a
fire in Charleston. It is stated on Confederate authority
that the whole number of our shells fired into the city
from August 21 to January 5 was 472, of which twenty-
eight fell short. They are said to have killed five persons.
Our opening thereupon from Cumming's Point was the
occasion of great dismay and confusion. A hegira to the
country took place, by railroad and every kind of vehicle
laden with household effects. Those who remained became
somewhat accustomed to our shelling. The collection of
old iron after each explosion was a regular business. Non-
exploded shells were purchased by the authorities. From
the "Battery" up to Wentworth Street, about the middle
of the city, nearly all the houses had been penetrated.

Wagner having been thoroughly prepared for our purposes and armed, on the 12th a distinguished company
assembled therein to witness the raising of the stars and

stripes on the high flag-staff erected. Captain Strahan, Third Rhode Island Heavy Artillery, was made commandant of the work. General Gillmore removed his headquarters from Folly Island to Hilton Head about this time. General Terry was given command of the Northern District from Charleston to St. Helena. Col. W. W. H. Davis, One Hundred and Fourth Pennsylvania, assumed control of Morris Island. His force was composed of one colored brigade and two white brigades, besides artillerymen and engineers.

During the time the Fifty-fourth had served with white troops a few officers and men manifested their dislike to the black regiment in various ways. Sometimes white sentinels would pretend not to see the approach of our officers, to avoid rendering the proper salute. Occasionally officers in charge of armed parties failed to give the marching salute to similar parties of the Fifty-fourth. In all such cases reports were made of the discourtesy. The following instance of preference given white troops, when on joint duty with blacks, occurred. Captain Emilio, with two hundred and fifty men and several officers, reported for grand-guard duty, and as the first on the ground, was entitled to the right of all others. This position, despite protest, was denied him by Maj. Michael Schmitt, Independent New York Battalion. When the tour of duty was completed, a report was made of the affair and forwarded to post headquarters. The discrimination did not occur again. By persistent and firm assertion of the rights of the men on the part of all the Fifty-fourth officers, a discontinuance of these and other discourtesies was at last obtained.

There arrived from Long Island, Mass., on the 20th, some one hundred and twelve recruits for the regiment, which served to fill the ranks nearly to the maximum. With a single exception they were all volunteers. By this date the Fifty-fourth was well clothed, fully equipped, and prepared for any service. The colder weather, although it brought some discomfort, served to lessen the number of sick. Food was better and more varied. Quartermaster Ritchie, assisted by Sergeant Barquet and Private King, secured bricks from the old lighthouse and constructed an oven which furnished soft bread. It had a capacity of two hundred loaves each baking.

Troops had been moving from various posts to Hilton Head during January, and on the 27th our brigade was ordered to embark as soon as transportation was provided. During the afternoon of the 28th everything but the tents was loaded upon two steamers assigned to the Fifty-fourth. As darkness fell, camp was struck; but as the vessels could not leave until the next forenoon, the regiment through the early part of the night remained on shore, gathered about small camp-fires.

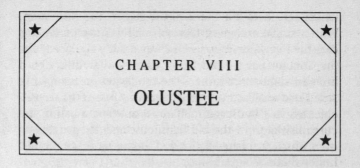

CHAPTER VIII
OLUSTEE

G ENERAL GILLMORE had resolved upon an expedition to Florida, which General Halleck approved, but remarked that such movements had little effect upon the progress of our arms. President Lincoln also desired to make Florida a loyal State. Gillmore's purposes were to secure an outlet for cotton, lumber, turpentine, and other products, cut off a source of the enemy's commissary supplies, obtain recruits for the colored regiments he was authorized to form, and to inaugurate measures to restore Florida to her allegiance.

In darkness, at 3 A.M., on January 29, Companies C, F, G, H, I, and K, embarked on the steamer "J. B. Collins," the remaining ones on the steamer "Monohansett." The departure took place at 10 A.M. It was not known that the regiment would ever return, so notwithstanding the uninviting aspect of the sandy island, its fading lines were scanned by all with mingled feelings of attachment and regret. Soon, however, the men began to chatter. Cheery voices exclaimed: "No more fatigue at the front!" "We'll have a rest from the sound of the guns!" "No more long-rolls," etc. Then they comfortably disposed themselves for the short voyage. Hilton Head was made at 3.45 P.M. by the "Monohansett," and at 7 P.M. by the "Collins," both vessels lying up at the pier. The companies on the former vessel landed at midnight, bivouacked in one of the streets, and early next morning marched a mile and a half to the Pope plantation outside the intrenchments, going into camp near the Second South Carolina and the Eighth United States Colored Troops,—the latter a new regiment from the North. Our other companies came to camp at 7 A.M. Tents were pitched on the 31st. A wood extended nearly to the camp, from which green boughs were brought for shelter and shade as well as fuel. All enjoyed the change of landscape,—green fields, trees, and herbage in place of the sand and sea wastes of Morris Island.

Around us troops were encamped or arriving daily. The Third United States Colored Troops joined on the 31st, uniting the brigade, which was enlarged by the assignment to it of the Eighth United States Colored Troops. Some fifty recruits for the Fifty-fourth came on February 1; but as the rolls were full, a provisional company, "L," was formed, and placed in charge of Lieut. T. L. Appleton. Service with the Fifty-fourth was eagerly sought for, and it was seen by Colonel Hallowell that several additional companies could be recruited. With the approval of General Gillmore, he therefore applied to Governor Andrew, on February 3, that the Fifty-fourth be placed on the footing of a heavy artillery regiment. This recommendation, however, bore no fruit.

Captain Partridge was discharged for disability January 19, and Captain Smith for the same cause January 25; Lieutenant Dexter having resigned, departed North, and

afterward became second lieutenant Sixty-first Massachusetts Infantry; Chaplain Harrison received sick leave, resigning at the North March 14. He was refused pay as
chaplain, because of his color. The matter received Governor Andrew's attention; and on April 23 Attorney-
General Bates rendered the opinion that the chaplain, because he was of African descent, could not be deprived of
the pay affixed to the office he lawfully held.

After a review by General Gillmore of all the troops on
February 4, on returning to camp the officers were informed that the regiment would embark the next day. The
sick, some recruits, and the camp were to remain in charge
of Lieut. T. L. Appleton. Captain Jones was too ill to accompany us.

Orders came to march at supper-time on the 5th; and
the Fifty-fourth proceeded from its only camp at Hilton
Head to the pier. Major Appleton, with Companies A, B,
and D, embarked on the steamer "Maple Leaf," which was
General Seymour's flag-ship. Captain Emilio, with Company E, some recruits, Quartermaster Ritchie, and the
stores, took passage on the schooner "R. C. A. Ward."
Colonel Hallowell, with the remaining companies, was assigned to the steamer "General Hunter."

Gillmore's Florida expedition was afloat, for the troops
comprising his force had embarked on some twenty-eight
transports, in darkness. It was probable that our point
of attack would be unknown. But General Beauregard
was aware of some movement, and notified General Gil-
mer at Savannah to prepare, and had troops ready to
move over the railroads to the southward. He personally
visited Savannah on January 16, returning to Charleston
February 3.

General Seymour, assigned to command the expedition,

was to have a force of about seven thousand men. His transports were ordered to rendezvous at the mouth of the St. John's River, Florida. Admiral Dahlgren was to co-operate, with some naval vessels.

It was most enjoyable voyaging down the coast. A few men were seasick, but soon recovered. The "Maple Leaf" arrived off the St. John's at 8.50 A.M. on the 7th, and the "General Hunter" at 9 A.M. Eleven steamers and smaller craft had arrived or were coming in; and as the transports passed one another, the troops cheered enthusiastically. There, too, the gunboats "Ottawa" and "Norwich" were found ready to escort the fleet. At about noon, the larger portion of the vessels started up the river for Jacksonville, some twenty-five miles distant.

Just three hundred years before, René de Laudonnière led a French fleet up the same river, known then as the "River of May," following the lead of the famous Ribaut the previous year. The beautiful and historic stream glided to the sea as placidly as then through the marshy lowlands, past the white bluffs and forests of pine and cedar. Amid the romantic scenery, through this historic region, on a delightful day, the fleet proceeded up the devious stream with the gunboat "Ottawa" in the lead, followed by the "Maple Leaf" and "General Hunter." Evidences of former Federal occupation or Rebel abandonment were seen in burned saw-mills, deserted houses, and decayed landings.

Upon rounding a point late in the afternoon, Jacksonville appeared in view, looking much like a devastated Northern city, with its ruined gas-works, burned saw-mills, and warehouses; but many residences and stores appeared in good repair. As the vessels approached nearer the town, some women and children were discovered, waving handkerchiefs from places near the water-front. A few men were also seen lurking about, as if fearing musket or cannon shots. When abreast of the place, the "Norwich" continued up the stream a short distance and anchored. General Seymour, on the "Maple Leaf," ran up to a wharf, and Major Appleton had his men ashore in a moment. A few cavalrymen had been discovered, who, as our Fifty-fourth men were formed, fired some shots, one of which wounded the mate of the "General Hunter," from which Colonel Hallowell and his six companies were disembarking. As the shots were fired, General Seymour ordered Major Appleton to "take his men and catch the Rebels." What followed, the major thus describes:—

"I tried, but our men with knapsacks were not fleet enough. I had a dark overcoat on, and was conspicuous. One 'Johnny' took deliberate aim at me over a fence. I saw him just as he fired. The ball came quite close, but did not hit me. By orders I placed men in each street, and pushed the command to the outskirts of the town, with no casualties on our side. We took a few prisoners, civilians, etc. Porter of Company A shot a Rebel through his leg, and got him and his horse."

While the major was thus engaged, the six companies of the regiment landed from the "General Hunter;" and Colonel Hallowell, also throwing out skirmishers, advanced through the town to the west side, where the regiment was reunited soon after. Pickets were thrown out, and the Fifty-fourth went into bivouac for the night.

The pursuit of the enemy was taken up and continued five miles by Major Stevens with his Independent Battalion Massachusetts Cavalry, which landed after the Fifty-fourth. They captured eleven Confederates, including some signal-men.

Transports which had been delayed having arrived with infantry, artillery, etc., on the 8th, at 4 P.M., General Seymour moved toward Baldwin. Much to the regret of all, the Fifty-fourth was ordered to remain behind. Colonel Hallowell was made commandant of Jacksonville. Captain Walton was appointed provost-marshal, with Company B as provost-guard. Company E, with the recruits, joined the regiment on the 9th. Lieutenant-Colonel Hooper, with details by companies, picketed the approaches to the town, holding a line mainly along two small creeks. For several days troops were landing and moving out to the advance.

Before the war Jacksonville contained some three thousand inhabitants, and was the key-point of Eastern Florida. It had been thrice before occupied by the Federal forces, and twice suffered from devastating fires. The enemy only held it in small force, their main body being at Camp Finegan, eight miles inland. It contained some tasteful residences, on wide streets densely shaded with old trees, the usual public buildings, churches, and stores. On the outskirts were old earthworks, facing cleared ground to woods beyond.

Col. Guy V. Henry's mounted troops, on the 8th, in darkness, flanked Camp Finegan, and at Ten-Mile Run captured five guns. Early on the 9th, he occupied Baldwin, capturing another gun and large stores. Our infantry, the first evening, entered Camp Finegan, whence some two hundred of the enemy fled. That night the steamer "St. Mary" was scuttled in a small creek, the navy securing a rifled gun, but her cargo, of two hundred and seventy cotton-bales, was burned. Our infantry advanced to Baldwin on the 9th, over bad roads, where both Seymour and Gillmore also arrived that day.

On the 10th the Light Brigade, consisting of the Massachusetts Cavalry Battalion, the Fortieth Massachusetts (mounted), and Elder's horse battery, First United States Artillery, some nine hundred men, under Colonel Henry, started out, followed by the infantry. About 11 A.M. the mounted force reached Barber's. A reconnoissance, with loss, disclosed the enemy, consisting of about one hundred and fifty men of the Second Florida Cavalry, under Maj. Robert Harrison, holding the south fork of the St. Mary's River. Henry, securing a position enfilading the ford, and the cavalry battalion charging across, drove the enemy in confusion, capturing their horses and arms. We lost four killed and thirteen wounded; the enemy, two killed and three wounded. Henry resumed the advance at 1 P.M., entering Sanderson three hours later. Gen. Joseph Finegan, the Confederate commander of East Florida, had retired, firing buildings and stores. The infantry column reached Barber's at midnight on the 10th. Henry, at Sanderson, rested until 2 A.M. on the 11th, when he again set out. No enemy was encountered until 11 A.M., when his skirmishers were found in the woods near Lake City. After developing his line, and a company had broken through the enemy's left, Henry, fearing to be outflanked by a stronger force, retired five miles. But the Confederate reports show that General Finegan had there in Henry's front only four hundred and fifty infantry, one hundred and ten cavalry, and two guns. Our loss was three men wounded; the enemy's, two killed and several wounded. The result of this affair was most unfortunate. It was the turning-point of the Florida expedition, for had the smaller Confederate force been driven by Henry's superior one, and followed up sharply at that time before Finegan's reinforcements had arrived, Seymour might have gone to the Suwanee River, a strong, defensive line.

Seymour arrived at Sanderson with Barton's brigade on the evening of the 11th, amid a torrent of rain. Gillmore on the 11th sent instructions to Seymour not to risk a repulse at Lake City, but to hold Sanderson and the south fork of the St. Mary's. Seymour withdrew to Barber's on the 12th.

From Jacksonville on the 10th, Major Appleton, with Companies C, D, F, and K, went to Camp Finegan, where the next day he was joined by Company E, and on the 12th his force marched to Baldwin. This hamlet was the junction of the Atlantic and Gulf, and Fernandina and Cedar Keys railroads. It consisted of a hotel, railroad depot, freight-house, and a few small, unpainted dwellings. The telegraph was in working order from there to Jacksonville. Supplies were brought up by means of captured cars drawn along the rails by horses.

Col. B. C. Tilghman, Third United States Colored Troops, with his regiment, and a company of the First New York Engineers, held the post. Work began and continued daily on intrenchments, block houses, and a stockade. Scouting parties and foraging details went out each day, the latter bringing in beeves, poultry, and potatoes. Pickets from the Fifty-fourth alternated with those from the Third United States Colored Troops, and furnished garrisons for the block houses and stockades.

From beyond the St. Mary's our advance forces had been all drawn back to Barber's by the 13th. Henry was sent to the southward. Capt. George Marshall, Fortieth Massachusetts, at Gainesville on the 15th repulsed the noted Captain Dickison, Second Florida Cavalry, with a superior force. From Barber's on the 14th a detachment went to Callahan Station and destroyed the railroad and bridges there.

This Florida expedition was a subject of Congressional inquiry. Seymour's letters disclose a most remarkable change of views and purposes. Gillmore was for holding Jacksonville as a base, and Baldwin, Pilatka, and other secondary posts with small garrisons and earthworks. After a conference with Seymour on the 14th at Jacksonville, Gillmore departed for Hilton Head. In his report to Halleck he says,—

"I considered it well understood at the time between General Seymour and myself that no advance would be made without further instructions from me until the defences were well advanced."

Seymour, left in command, at once issued a number of orders for the governing of his territory. One of these honored the memory of the regiment's first commander in the following words:—

HEADQUARTERS DISTRICT OF FLORIDA, DEP'T OF THE SOUTH,
JACKSONVILLE, FLA., Feb 16, 1864.
General Orders No. 2.
The Camp of Instruction, established by direction from Department headquarters on the railroad eight miles from Jacksonville, will be known as Camp Shaw, in memory of the young and devoted patriot who fell in the assault of July 18, 1863, upon Fort Wagner, S.C., and whose name will constantly suggest to the troops of this camp all that is honorable and meritorious.

By order of
BRIG.-GEN. T.SEYMOUR.
R. M. HALL, *1st Lieut. 1st U.S. Art'y, Act. Ass't-Adj't-Gen'l.*

Disregarding his instructions, Seymour prepared to execute the advance which he had resolved to make, seem-

ingly in complete ignorance of the enemy's force. Disaster
and failure were inevitable. By letter on the 17th, he informed Gillmore that he would move to the Suwanee River
to destroy the railroad. His letter closed with a postscript
reflecting upon all his higher officers in these words: "Send
me a general for the command of the advance troops, or
I shall be in a state of constant apprehension." On the
18th Gillmore did send him a general in the person of
General Turner, his chief of staff, not for the purpose
requested, but to suspend the movement, bring Seymour
back to Baldwin, and deliver letters expressing his surprise
at the advance. When Turner, delayed many hours by
stormy weather, reached Jacksonville, Seymour was engaged with the enemy.

In response to calls in every direction for help, General
Finegan began to receive aid immediately after our retirement from Lake City. On the 13th, with a force numbering two thousand men, he moved forward toward
Sanderson, taking post at Olustee, where he constructed
strong works, to better defend his position. Reinforcements continued to join, so that on the 18th he had forty-
six hundred infantry (largely veterans), about six hundred
cavalry, and three batteries of twelve guns. The enemy's
knowledge of our force was accurate, and of our plans
considerable, for despatches from Gillmore to Terry at
Folly Island were intercepted and deciphered. Beauregard
therefore stripped his garrisons elsewhere to meet us in
Florida.

A diversion made by General Schimmelfennig on John's
Island, S.C., occurred too early, and another by Col. J. B.
Howell, Eighty-fifth Pennsylvania, at Whitmarsh Island,
Ga., too late to serve Seymour.

Colonel Hallowell, commanding Jacksonville, occupied

the Crespo house as headquarters. The Fifty-fifth Massachusetts arrived on the 14th, and the next day relieved the Fifty-fourth from picket and provost-guard duty. Colonel Hartwell succeeded Colonel Hallowell in command of the post. Second Lieut. Thomas S. Bridgham, a brother of our assistant-surgeon, first joined at Jacksonville.

With Companies A, B, G, and H, at 8 A.M., February 18, Colonel Hallowell set out from Jacksonville for Baldwin. A march of some eighteen miles was made that day, and the next morning at 8.30 o'clock the Fifty-fourth was again reunited. Our pickets and details were relieved, rations of coffee and sugar issued, knapsacks lightened of much clothing, which was stored, and the regiment moved at 10 A.M., with orders to report at Barber's. The distance of twelve miles was compassed with four halts for rest. Mile after mile of pine barren was passed through, bounding the sandy road on either side, many of the trees bearing the scarification of the axe made to secure the resinous sap. But few habitations were encountered, and those seen were small log or slab huts, in cleared spaces, whose only touch of beauty were the apple and peach trees in blossom.

About 6 P.M. the Fifty-fourth arrived at Barber's, bivouacking in the woods on the left of the road near the First North Carolina. Fires were made; and the quartermaster having borrowed four days' rations of hard bread, the men made a hasty meal, and turned in for the night. There had been no time or inclination to look about, but there around Barber's house lay Seymour's little army of some five thousand men resting beside the flickering camp-fires.

Reveille sounded at 5 A.M. on the eventful Feb. 20, 1864, and at seven o'clock the troops began to move,—the Light Brigade in advance, followed by Hawley's, then Barton's, the Artillery, and Montgomery's in rear guarding the train. Just before the Fifty-fourth started, Major Appleton was ordered to remain in command at Barber's with Company E on picket, covering the railroad trestle, and Company A at Barber's house. Lieut. Lewis Reed, with thirty men, was to protect the telegraph line as the column advanced.

In fine spirits, the Fifty-fourth, followed by the First North Carolina, began the march, while the men sang, "We're bound for Tallahassee in the morning." The country was more open than that below. The road ran for long distances beside the railroad. Occasionally the forest widened out into savannas yellow with grasses and dotted with hemlock patches. From a clear sky the warm sun glistened and gleamed through the tall pines bordering the pathway. About every hour the brigade halted for a short rest.

Sanderson, some nine miles from Barber's, was reached by our advance before noon. People there stated that the enemy were in force beyond, and truly predicted our defeat; but their words were little heeded. Near an old mill beyond Sanderson, Henry's men came upon a few cavalry of the enemy, who fled when fired upon. Henry halted there until Hawley's infantry and Hamilton's battery came up, when the advance was resumed, the Seventh Connecticut, as skirmishers, leading.

Meanwhile, General Finegan at Olustee, receiving word that we were approaching in small numbers, sent out his cavalry under Col. Carraway Smith, with orders to skirmish and draw us on to the works at Olustee. As support he sent the Sixty-fourth Georgia and two companies of the Thirty-second Georgia. Moving forward two miles, where the wagon-road crossed the railroad, the infantry halted, the cavalry proceeding until near a point where the railroad recrossed the country road. The intervening ground, between the two crossings, was the battlefield of Olustee. The Confederates call the action the battle of Ocean Pond, from the extensive lake near the field on the north.

Over the last-mentioned crossing our skirmishers advanced at about 1.30 P.M., Elder's battery occasionally shelling the woods. The enemy's cavalry fell back, as instructed, to their infantry, at the crossing. At that point, Brig-Gen. A. H. Colquitt had arrived with the Sixth, Nineteenth, and Twenty-eighth Georgia, and ordering the cavalry to his flanks, threw out skirmishers and formed line of battle. Perceiving our strength, he sent for reinforcements and ammunition.

Moving through open pine woods, our advance now met firm resistance for the first time. By General Seymour's direction, Hawley moved his brigade into line. Personally leading the Seventh New Hampshire by the flank to the right, to avoid a small pond, he ordered a deployment under fire. He supposed the noise and confusion caused his order to be misunderstood, for the Seventh scattered, and went drifting to the rear notwithstanding the efforts of Colonel Abbott, his officers, and the gallant color-bearer, Thomas H. Simington. Hamilton placed his six guns under heavy fire within one hundred and fifty yards of the enemy; and the Eighth United States Colored Troops went into line on the left. Henry, with the Fortieth Massachusetts (mounted) and the Massachusetts Cavalry Battalion, held the flanks. Opposed to a superior force and murderous fire, the Seventh Connecticut and Eighth United States Colored Troops were, after excessive losses, forced to give ground. Hamilton, who was wounded, bravely supported the line with his guns, but was finally obliged to abandon two pieces for want of horses to bring them off. Col. Charles W.

Fribley, of the Eighth United States Colored Troops, after displaying the utmost gallantry, was mortally wounded.

But fresh troops were at hand, for Barton's brigade was coming up, supported by Elder's battery of four pieces on the right, and Langdon's battery of six guns, with a section (two guns) of Battery C, Third Rhode Island Artillery, under Lieut. Henry Metcalf, on the left. Barton formed on the right of the road at the new position taken up by Hawley. Colquitt, however, had received reinforcements, putting the Sixth Florida Battalion and Twenty-third Georgia into line, and the First Georgia (regulars) and the Thirty-second Georgia, which arrived shortly after, to prolong his left. He then advanced with the Chatham Artillery in rear of his centre, opening a destructive fire along the whole front. Finding feeble opposition on his right, he threw the Sixth Florida Battalion forward to enfilade our line. Barton now only maintained his position at a terrible cost of officers and men, and all his regimental commanders—Col. Henry Moore, Forty-seventh, Major W. B. Coan, Forty-eight, and Colonel Sammon, One Hundred and Fifteenth New York—wounded. Colquitt's men were out of cartridges for a time; but supplies came, and fresh troops also, composed of a section of Guerard's Battery, Bonaud's Battalion, the Twenty-seventh Georgia, and Second Florida Battalion. The enemy's artillery too was supplemented by a heavy gun mounted on a railroad car. With these accessions to his force, Colquitt moved the Sixth and Thirty-second Georgia to flank the right of Barton's brigade, and notwithstanding stubborn resistance, was gradually forcing it back.

General Seymour throughout these events was present on the field, exhibiting great personal gallantry. Discerning that victory was not for him, after such grievous losses, he sent to hasten the colored brigade into action, and made disposition to retire under cover of Montgomery's attack.

About 2.30 P.M. the colored brigade was resting,—the Fifty-fourth in the shade on the left of the road at a place where wood had lately been felled. Musketry firing had been heard in the distance, but after a time there came the sound of cannon. "That's home-made thunder," said one man. "I don't mind the thunder if the lightning don't strike me!" was the response. Another remarked, "I want to go home!" "You'll stay forever, maybe!" was the reply. Soon an orderly rode up at full speed, calling for the commanding officer. Colonel Hallowell sprang to his feet, and received an order for his rapid advance. In a few moments the regiment was moving at the double-quick, urged on by the heavier sound of battle. When the pace began to tell on the men, knapsacks, blankets, and even haversacks were cast away to lighten their load. At the railroad crossing, Colonel Montgomery, who was leading, was met by a staff-officer from General Seymour, bringing the order to move forward he had anticipated.

Nearing the battleground, resounding with cannonshots and musketry, the dispiriting scene so trying to troops about to engage, of hundreds of wounded and stragglers, was encountered. All sorts of discouraging shouts met the ear as the regiment speeded onward, as, "We're badly whipped!" "You'll all get killed." Still farther on was part of a disabled battery also going to the rear. But through this rift and drift of conflict the tired and panting men pressed on, and led by Sergeant Cezar of Company D, found breath to shout their battle-cry, "Three cheers for Massachusetts and seven dollars a month!" As the Fifty-fourth advanced, the field hospital of the Eighth United States Colored Troops was passed, which its coming saved from the threatening enemy. Adjutant Howard relates that as he was riding over the field beside Colonel Hallowell, General Seymour rode up to that officer and told him in substance that the day was lost, and that everything depended on the Fifty-fourth.

When the regiment arrived at the battle-front, it was about four o'clock. Colonel Hawley in his report thus describes the event:—

> "Colonel Montgomery's brigade had come up. The Fifty-fourth Massachusetts, Colonel Hallowell, went into action on our left, the First North Carolina on our right between us and Barton's retiring brigade, halting and firing fiercely, with its right well forward so as to form an angle of perhaps 120° with the line of the Fifty-fourth."

He further says,—

> "About that time an aid came to say that the general wished me to fall back, as the enemy were only feinting on our right, and were preparing to flank us in force."

This, then, was the situation as the Fifty-fourth took position: Barton retiring; the only other infantry—the Seventh Connecticut Battalion—ordered to fall back; and Seymour believing that the enemy were preparing to flank us on the left, where the Fifty-fourth alone were taking post. Well might Seymour think that everything depended on our regiment. Under these adverse conditions the colored brigade was to hold the enemy in check until a new line could be formed in the rear.

Colonel Hallowell led his regiment by the flank into the woods on the left of the road, and forming by file into line, immediately opened fire. The Fifty-fourth had thirteen officers and 497 men in action, with a formation as below, Company D being on the left,—

D B H F K C G I

The following-named officers were present,—Colonel Hallowell, Lieutenant-Colonel Hooper, Acting Adjutant Howard; Company I, Lieutenant Homans; Company G, Lieut. David Reid; Company C, Lieutenant Tomlinson, commanding, and Lieutenant Bridgham; Company K, Lieutenant Littlefield, commanding, and Lieutenant Leonard; Company F, Captain Bridge; Company H, Lieutenant Chipman; Company B, Lieutenant Newell; Company D, Lieutenant Duren. Assistant-Surgeons Bridgham and Pease, and Quartermaster Ritchie, were on the field. Sergeant Wilkins, of Company D, bore the national flag in the ranks of Company K, and Corporal Peal, of Company F, the State color. Captains Pope and Jewett, of the Fifty-fourth, on Colonel Montgomery's staff, took part in the action.

About the same time the First North Carolina went into action on the right of the road. The Fifty-fourth formed in a grove of pine extending around on every side over ground nearly level. So open was the forest that the enemy's line and colors could be seen about four hundred yards distant, with two guns in front of our right well advanced, apparently without much support. On the extreme left front were guns covered by the railroad embankment. A Confederate plan of the battle shows Bonaud's battalion advanced, supported by the Nineteenth Georgia and Sixth Florida, all between the wagon-road and the railroad, while beyond the railroad to their right were two guns of Guerard's battery and some cavalry. Only the Fifty-fourth in the latter part of the action was on our left of the wagon-road in the battle-front.

Upon taking position the regiment received a steady but not severe musketry fire, with a flanking fire of shell from the artillery on our left front. The horses of the field and staff had been sent to the rear. Colonel Hallowell mounted the stump of a tree some fifty feet in rear of his centre to oversee his men and the position. After a time Companies D and B on the left were thrown back to present a better front and guard that flank. While retiring from making report of this to Colonel Hallowell, Acting Sergeant-Major Swails was wounded.

On the extreme right, Lieutenant Homans, an impetuous and brave officer, noticing the exposed position of the two pieces, sprang in front of his line, and shouting, "Now is a good opportunity; we'll try and take those guns!" led his men forward; but he was soon ordered back into line.

In the centre, where Captain Bridge was prominent, our companies were enduring an increased musketry fire from front and flank. Sharpshooters were observed perched in the trees, but a few volleys brought them down. We were sustaining casualties every moment; but most of the missiles passed overhead.

Assistant-Surgeons Bridgham and Pease brought their ambulance to the field and proceeded to establish themselves not far from the line. After some time, and a shell having fallen near by, they retired to a less exposed place. Colonel Montgomery, accompanied by his staff, was round and about the Fifty-fourth line exposing himself freely; perceiving the strong fire coming from the direction of the railroad, he shouted, "Fire to the left! Fire to the left!"

Under such conditions after a while the men began to

chafe, and exhibit a desire for aggressive action. Already Warren Moorhouse, of Company E, and another man had crept out as sharpshooters. Sergeant Stephens, of Company B, remembered distinctly that "a little black fellow, whose name I cannot recall, would run forward beyond the line in his excitement, discharging his piece, fall back and load, and then rush out again. Our line was doing its level best. Shortly, this man I speak of fell, shot through the head."

Now there occurred an episode which shows that the colored soldiers, of the Fifty-fourth at least, possessed other than passive courage. They had, as stated, endured the situation with growing impatience. Suddenly Sergeant Wilkins, with the national flag, was seen advancing, followed by the men about him. They had proceeded some one hundred and fifty paces when Colonel Hallowell, realizing that the regiment without orders might follow them into a dangerous position unsupported, sent word for a return.

Meanwhile in the action Captain Jewell (who had been relieved from staff duty at his own request), Lieutenants Littlefield and Tomlinson, and many men had been wounded, and some killed. The regiment had been firing very rapidly; for many of the men, by jarring their pieces on the ground, sent the loads home without using the ramrods. It was observed that the musketry fire of the enemy was more effective than that of their artillery. Their shells were fired too high, passing over into the trees back of the Fifty-fourth. From the heavy gun on the railroad car came reports which dominated all other battle sounds.

This spirited movement into action of the colored brigade is acknowledged to have caused the enemy's right to give way somewhat, and imperilled the guns of Captain

Wheaton's Chatham Artillery. Under cover of its onset Seymour withdrew his white troops to a new line some one hundred yards in the rear,—Langdon being forced to abandon three of his guns. This retirement was continued in successive lines of battle. A newspaper correspondent, writing of the action, said, "The two colored regiments had stood in the gap and saved the army." But the cost had been great, particularly to the First North Carolina, for it lost Lieut.-Col. Wm. N. Reed, commanding, mortally wounded; Maj. A. Bogle, Adjt. W. C. Manning, three captains, and five lieutenants wounded; one captain killed, and some two hundred and thirty enlisted men killed, wounded, or missing. Having maintained the contest for some time, it was withdrawn.

Every organization had retired but the Fifty-fourth, and our regiment stood alone. From the position first taken up it still held back the enemy in its front. What had occurred elsewhere was not known. Why the Fifty-fourth was left thus exposed is inexplicable. No orders were received to retire. No measures were taken for its safe withdrawal. It would seem either that the position of the regiment was forgotten, or its sacrifice considered necessary.

Darkness came on early amid the tall pines. It was now about 5.30 P.M. The Fifty-fourth had lost heavily. Corporal Peal, with the State color, was mortally wounded, and from his hands Corp. Preston Helman, of Company E, received the flag. Of the color guard Corporal Gooding, of Company C, was mortally wounded, and Corporals Glasgow of B and Palmer of K were also wounded. One other noncommissioned officer was killed, and seven wounded. Only a few cartridges remained in the boxes; more were brought, but they proved to be of the wrong calibre.

From the sounds of battle extending behind our right, it at last became apparent that our forces had fallen back. Colonel Montgomery was with the Fifty-fourth, and seems to have determined to retire it in his bushwhacking way. This he did, as his staff-officer Captain Pope relates, by telling the men to save themselves. Lieutenant-Colonel Hooper recalls that the men informed him that Montgomery said, "Now, men, you have done well. I love you all. Each man take care of himself." But this plan did not please Lieutenant-Colonel Hooper, so telling Color Sergeant Wilkins to stand fast, and securing the co-operation of officers and reliable men near at hand, he shouted, "Rally!" and a line was again formed.

At this time Colonel Hallowell with others became separated from the main portion. Lieutenant-Colonel Hooper, thus in command, briefly addressed the men, ordered bayonets fixed, and exercised the regiment in the manual of arms to bring it completely under control. Lieutenant Loveridge of Montgomery's staff at Lieutenant-Colonel Hooper's request rode out to the right, and returning, reported the enemy following our forces without order. The regiment was then directed to give nine loud cheers to make it appear we were receiving reinforcements. In line of battle faced to the rear the Fifty-fourth then marched off the field, stopping every two or three hundred yards and retiring again. The enemy did not follow closely, but some of their cavalry were on the right flank. Stray cannon-shots and musket-balls occasionally fell about. After thus moving back some considerable distance, the Fifty-fourth, passing through woods, came in sight on the left of part of a regiment armed with breech-loaders. This body of men retired, and soon another body of men was encountered, which also retired. At last the regiment came up with Seymour's main force, where Colonel Hallowell found it, and assumed command.

Before the Fifty-fourth retired, the boxes of unused ammunition of the wrong calibre were thrown into mudholes. Assistant-Surgeon Bridgham also sent on before his only ambulance with wounded officers and men. Lieutenant Leonard, when leaving the field, found Adjutant Manning, First North Carolina, helplessly wounded; so swinging his friend upon his back, he carried him to a point of safety. Sergeant Swails, wounded in the head, set out toward Sanderson, but soon fell exhausted beside the road, unable to make himself known. Lieut. Lewis Reed, passing by, recognized him, and had him placed on a cart. Sergeant Vogelsang relates that Colonel Hallowell had, in charge of a servant, a mule laden with his camp kit, etc., packed in two champagne baskets. Upon going to the rear, some guards would not allow the servant and his mule to pass. The servant pleaded with them, saying, "Gentlemen, for God's sake, let the mule go!" and while doing so, the mule, taking matters into its own hands, kicked up its heels and broke through the line, strewing the path with pots, kettles, and pans, tipped out of the overturned baskets. This caused great merriment; and "Let the mule go!" became a saying in the regiment.

From the general field hospital, established behind a small stream, Seymour made his final retirement. Some forty men severely wounded were left in charge of Assistant-Surgeon Devendorf, Forty-eighth New York, there; and at Sanderson some twenty-three more remained. Moving toward Sanderson, the narrow road was choked with a flowing torrent of soldiers on foot, wounded and unwounded, vehicles of every description laden with wrecks of men, while amid the throng rode others, many of whom roughly forced their jaded animals through the crowd. In this throng generous and self-sacrificing men were seen helping along disabled comrades, and some shaking forms with bandaged heads or limbs, still carrying their trusty muskets. About the sides of the road exhausted or bleeding men were lying, unable to proceed, resigned, or thoughtless of inevitable captivity.

While our advance presented these deplorable scenes, the rear-guard was still full of courage and obedient to command. Notable among these organizations were the Seventh Connecticut, the Fifty-fourth Massachusetts, and Henry's brigade. When Sanderson was reached, the troops halted until the place was cleared of wounded and vehicles, when fires were set to stores previously spared, and it was abandoned. With the Seventh Connecticut deployed in rear of the infantry, and Henry's mounted men covering all, the army retired to Barber's, destroying bridges and the railroad as they proceeded.

General Finegan, who came upon the field during the later part of the action, ordered Colquitt to pursue and occupy Sanderson. Colquitt representing that his men were fatigued and without food, and that reports had come in that we had gone into camp and were in good order, these instructions were countermanded. Finegan states that although he gave repeated orders for his cavalry under Colonel Smith to press our flanks and pursue, it was not done except by two companies on our right for a short distance. All the Confederates, except one regiment, retired to Olustee that night, and no advance was made in force by the enemy until February 22.

Major Appleton at Barber's was relieved just after dark by Colonel Hartwell with six companies of the Fifty-fifth Massachusetts. He then set out, as instructed, to join the regiment with the two companies, and Lieut. W. B. Pease and twenty-five men of the Eighth United States Colored Troops, who had come up. Ten miles on, a surgeon with wounded gave the first intimation of defeat, although the firing had been heard at Barber's. Hastening onward through an ever-increasing throng, when within one mile of Sanderson Major Appleton halted, disposing his men to restore order. The sight of his compact little force was encouraging; and the unwounded, when approached, readily placed themselves in line until some six hundred men were collected. Major Appleton soon received orders to escort the train to Barber's, and did so, arriving at 2 A.M. on the 21st.

Forming part of the covering column, the Fifty-fourth made the night-march over the littered road until at 2 A.M. the bivouac fires of the Fifty-fifth at Barber's were reached. Then the regiment, worn out with the enervating events of the day, and the march of thirty-two miles since the preceding morning, went to rest on the ground previously occupied. Soon, however, Companies A and E were detailed for picket across the St. Mary's,—the former on the line, and the latter occupying a block house. Pickets from the Fifty-fifth were also put out. An attack was of course expected; but notwithstanding the probable danger, it was difficult for the officers to keep their exhausted men awake. But the night passed without alarm of any kind. Throughout those hours the wounded and stragglers kept coming in. Barber's house and outbuildings were used to shelter the wounded, while others were taken to or gathered about the large fires Colonel Hartwell caused to be made. Assistant-Surgeon Bridgham sheltered the wounded of the Fifty-fourth in an old house, and never ceased to care for them till morning.

Olustee was the most sanguinary engagement in which the troops of the Department met the enemy. Our loss was greater than in many better-known actions elsewhere. Fought without the shelter of earthworks, with nearly equal numbers on each side, it was a fair field fight. Our force was beaten in detail, as they came up, Seymour repeating his error committed at the assault of Wagner. It is natural to speculate as to the result, had he amused the enemy with skirmishers until all his troops arrived on the field, and then attacked, or attempted to draw the enemy on to a selected position; but had Seymour prevailed at Ocean Pond, there still was the strong intrenched position at Olustee Station to encounter.

Phisterer's Statistical Record gives the Union loss as 193 killed, 1,175 wounded, and 460 missing, a total of 1,828. Many of the wounds were slight, however. Our losses in the Fifty-fourth are given by the Adjutant-General of Massachusetts as three officers wounded, and of enlisted men thirteen killed, sixty-three wounded, and eight missing. It is probable that besides Corporal Gooding, of Company C, who died at Andersonville Prison, several others of the Fifty-fourth reported missing were there confined. General Finegan gives his casualties as 93 killed and 841 wounded. His killed included Lieutenant-Colonel Barrow, Sixty-fourth Georgia, Captain Cameron commanding, and Lieutenants Dancy and Holland, First Georgia (regulars). Among his wounded were Colonel Evans, Sixty-fourth Georgia, Col. D. L. Clinch, Fourth Georgia Cavalry, and Captain Crawford, Twenty-eighth Georgia. After the war in 1867 or 1868 the remains of Union soldiers buried on the field of Olustee were taken to the National Cemetery at Beaufort, S. C., for reinterment. The battlefield remains in much the same state as in 1864,—an open pine barren with many trees bearing the scarifications of shot and shell.

Provision was made for carrying the wounded from Barber's, February 21, by placing them on wagons, and on cars drawn by animals over the railroad. Our army followed in three parallel columns. The Fifty-fourth, placed under Colonel Hawley's command, moved at 9 A.M. When relieved from picket, Companies A and E were temporarily attached to the Fifty-fifth Massachusetts, which, with two other regiments, retired from Barber's in line of battle for some distance, covering the other infantry. In rear of all was the Light Brigade. Passing through Darby's, where an immense pile of barrels of turpentine was flaming and smoking, the regiment arrived at Baldwin about 4 P.M. The Fifty-fourth was not allowed to take the clothing left there, which was destroyed with other stores. There Companies A and E re-joined, and the regiment continued on to near McGirt's Creek, where it halted for the night after throwing out pickets. A twenty-two mile march had been made that day. Barton's brigade and Montgomery with the First North Carolina continued on farther.

At 4 A.M. on the 22d the Fifty-fourth stood to arms until daylight. Hawley, with the Fifty fourth, Seventh New Hampshire, and Eighth United States Colored Troops, moved on at 7 A.M., the Seventh Connecticut having been left at Baldwin to support the Light Brigade. Four miles farther on, Colonel Hallowell received orders from General Seymour to march his regiment back to Ten-Mile Station, and bring on the railroad train, as the locomotive had broken down. It was a hard trial for the footsore and hungry men to retrace their steps; but the thought of the cars laden with wounded nerved them to the task, so they faced about cheerfully. Upon arriving at the station, Quartermaster Ritchie found some hard bread on the train which he distributed to our men, sadly in need of food. Then ropes were attached to the engine and cars; and the Fifty-fourth furnishing the motive-power, they were pushed and dragged over the rails to Camp Finegan, where horses were provided for further progress.

Dr. Marsh, of the Sanitary Commission, who was present, thus describes this event:—

> "Through eagerness to escape the supposed pursuing enemy, too great pressure of steam was employed, and the flue collapsed; and here the immortal Fifty-fourth (colored) did what ought to insure it higher praise than to hold the field in the face of a victorious foe,—with ropes it seized the engine (now useless) and dragged it with its doomed freight for many miles. . . . They knew their fate if captured; their humanity triumphed. Does history record a nobler deed?"

During our short halt at Camp Finegan the men rested after their exhaustive efforts. Lieutenant Knight, Second South Carolina, kindly brought refreshments for the officers; and the men were supplied with some rations. The march was resumed at 4 P.M., and the Fifty-fourth without further incident arrived at Jacksonville about 8 P.M., going into camp on the old ground outside the town. Nearly one half the regiment was without shoes; their blankets and knapsacks were sacrificed to get speedily into action; they had no rations or shelter, so with crippled feet and weary limbs they cast themselves on the bare ground for rest after the march of twenty-two miles that day. The Adjutant-General of Massachusetts reported that "the Fifty-fourth marched 120 miles in 102 hours, yet the roll-call showed no stragglers;" and it should be added, of this time forty-four hours were given to sleep.

Seymour's infantry was all back at Jacksonville or vicinity by the 22d; his mounted force was in advance at Cedar Run. As it was feared the enemy would attack Jacksonville, reinforcements arrived daily, including Brigadier-General Vogdes with Foster's and Ames's brigades. An extensive line of earthworks was begun, encircling the town.

General Finegan, having repaired the railroad, advanced, occupying the territory to within ten or twelve miles of Jacksonville. He was soon succeeded by Brig.-Gen. W. M. Gardner. By March 3 the Confederate force in front numbered some eight thousand men. Their position was soon protected by earthworks, and was called Camp Milton.

A mail received February 24 brought news of the discharge of Captain Higginson for transfer, and Adjutant James and Lieutenant Pratt for disability. Assistant-Surgeon Bridgham resigned, and departed on the 26th. In accordance with the desire of his officers as well as his own, Colonel Hallowell on the 24th recommended to Governor Andrew that Sergeant Swails be commissioned, in recognition of many soldierly qualities and his gallantry at Olustee.

Our short season of quiet was disturbed on the 25th, when, in the morning, camp was moved to a point south of the railroad near the cemetery, in a grove and partly in a brickyard, next the Fifty-fifth Massachusetts. Soon both regiments were ordered back as the pickets were retiring. The Fifty-fourth took post on the left of the railroad in prolongation of the earthworks, and after two hours' work its front was covered by a good parapet. Quartermaster

Ritchie hauled out ammunition, and then as no crackers were to be had, finding an old oven, had soft bread baked. The worthy quartermaster describes his first batch as "a sort of indigestible paste very good for diarrhoea."

Our wounded were first cared for at Jacksonville, and then sent to Hilton Head and Beaufort. Major Appleton, on the 26th, with Companies A, B, and E, was sent to occupy works at the front as a reserve, should the cavalry be forced back. That day the Fifty-fourth and Fifty-fifth Massachusetts were brigaded together for the first time, under Col. M. S. Littlefield, Twenty-first United States Colored Troops. Our camp was again shifted to the brickyard on the 27th. Late that day Company E and thirty men of Company F, with Lieutenants Lewis Reed and Knowles, under Captain Emilio, were sent to guard the railroad and telegraph to Cedar Run. Messrs. Jones and Whitfield, sutlers, arrived with a cargo of goods on the 28th, and as they gave credit to the men, were well patronized.

About this time a corporal and private of the Fifty-fourth, posted on the railroad, while firing at a stray hog accidentally wounded a bandsman of the Fortieth Massachusetts. Col. Guy V. Henry sent for the men, took them to his camp, and there tied them up in a manner which caused great suffering. General Seymour expressed his intention to have the men shot. Such threats for trivial offences were frequent during General Seymour's command in Florida. An officer of the One Hundred and Fifteenth New York relates that a man of his regiment was ordered to be shot in three hours, for firing his musket. The provost-marshal asked him if he was ready to die, and the poor fellow with streaming eyes inquired if there was no hope. Only the pleading of his officers saved his life.

Another man of the same regiment for taking a chicken received a similar sentence, but was pardoned.

By the last of February the number of troops at Jacksonville was quite large. They were encamped beyond the earthworks, which extended about a mile and a half around. In the river the gunboats "Mahaska," "Ottawa," and "Pawnee" were ready to aid in the defence. Churches in the town were opened, wharves were repaired, and warehouses put in order. Bay Street along the river-front was teeming with busy life. Vessels were arriving and departing. Stores were opened by sutlers and tradespeople, and a newspaper, "The Peninsula," was printed. Never before had Jacksonville held so many people. All enjoyed the charming weather of those warm and balmy spring days.

Colonel Hallowell was given command of our third brigade of Ames's division on February 29, making his headquarters at the Florida House. The next day General Gillmore reviewed all his troops at Jacksonville. On the same date, from their strong defensive line at McGirt's Creek, Colonel Zachry, Twenty-seventh Georgia, with infantry and artillery, started out to advance the enemy's picket. He was met by Colonel Henry with two companies of the Fortieth Massachusetts and one gun, and our force was obliged to retire to Cedar Run. After a sharp skirmish there, we fell back still farther to Three-Mile Run. Henry lost one man killed, four wounded, and five captured; the enemy seven killed and more than thirty wounded. Captain Emilio, with the Fifty-fourth men, on the railroad, retired with the cavalry. In consequence of this affair all the troops were drawn back to the lines, as an attack was expected.

Camp was again changed to the brickyard from the lines on the 3d, where the regiment remained until its departure from Florida. On this date we had thirteen officers and

725 men present. Thereafter three companies were furnished for picket every third day.

General Beauregard arrived at Camp Milton March 2, and inspected the lines. Maj.-Gen. J. Patton Anderson assumed immediate command there the succeeding day. Beauregard telegraphed the War Department that he would endeavor to draw us out for battle. He gave our force as twelve thousand and his own eight thousand. In reply he was told that we were overestimated, and he was ordered to attack. Now was the opportunity for the offensive he so many times had fruitlessly recommended against the "Abolitionists," as he was wont to call us. But he only informed the Department that he should not attack, and that he was willing to turn over the command to General Anderson, who would attack, if ordered. Then the War Department seems to have done nothing further about the matter.

Barton's brigade, with some artillery and cavalry, embarked for Pilatka up the St. John's on the 9th, and occupied the place the next day.

With a return to the monotony of camp the question of pay again became a source of discontent. False rumors of Congressional action in behalf of the men came, but to be soon contradicted. By every mail they received letters setting forth the sufferings of their families. The officers, jealous of the good name and behavior of the regiment, were in fear of some overt fact such as had occurred in other regiments, where colored soldiers had refused duty and suffered punishment. At this time an officer of the Fifty-fourth wrote,—

"Sometimes we almost despair about our men in the matter of pay and proper recognition. We cannot but think it needs only to be thoroughly understood—this case of ours—to have justice done us.... These men were enlisted either legally under the Act of July, 1861, and they should then be paid as soldiers, or illegally, and then they should be mustered out of the service.... Think of what the men do and suffer; think of their starving families. There is Sergeant Swails, a man who has fairly won promotion on the field of battle. While he was doing the work of government in the field, his wife and children were placed in the poorhouse."

In a letter to Hon. Wm. Whiting, Solicitor of the War Department at Washington, Lieutenant-Colonel Hooper wrote,—

"The question whether the men of the Fifty-fourth were legally enlisted into the service of the United States is about to be put before a court-martial here,—that is, a man of the regiment is to be tried by a court-martial for a military offence, and he will put in a plea in bar of trial, on the ground that he is not amenable to a court-martial because he is not a soldier; that he is not a soldier because he was illegally enlisted,—hence he is no soldier."

Lieutenant-Colonel Hooper then recited the Act of July 22, 1861, saying that its provisions were read to the man and subscribed to by him. But the Government instructed its agents that it could only pay the Fifty-fourth (to which this man belonged) according to the provision of the Act of July 17, 1862. He asked assistance in solving the question in behalf of his men, and further asked for a decision from Judge Holt bearing upon the point at issue.

Advices from the North informed us of the efforts of the Massachusetts Congressmen in Washington to equalize the pay of colored and white troops. The first bill offered by Senator Wilson was not retrospective, and received the opposition it merited in Congress and by the press. To remedy this defect the senator reported a joint resolution on February 3, which, variously amended, came up until March 2, when it was returned to committee. Senator Fessenden, of Maine, led the opposition. The key-note of his remarks in debate was: "What propriety is there in our going back and paying them for services already rendered?" The Maine senator's course received the merited scorn of Wendell Phillips at a meeting of the Antislavery Society. He said,—

"Senator Fessenden was the son of one of the first Abolitionists of that State, the ablest debater in the Senate, the leader of that body. Governor Andrew's proclamation was published in one hundred papers of the United States calling colored men to arms for Massachusetts. The War Department knew of it. It was a government contract. The Government, accepting these men, accepted the contract. Wilson said to Fessenden, 'Will you fulfil it?' This pettifogger, representing the State of Maine, replied, 'I would like to see Governor Andrew's written authority!' "

Mr. Wilson on March 2 reported a new bill equalizing soldiers' pay. By one section colored soldiers were given the same pay as whites from Jan. 1, 1864; another section gave the same bounties to colored as to white volunteers in the loyal States, enlisted under the Act of October, 1863; and still a third gave the same pay to colored soldiers as other volunteers from muster-in, if so pledged to them by authority of the War Department, the Secretary of War to determine the question of fact. This bill passed the Senate March 10, and went to the House. There was still to be the struggle amending the Army Appropriation Bill, that the provisions of the Equalizing Bill could be carried out, if agreed upon by the House. Copies of Mr. Wilson's bill were received by Colonel Hallowell soon after its presentation; and it was ordered read to the enlisted men of every company of the Fifty-fourth, which was done.

In Massachusetts the friends of the regiment were, through the committee, doing much to aid the distressed families within their reach, by contributions of money and clothing. Those in other States were numerous, and the story of their sufferings would fill a volume.

General Seymour issued the following order, which was read to the regiments of his command,—

HEADQUARTERS DISTRICT OF FLORIDA, DEP'T OF THE SOUTH,
JACKSONVILLE, FLA., March 10, 1864.

General Orders No. 13.

The brigadier-general commanding recurs with great satisfaction to the conduct of his troops in their late battle, and desires to convey to them in the most public manner his full appreciation of their courage on that well-contested field.

Against superior numbers holding a position chosen by themselves, you were all but successful. For four hours you stood face to face with the enemy; and when the battle ended, and it ceased only with night, you sent him cheers of defiance.

In your repulse there was perhaps misfortune, but neither disaster nor disgrace; and every officer and soldier may remember with just pride that he fought at Olustee.

By order of
BRIGADIER-GENERAL SEYMOUR.

Lieut. Thos. L. Appleton re-joined on the 11th, bringing on the steamer "Boston" the camp equipage; and tents were put up on the 14th. Although there was more rain in March than during the preceding month, the weather in the main was most enjoyable, and camp-life under canvas a pleasure. Our frequent tours of picket duty in the pine woods were always delightful, amid the trees, vines, and beautiful ferns.

Deserters came in occasionally. From them it was learned that the enemy was fortifying a strong position in front of Baldwin. Most of their cavalry was ordered elsewhere in March. Both forces were apprehensive of attack, and alarms occurred frequently, occasioned by picket firing and reconnoissances. On the 23d the prize steamers "Sumter" and "Hattie Brock," captured at Deep Creek on the 14th, were brought to Jacksonville.

During March, Lieutenant Howard was made adjutant. Captains Jones and Walton re-joined. Lieutenants Chas. Jewett, Jr., and Daniel G. Spear, newly appointed, joined. Assistant-Surgeon Pease went North sick, and never returned. News of a number of promotions came on the 26th. Lieutenant Homans was made captain of Company C, *vice* Partridge; Lieutenant Tucker captain of Company H, *vice* Higginson; Lieut. T. L. Appleton captain of Company G, *vice* Smith. Second Lieutenants Chipman, Lewis Reed, Leonard, Knowles, Duren, and Newell were promoted first lieutenants. Sergt. Stephen A. Swails, of Company F, was commissioned second lieutenant.

Brig.-Gen. John P. Hatch relieved General Seymour of the command in Florida, March 28. He was a West Point graduate, who had served with the Third Infantry and Mounted Rifles in Mexico and on the frontier. His commission dated Sept. 28, 1861, and he had been connected with the Army of the Potomac. Colonel Henry, with the Fortieth Massachusetts, Seventy-fifth Ohio, and One Hundred and Sixty-ninth New York, went upon a reconnoissance April 2. He found the enemy's outposts a mile beyond Cedar Run, and drove them until a strong skirmish line was shown, when he retired, with four men wounded.

General Anderson courteously sent to us on the 6th a list of our wounded and captured at Olustee, giving 449 names, nine of which purported to be Fifty-fourth men. In the Record of Massachusetts Volunteers but five of these names are found; namely, Corp. J. H. Gooding, Company C, who is given as having died at Andersonville; Private Isaac H. Hawkins, Company D, who was discharged June 20, 1865; Private Wm. Mitchell, Company F, discharged as a prisoner of war; and Jason Champlin and Wm. H. Morris, of Company K, whom the Record reports as missing, but who probably died in prison.

At the camp, drills and parades had been resumed for some time. On April 3 the number of officers was increased by the arrival of Lieut. Edward L. Stevens, newly appointed. On April 12 the Eighth United States Colored Troops was added to our brigade. The Fifty-fifth Massachusetts since March 11 had been detached at Pilatka.

By this period in April regiments began to move from Florida. Pilatka was evacuated on the 14th. Several transports were sailing away daily, the men cheering, bands playing, and flags fluttering, as they departed. In the public square regiments drawn from the lines were bivouacked, awaiting embarkation. News was received that the steamers "General Hunter" and "Maple Leaf" had been blown up by torpedoes at Buckle's Bluff. Thus the two transports which had brought us to Florida were sunk in the St. John's.

April 17 was the last day of our sojourn in Florida. Line was formed at 9 A.M., and the march to the transport began. Passing into town, the regiment halted and presented arms at the headquarters of General Hatch, the district, and General Ames, the division commander. Embarkation was speedily effected. Major Ten Eyck paid the officers on board. At 11 A.M. the "Cosmopolitan" steamed down river. Our transport was a noble craft, the hospital steamer of the department. As on our advent, the day of departure was delightful; and the vessel glided over the waters of the majestic river steadily and swiftly. Those few weeks in the "land of flowers" left recollections never to be effaced of soft skies, beautiful plants, perfume of orange and magnolia, the resinous odor of the pines; of battle and defeat, severe marches, midnight alarms, and long hours of picket in woody solitudes. But speculations as to where we were going were then uppermost in our minds. Were we to join the armies of the North with a prospect of military glory and its accompanying danger, or to be doomed to comparative inaction in the Department of the South, depleted of its troops? Musing thus, we ran past part of our sister regiment, the Fifty-fifth, at Yellow Bluff, continuing down the river to its junction with blue water. There the tide was found not to be serving; and our transport lay swinging and rolling lazily in unison with other craft, similarly detained, until the bar could be safely crossed and the open sea gained.

In the North great movements were preparing. Lieutenant-General Grant had been appointed to the chief command of the armies. A combined movement of the Army of the Potomac and the Army of the James against Richmond was determined upon, and General Gillmore was ordered to join the latter army with the divisions of Terry, Turner, and Ames, of the Tenth Corps, as rapidly as they could be transported. General Hatch was to take command of the Department of the South.

Aware of the impending stroke in Virginia and the with-drawal of our main force from Florida, by April 18 the enemy had sent away the larger part of his troops. General Beauregard had been relieved of the command on April 20 by Maj.-Gen. Samuel Jones, and departed for Weldon, N.C.

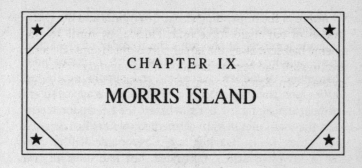

CHAPTER IX

MORRIS ISLAND

Oᴜʀ ᴠᴏʏᴀɢᴇ ꜰʀᴏᴍ Fʟᴏʀɪᴅᴀ terminated at Stono Inlet on the morning of April 18. The steamer thence proceeded up Folly River, but running aground, the left-wing companies were transferred to the steamer "Canonicus." Disembarking at Pawnee Landing about 3 ᴘ.ᴍ., the Fifty-fourth at once marched to Lighthouse Inlet in a heavy rain-storm, and there crossed on a large flat boat to Morris Island. Shelter for the night was provided in the ordnance building for the men, the officers finding accommodations with friends. That evening Captain Emilio was ordered to command the outpost of Black Island with Companies C, E, and H, as the garrison.

Camp was established where the receding sand-hills formed a sort of natural amphitheatre, at a point about a mile up the the beach, near the signal hill. There the regiment remained during its continuance on Morris Island. A company was sent to Fort Wagner that evening, and the next day suffered the loss of one man, killed by a shell.

Again the Fifty-fourth was upon the sand isle, which the winds and tides had perceptibly encroached upon during our absence. At the front the thunder of great guns rang out only occasionally, in place of incessant bombardment. Monitors, gunboats, and supply-vessels still rode upon the near waters; and blockaders appeared and disappeared along the horizon before the beleaguered port. But the thousands of blue-garmented soldiery had departed for other fields, leaving but a remnant behind. Col. W. W. H. Davis still commanded, but had only his own regiment,—the One Hundred and Fourth Pennsylvania,— the Fifty-second Pennsylvania, and five companies of the Third Rhode Island Heavy Artillery on Morris Island, and the Eleventh Maine on Black Island. Few events of importance had occurred during the winter months. Vessels still ran the blockade, but sometimes came to grief, as did the "Presto," which went ashore on Sullivan's Island February 2, and was destroyed by our guns. The navy lost the "Housatonic" on February 17, sunk by a torpedo boat, the latter also going to the bottom with all on board. Sumter had been made stronger against assault, and a few guns were mounted on its channel face.

Black Island was reached by the three companies, after laboriously rowing up Lighthouse Inlet and the creeks, on the evening of the 18th. The Eleventh Maine was relieved there and departed the next day. This outpost, occupied by a portion of the Fifty-fourth until Charleston was evacuated, merits description. It was of small extent and almost the only dry spot amid the marshes between Morris and James Islands. The safety of Lighthouse Inlet and the inland channel from Stono depended upon its safe maintenance. Our heavy guns, mounted there in August, 1863, had been removed. There was an enclosed work holding a single Wiard rifle-gun. As it was within range of the lower James Island batteries, bombproofs had been constructed. From a platform near the top of a tall pine-tree called the "Crow's Nest," commanding a fine view of the whole region, a constant watch was kept. Messages were sent to and received from Morris Island by signal flags and torches. A foot-bridge over the marshes connected it with the main post. Stores had to be brought in rowboats. Much vegetation covered the ground, rendering it altogether a pleasanter spot than Morris Island. Some twenty-five men were detailed daily for guards and pickets. A non-commissioned officer and five men in each of two boats were sent at night to guard the water-ways toward James Island. Sergt. Joseph Sulsey of Company E was appointed acting sergeant-major. A detail of twenty-three non-commissioned officers and men was placed under instruction until proficiency was attained in artillery practice.

Colonel Hallowell assumed command of Morris Island on the 20th, relieving Colonel Davis, who, with the Fifty-second and One Hundred and Fourth Pennsylvania, departed for Hilton Head. The next day Colonel Montgomery arrived and relieved Colonel Hallowell. He brought the Thirty-fourth United States Colored Troops (formerly the Second South Carolina) and the Twenty-first United States Colored Troops. Col. William Gurney, with his regiment, the One Hundred and Twenty-seventh New York, came on the 23d, and in turn relieved Montgomery. In consequence of these frequent changes of post-commander some of the Fifty-fourth companies were as often shifted from one duty to another. On the 23d Companies B and G were made the provost-guard at Morris Island; but Company B was relieved therefrom in two or three days. Companies A, I, and K, under Lieutenant Leonard, were detailed for a few days as boat infantry. Captain Jones, with Company D, relieved a company of the Thirty-fourth United States Colored Troops as the garrison of Fort Shaw.

A very heavy wind swept the island on the 25th, which blew down the Beacon house on the beach-front. This prominent landmark was a frame building, resting on a masonry foundation. On the northerly end was the chimney-stack, and surmounting the roof was a cupola. It had long been stripped of weather boarding, and stood, skeleton-like, in our daily pathway to and from Cumming's Point.

General Schimmelfennig, commanding the Northern District, and Colonel Gurney visited Black Island May 1, and after inspecting the post, viewed the enemy's lines beyond. About this period the commanding officer thus wrote:—

> "So near are we to the enemy on this island that we can distinctly hear the bands and drums on James Island, and see them drilling in the daytime. For the past few nights we could hear them having jolly times at Secessionville, cheering, etc., and from seeing regiments leaving in heavy marching order, with baggage-wagons in the rear, judge that the uproar was occasioned by these departures of troops, probably to join Lee."

General Gillmore, on May 1, formally relinquished command of the department to General Hatch. Admiral Dahlgren, who had been North, returned that day and records in his journal: "Hatch says that Gillmore has taken off twenty thousand men, and leaves him no more than enough to hold on." On the 17th Dahlgren writes that Hatch had some fourteen thousand men remaining, "which were barely sufficient for the defensive."

No mails came to Morris Island for many days, while the steamers were all employed in transporting troops North. The infantry regiments went out in regular turn for grand guard, and fatigue work, at the front, or at the ordnance and quartermaster's depots. Our artillerymen were throwing about a dozen shells into Charleston daily. Against Sumter they were firing mainly with mortars at night. A new commander was in charge of the Confederates there, for Capt. John C. Mitchel, First South Carolina Artillery, relieved Colonel Elliott on May 4.

For some time a very few men of the Fifty-fourth had manifested sullenness and an indisposition to promptly obey orders, justifying their actions to themselves and others on the ground of non-payment. Advices from the North regarding Congressional action were surely discouraging. Mr. Wilson, on April 22, had moved to add the Equalizing to the Appropriation Bill, which was finally agreed to by the Senate; but the House amended it as to the amount of bounty and the clause authorizing the Secretary of War to allow full pay to those colored soldiers who had been promised it. In place, the House inserted a provision allowing full pay only to free persons of color who were enlisted. This the Senate refused to agree with on May 3. Two conference committees were appointed, but the House rejected their reports. Colonel Hallowell used every means to secure the just claims of the men by letters to their friends. His frequent applications for leave of absence upon this business had not been granted. When informed of the threatening disposition of the few men referred to, he visited each post, addressed the companies, explaining the causes of delay, and counselling patience still longer; but he warned the disaffected that orders must be obeyed, and set forth the sure penalty of disobedience.

His words were disregarded in but two instances. On May 12, a private of Company B, for refusing duty, was slightly wounded by a pistol-shot from an officer; and on the 21st another man (of Company H) was shot at and slightly wounded by an officer for a similar offence. This summary punishment inflicted was effective in its results to the command.

Colonel Hallowell on June 4 informed Governor Andrew that the regiment had not been paid, and requested that he demand of the Secretary of War that the Fifty-fourth be paid or sent to Massachusetts for muster-out, as the contract was broken.

For the further security of Black Island, early in May, Company E was ordered to encamp within the fort to guard against sudden attack; and Lieutenant Spear, in charge of the picket-boats from there, placed a boom of barrels, connected by chains, across the creek, in advance of his night stations. While visiting the pickets in the patrol-boat after dark, Captain Homans on one occasion discovered a floating torpedo, which he secured and brought to Black Island. It was made of staves, cigar-shaped, with a large cap to explode by contact.

Lieutenant-Colonel Hooper assumed command of the "Defences of Lighthouse Inlet" on May 7. They included Black Island, Battery Purviance, and Fort Green, on Folly Island, opposite Purviance. These two batteries mounted thirty-pounder Parrotts for offensive purposes against James Island. Lieutenant-Colonel Hooper made his headquarters at Fort Green. Captain Tucker, with Company H, left Black Island and relieved Lieutenant-Colonel Fox and Companies A and F, Fifty-fifth Massachusetts, at Fort Green on the 7th. Company I, under Lieut. Lewis Reed, took the place of Company H at Black Island.

A rude structure of logs raised above the marsh had been built by the Confederates near the water-ways toward James Island. We called it "Block House No. 1." Lieutenant Spear made a reconnoissance of it on the night of the 8th, and was twice fired upon. Capt. T. L. Appleton, provost-marshal on Colonel Gurney's staff, had been for some time making preparations to capture this block house. With a party of Fifty-fourth men he went there on the night of the 14th, only to find it unoccupied. It was visited a number of times afterward by our officers from Black Island.

There was an utter stagnation of active operations in the department. Hatch was considering a plan of moving up the Wando River in connection with the ironclads, and a foray at Murrell's Inlet and Georgetown. Admiral Dahlgren had convened another council of his chief officers when the project of attack on Sumter was again negatived. He was contenting himself with a sharp bombardment of the fort with an ironclad or two for the purpose of preventing work there. The land forces were firing more briskly in unison with the navy. High tides somewhat damaged our works at Cumming's Point toward the close of May.

Further changes of station occurred for some of our companies, as, on the 18th, Captain Emilio, with Company E, relieved Company H at Fort Green, and the succeeding day Captain Bridge, with Company F, took post at Battery Purviance. Company H returned to Black Island, where Captain Homans was in command; and the garrison there was increased toward the last of May by a portion of Company F, under Lieutenant Edmands. Then the Fifty-fourth held all the posts about Lighthouse Inlet. Our men at Green and Purviance in a short time became efficient artillerists, as had those of Company H.

Both works on Lighthouse Inlet were frequently engaged
with the lower James Island batteries about Secessionville, at long range.

General Hatch, having concluded to try to cut the railroad at Ashepoo, sent Brig.-Gen. William Birney with some
sixteen hundred men to make the attempt. He landed at
the mouth of Mosquito Creek on May 25, advancing about
six miles in the evening. The naval vessels landed a force
to co-operate on Johassie Island. The steamer "Boston,"
on which were Colonel Montgomery and the Thirty-fourth
United States Colored Troops, ran aground and was fired
upon by the enemy with artillery, compelling her abandonment and destruction by fire. General Birney's force
retired to Port Royal on the 27th.

Maj.-Gen. John G. Foster, a distinguished officer, who
graduated from West Point in 1846, took command of
the Department May 26. He was no stranger there, for
in April, 1861, he was the engineer officer at Moultrie
and Sumter, and in January, 1862, brought a large part
of the Eighteenth Corps to South Carolina. Throughout
the Civil War he suffered from a wound received in
Mexico.

As Lieutenant-Colonel Hooper was detailed for court-
martial duty and Captain Emilio as judge-advocate at Hilton Head, on May 29, Captain Bridge took command of
Lighthouse Inlet and Capt. T. L. Appleton of Fort Green.
During the ensuing night some of our officers perpetrated
a great joke on the Johnnies. Making the stuffed figure of
a soldier, they took it out in a boat and stood it on top of
Block House No. 1, placing an imitation gun in its hands.
When morning broke, the Johnnies espied the supposed
sentinel, and fired at him for half an hour, through which

he seemed to bear a charmed life. When they opened, we replied from Green and Purviance.

Lieutenant Swails, when commissioned, was placed on duty as an officer, but the application for his muster inaugurated a new struggle with the War Department. When the usual request was made, it was refused on account of Lieutenant Swails's African descent, although to all appearances he was a white man. After the regiment came under Colonel Gurney, Swails was ordered to discard his officer's uniform and take duty as an enlisted man. Colonel Hallowell, however, procured him a furlough, and sent him, provided with the necessary papers, to see General Foster at Hilton Head. There Lieutenant Swails presented his claims in person and received the general's recommendation for muster, to be forwarded to higher authority.

We had only seven monitors before Charleston June 1, with but four of that number serviceable, while the enemy had four ironclads. Their garrisons were depleted to the last man, artillerymen holding their forts with feeble supports. On James Island there was not a single infantry regiment; and for some time the Citadel Cadets, composed of youths, and some companies of city firemen, armed for the duty, served at that point. One of their supply-steamers grounded during the night of the 4th between Sumter and Johnson, and the next morning Gregg opened on her, and soon destroyed the craft. A few vessels, under skilful and daring officers, managed to run the blockade into Charleston. From first to last some sixty-seven steamers and twenty-one sailing-vessels eluded us, of which a large proportion were owned by J. Fraser & Co. With spool-cotton at $12.50 per dozen, sole-leather $9.25 per pound, writing-paper $72 per ream, steel pens $8.50 per gross, and other foreign goods in like proportion, enormous profits were realized, as the cotton exported cost but little over the ordinary price. A clear profit of $150,000 for the round trip was not unusual. Captains of vessels frequently realized $5,000 for the voyage.

Colonel Hallowell having at last received permission to proceed North to press the claims of the regiment in person, left Morris Island on June 6, and Major Appleton assumed command. On the same day the great ironclad, "New Ironsides," steamed away for the North. Our boat parties were spurred on to activity by General Schimmelfennig, who was desirous of obtaining information of the enemy's lines by such means, or from prisoners who might be secured. A steadier and increased fire on the city was ordered by General Foster.

General Jones, the Confederate Department commander, about this time bethought himself of an expedient by which he hoped to cause a cessation of our bombardment. He set forth his inhumane plan as follows:—

> CHARLESTON, June 1, 1864.
> GENERAL BRAGG,—The enemy continue their bombardment of the city with increased vigor, damaging private property and endangering the lives of women and children. I can take care of a party—say fifty—Yankee prisoners. Can you not send me that number including a general— Seymour will do—and other officers of high rank, to be confined in parts of the city still occupied by citizens under the enemy's fire?
>
> S. JONES.

In response to this telegram, Generals Wessells, Scammon, Shaler, Seymour, and Heckman, and forty-five field-officers were sent to Charleston and placed under fire,

General Jones notifying General Foster of the fact on June 13. In compliance with General Foster's request to the President, on the 29th Generals Gardner, Steuart, Archer, Jeff. Thompson, and Edward Johnson, besides forty-five Confederate field-officers, were received at Hilton Head and confined on the brig "Dragoon" there. It was General Foster's purpose if necessary to imprison these officers under fire in retaliation.

Our Morris Island garrison was reinforced on June 13 by the return of the Fifty-second Pennsylvania, Col. H. M. Hoyt; and the next day the Thirty-third United States Colored Troops landed and camped above the Fifty-fourth. A company of the One Hundred and Twenty-seventh New York relieved Company G, of our regiment, from provost duty on the 15th. On the next day at 5 P.M. the enemy fired salutes of shotted guns from every battery in view, besides two rams, probably in honor of some success to their arms.

Lieutenant-Colonel Hooper returned on the 18th and took command of the regiment, Major Appleton assuming charge of the defences of the inlet. During May and June the following changes took place among the officers: Surg. Chas. E. Briggs and Lieutenants Fred. E. Rogers, Joseph E. Cousens, Chas. O. Hallett and Benj. B. Edmands, newly appointed, reported; Capt. R. H. L. Jewett and Lieutenant Littlefield re-joined from the North; Assistant-Surgeon Pease resigned; Assistant-Surgeon Bridgham, who had been reappointed, reported June 5, but went to Beaufort, sick, resigning there on the 16th. Lieutenant Tomlinson was discharged at the North.

There was variable weather the second week in June, but remarkably cool for three days previous to the 15th, with rain. Then the hot weather set in, the temperature often being 90° in the shade. Orders were given for thorough policing, the burial of garbage, and the free use of disinfectants. Every man was required to bathe twice each week. Where practicable, sentry-boxes were built for shelter. The troops suffered from want of ice. Desiccated vegetables, soaked overnight and boiled with fresh beef, were issued twice a week. As fresh vegetables were sorely needed, Commissary-Sergeant Lee was sent to Beaufort and brought back a limited quantity.

Our daily duties of fatigue and grand guard went on unvaryingly week after week. The troops only looked forward to the arrival of the mails to bring news of events taking place elsewhere. Some sick and wounded comrades returned; and on June 20 we received twelve recruits for the regiment. That same day Quartermaster Ritchie recorded in his journal that he saw and talked with "Washington Smith just escaped from Charleston," who told him about the Fifty-fourth prisoners there. This seems to be the first news received of these men, then confined nearly a year.

Until late in June it was not expected that any active operations would be attempted, at least during the summer months. But on the 19th there were demonstrations made by our troops from Folly Island about the Stono. By the 29th evidences of some projected movement became apparent. Our scouting parties were urged to greater activity; boats were put in order, bridges toward James Island were laid, and ammunition was served out. The time seemed favorable, for the enemy were few in number, and did not expect attack.

Major Appleton, commanding Lighthouse Inlet, made a boat reconnoissance on the night of the 29th, nearly up to the enemy's lines at Secessionville. Orders were received on the 30th for the Fifty-fourth, except Companies C, H, I, and part of F at Black Island, to move at sunset, with arms and intrenching tools. But at 9 P.M., after waiting three hours, the orders to march were countermanded for twenty-four hours.

CHAPTER X

ATTACK ON
JAMES ISLAND

ADMIRAL DAHLGREN on June 20 received a letter from the Navy Department, informing him that the enemy was preparing to attack his fleet, inside and outside, to facilitate the shipment of a large amount of cotton from Charleston. He conferred with General Foster, and it was arranged to engage the enemy in maintaining his own lines by simultaneously attacking several points. It was hoped that the Charleston and Savannah Railroad might be cut, and a nearer and better position gained in front of the city. Brig.-Gen. Wm. Birney, ordered to Port Royal from Florida with a brigade of colored troops, was to ascend the North Edisto and destroy the railroad at Adam's Run. General Hatch with two brigades was to land at Seabrook Island, cross to John's Island, and be at the ferry near Rantowle's Bridge the succeeding night, to demonstrate against the city and Fort Pemberton from across the Stono. General Schimmelfennig's force, landing on James Island, was to front Secessionville; and he was also to send troops to John's Island to open communication with General Hatch. The navy was to assist at all these points, but more strongly in the Stono. Our batteries at Cumming's Point and on Lighthouse Inlet were to engage the enemy's attention.

July 1, at 6 P.M., the Fifty-fourth moved to the landing, crossed to Folly Island on pontoon-boats and scows, and Companies E and F having joined, marched to Stono. Although the men were lightly equipped, it was warm and exhausting. Arriving at 2 A.M., the regiment embarked on the steamer "Fraser;" and after provoking delays, which enabled the other regiments to precede us, we landed on Cole's Island at 4 A.M., on the 2d. Marching just after daybreak, the Fifty-fourth crossed to James Island over the route traversed a year before in the opposite direction. As the road and bridges had been repaired, there was little to remind us of the old pathway. While advancing, skirmish firing and cannon-shots were heard in the front.

Colonel Hartwell, ordered to attack on the right, with his regiment,—the Fifty-fifth Massachusetts,—the Thirty-third United States Colored Troops, and the One Hundred and Third New York, passed from Long to Tiger Island in darkness, and at daylight on the 2d crossed the marsh to James Island and advanced to surprise Fort Lamar. His skirmishers received the fire of the enemy's vedettes, drove them, and captured some prisoners and horses. Unknown to us, a force of the enemy was stationed every night at Rivers's Causeway, which this morning was composed of two guns of Blake's Battery under Lieutenant De Lorme, posted in a small fieldwork and supported by fifteen men of the Palmetto Siege Train under Lieutenant Spivey, besides the picket reserves. Our force was received with an unexpected fire of grape-shot and musketry, which caused

some losses and created confusion in the Thirty-third and
One Hundred and Third. But Colonel Hartwell, promptly
deploying the Fifty-fifth under Lieutenant-Colonel Fox,
pushed it rapidly forward in spite of a severe fire, drove
off the supports, and gallantly captured De Lorme's two
twelve-pounder Napoleons. In this charge the Fifty-fifth
had seven men killed, and Captains Thurber and Goodwin
and nineteen men wounded. The guns were manned and
fired at the retiring enemy. Colonel Hartwell moved beyond the fieldwork a short distance, and strengthening a
hedgebank and ditch, held this position throughout the
day under fire from Lamar and other works. As all hope
of a surprise was over, orders were signalled to make no
farther advance at that point.

Lieutenant-Colonel Bennett with his Twenty-first
United States Colored Troops and two guns under Lieu-
tenant Wildt, of Battery B, Third New York Artillery, landed
on John's Island to open communication with General
Hatch's force. Col. Wm. Heine (One Hundred and Third
New York), with the Fifty-fourth New York, Seventy-fourth
Pennsylvania, a section of Battery B, Third New York Ar-
tillery, and a rocket battery, moved from Cole's Island to
James Island, driving the enemy's pickets under Major
Managault. His force started at the same time as Colonel
Hartwell's, and advanced to the lines of the previous year
at the head of Grimball's Causeway. Only the gunboat
"McDonough" was ready to co-operate, for the monitors
were not on hand.

Even during these early hours the troops suffered
greatly from the heat, and in moving over Cole's Island
several men of the Fifty-fourth fell exhausted, and one
dropped senseless. The bridge to James Island was crossed
at 6 A.M., bringing us upon familiar ground. Captains Wal-

ton and Appleton, of General Schimmelfennig's staff, were
greeted as they passed by the officers. Some prisoners were
encountered going to the rear under guard. Passing our
old camp-ground and bearing to the left, the Seventy-
fourth Pennsylvania (a German regiment, as was the Fifty-
fourth New York) was seen deployed as skirmishers. About
a mile and a half from the bridge the low ground was
crossed; and Lieutenant-Colonel Hooper deployed the regiment under artillery fire. The line was formed as below,
with Company D on the right,—

F G B E A K D

and with the following officers present; Lieutenant-Colonel
Hooper, commanding; Major Appleton; Adjutant Howard;
Company D, Captain Jones and Lieutenant Swails; Com-
pany K, Lieutenant Leonard, commanding, and Lieutenant
Chas. Jewett, Jr.; Company A, Lieutenant Knowles; Com-
pany E, Captain Emilio and Lieutenants Chipman and Cousens; Company B, Lieutenant Newell, commanding, and
Lieutenant Hallett; Company G, Lieut. David Reid; Company F, Captain Bridge and Lieutenant Duren. Sergt. Chas.
A. Lenox, of Company A, bore the national flag, and Corp.
Jos. Stiles, of Company F, the State color, in the ranks of
Company E. There were 363 enlisted men present. Quartermaster Ritchie was also on the island. Surgeon Briggs
was detailed on Morris Island, and an assistant-surgeon
(whose name is not known), was temporarily assigned to
the regiment. All the horses had been left at Stono.

Though partially concealed by woods and irregularities
of the ground, we of the Fifty-fourth knew the formidable
character of the enemy's works in our front, for from the
"Crow's Nest" on Black Island we had seen in reverse the
line constructed since the previous summer in advance of

the older works. Fort Pemberton and Batteries Pringle and Tynes were on the Stono to our left front; and from there to Fort Lamar and Secessionville were mutually supporting and detached fieldworks for artillery united by curtains for infantry. The enemy's force comprised some Georgia Volunteers, Lucas's battalion, the South Carolina Siege Train, detachments of the Second South Carolina Artillery, Blake's battery, and the Chatham Artillery. Brig.-Gen. Wm. B. Taliaferro, commanding James Island, made drafts on the garrisons of Fort Johnson, and Batteries Haskell and Tatom, to supplement the small force on the lines. He states that his available troops that day, other than artillerymen, did not exceed three hundred men.

Moving slowly, the Fifty-fourth advanced in line of battle over open and rising ground. Some distance to the right was another regiment and the rocket battery. Our movement caused the retirement of the enemy; but the Chatham Artillery in rear of their skirmish line fired briskly on the Fifty-fourth. We had no field-guns with which to reply; but the missiles from the rocket-stands on our right, while they did no damage, served to frighten the enemy's artillery horses. To avoid casualties from this artillery fire, Lieutenant-Colonel Hooper kept shifting the position of the Fifty-fourth as the enemy secured the range; and the necessary movements were effected with admirable precision and promptness, as on ordinary exercise. Progress forward was made to within some six hundred yards of the enemy, while solid shot came bounding and ricochetting over the intervening space toward the line. Some shells too from guns on our right front dropped unpleasantly near. The regiment in this advance passed to the right of a small fieldwork, or redoubt. A little distance beyond it the Fifty-fourth was halted and ordered to lie down in perfectly open ground, exposed to the hot rays of the sun and the dropping fire of the enemy.

Though many solid shot fell about or passed through or over the line, only Private Cornelius Price, of Company A, was mortally, and Sergeant Palmer, of Company K, slightly wounded. There were many narrow escapes, however; among them, a corporal, of Company E, had his canteen struck from his side, and his musket doubled up. Colonel Heine, commanding at that portion of the field, was a large man, rendered more conspicuous by white clothes, and was noticeable the whole day for activity and personal gallantry. He came to our line and directed Lieutenant-Colonel Hooper to draw back the Fifty-fourth to the old fieldwork. Captain Jones, with Companies A, D, and K as skirmishers, advanced and took position well to the front of the work, and to the right and left of a hedge, where the men were ordered to lie down in the grass and weeds which grew waist high. This position the skirmish line kept till relieved, unmolested by the enemy's infantry, but subjected to cannon-shot whenever our men exposed themselves. No opposing skirmishers were seen. Our men held their fire so as not to disclose their location. Captain Jones's line did not immediately connect with any other; but some distance to the left were troops.

At the old redoubt the men were put to work with the tools they carried, extending the flanks of the intrenchment for better protection. With excessive heat during the morning hours, by midday it became almost unbearable to the skirmishers, stifled in the high grass on the line, who were compelled to maintain a prostrate and immovable position, and to the support at the fieldwork, obliged to sit crowded for space. Throughout that whole day, with a temperature at 110°, officers and men on James Island, both Union and Confederate, were succumbing to the heat of the sun. More than fifty men of the Fifty-fourth were affected to a greater or lesser degree; and Private John Hale, of Company D, died at his post with the skirmishers. Major Appleton was completely prostrated, and while lying on the ground received a contusion from a solid shot which ultimately forced him to leave the service. Captain Jones, commanding the skirmishers, was compelled to retire, and was taken to the rear delirious. He suffered all his life thereafter in head and brain, and died from the effects in 1886. Lieut. Chas. Jewett, Jr., was seriously injured from the same cause, and died from it in 1890. Lieutenants Newell, Chipman, and David Reid were also badly affected. Most of those prostrated were on the skirmish line. So great were their sufferings that at last word was sent to Lieutenant-Colonel Hooper that they could no longer endure it, and that many men were lying unconscious and helpless, for their stronger comrades could not leave their positions. It was not possible to send a relieving force without sustaining heavy casualties, so stretchers were taken out, and upon them a number of men were brought back.

Under such conditions hour after hour of that seemingly interminable day wore on. Our position was isolated; there appeared to be momentary probability of attack by an overwhelming force; but Colonel Heine's orders were that the position must be held at all hazards. The officers by confident bearing did their best to make light of the situation, and Colonel Heine's actions helped greatly. He was about the skirmish line and the fieldwork, and at one time mounted the parapet of the redoubt and therefrom facetiously harangued the Rebels, to divert the men. Soon after dark the Chatham Artillery in our front withdrew to their lines, as General Taliaferro feared a sudden dash. There were no further infantry movements or fighting during the remainder of the day; but from the river the gunboat continued to fire, and receive shots from Battery Pringle. During these events a force of the First New York Engineers and civilian employees had thrown up a defensive line along our margin of the low ground; and to it General Schimmelfennig ordered all his troops in advance to retire after nightfall. It was not until 11 P.M., however, that the Fifty-fourth called in its skirmishers and silently withdrew to the main line. Bivouac was made in a cornfield just at the general's headquarters. Lieutenant Leonard and a large part of Company K were in the darkness inadvertently left on post until Lieutenant Swails, who was sent back with ten men, brought them in.

Thus ended a most memorable day for the regiment, not sanguinary, but full of trials requiring not only courage, but constancy to suffer and endure. Having drawn the enemy to the south lines of James Island, General Schimmelfennig prepared a daring attack on Fort Johnson. Colonel Gurney commanded; and his force was the Fifty-second Pennsylvania, One Hundred and Twenty-seventh New York, and a detachment of the Third Rhode Island Artillery. It left Payne's Dock in twenty-eight barges at 2 A.M., July 3, but was delayed in crossing the harbor and bar. The boats were observed and fired upon. A portion, however, landed near Battery Simkins, and was at once repulsed. Colonel Hoyt, Fifty-second Pennsylvania, and a number of his officers and men, were not supported by their comrades, but landing, captured the Brook's gun battery. They then pressed on toward Johnson under heavy fire, before which they were obliged to retire to the captured battery where they all surrendered. The retreating boats communicated their disorder to those carrying the One Hundred and Twenty-seventh; and they too fell back against the peremptory orders of Maj. Edward H. Little, commanding, and Captain Little and Lieutenants Little and Abercrombie, who brought their men of the One Hundred and Twenty-seventh to land. This surprise, which, if successful, might have sealed the fate of Charleston soon after, thus failed. A military court, on Nov. 7, 1864, found that—

"Colonel Gurney, One Hundred and Twenty-seventh New York Regiment, commanding Morris Island, who was charged with sending the expedition, did not accompany it, but remained at Payne's Dock. There seems to be no sufficient reason for this conduct."

The report further says,—

"The chief cause of failure was the lack of spirit, energy, and power of command on the part of subordinate officers."

Captain Homans with the Fifty-fourth companies at Black Island was ordered to cross in boats to James Island, and attack toward Secessionville, to co-operate with the movement against Johnson. Preparations were made, and the boats transported across the island in accordance with specific instructions; but in transit, without proper means, they were so damaged as to make their use impracticable, and the expedition necessarily impossible.

At Port Royal three brigades of troops embarked on transports and sailed for the Edisto on the evening of July 1, arriving early on the 2d. There General Hatch, with Saxton's and Davis's brigades, landing at Seabrook, crossed to John's Island at the Haulover Bridge, and bivouacked some distance beyond for the night. General Birney, with his brigade and a marine battery, went up the North Edisto and landed at White Point. He then moved toward Adam's Run, but meeting the enemy in small numbers, halted for the night, after marching but two miles. Resuming the advance early on the 3d, Birney drove the enemy's light troops some five miles to King's Creek, where on the opposite bank the Confederates under Gen. B. H. Robertson had a battery which opened on our force. General Foster, with two armed transports, ran up the Dawhoo River, and co-operated by throwing shells across the intervening ground. After two or three hours of cannonading and skirmishing, and as General Birney reported that it was expedient to withdraw, General Foster ordered a retirement to White Point, where the force took transports for James Island.

In response to General Jones' requests for reinforcements, the First Georgia (regulars) Fourth Georgia Cavalry, and three companies of the Third South Carolina Cavalry, all dismounted, were sent to John's Island from Savannah, for news had been received of the landing of Hatch's and Birney's forces. The enemy was apprehensive of attacks by way of the Stono, which was the route taken by the British in 1780. During the night of the 2d the Thirty-second Georgia, Col. Geo. P. Harrison, reported to General Taliaferro; and every available man was taken from other points to reinforce the southern lines on James Island.

Supposing that we still held the positions of the previous day, Colonel Harrison, with several companies of his regiment and two guns, was ordered to ascertain our strength. About 9 A.M. on the 3d, this force was discovered advancing, and our pickets retired before it. Then the monitors "Mon-

tauk" and "Lehigh" and the gunboat "Pawnee," having
taken position in the Stono the previous evening, opened,
preventing their farther advance, and causing a retirement
at 11 A.M. But they manœuvred in our front the whole
day, with skirmishers established about the old fieldwork
we held on the 2d. Our rifle trenches were strengthened
with two guns posted on Colonel Heine's front; and Colonel
Hartwell's captured pieces were also in position. The naval
vessels slackened fire in the afternoon. Excessively warm
weather continued. No service was required of the Fifty-
fourth during that day. Surgeon Briggs reported for duty,
and Lieutenant Newell was sent to hospital. At dark the
Fifty-fourth relieved the Seventy-fourth Pennsylvania. Our
main body occupied the rifle trenches, with Captain Emilio
and seventy-five men, supported by one gun thrown forward upon the causeway within three hundred yards of the
enemy's line, and Lieutenant Cousens and twenty-five men
still farther advanced. Our line was quiet, but on the right
there were frequent shots, and a few rifle-balls fired by our
own troops in rear of our flank fell near. Our mortar
schooner "Racer" kept firing slowly. So the night passed
with but one man of another regiment killed. General
Hatch on John's Island that day advanced on the road
running parallel with Bohicket Creek and halted at Parker's, where a road branched to Stono on the right. The
march, though short, was severe because of the heat.

Just at dawn on Independence Day, the Fifty-fourth was
reduced one half for the day. We could see that the enemy
had fortified their line at or about the old redoubt. They
occasionally showed themselves, and threw out a skirmish
line whenever we advanced. In the Stono the naval vessels
at 8 A.M. were dressed with flags at the signal given from
the admiral's flagship, "Philadelphia." Pringle opened im-

mediately after, and some of our vessels replied, occasioning a lively duel. Birney's brigade, of the Seventh, Thirty-fourth, and Thirty-fifth United States Colored Troops, landed on James Island that day, occupying a second line in rear of our right. Two thirty-pounder Parrotts were placed on the lines. Refreshing rain with a strong wind came in the afternoon. At the rifle trench held by the Fifty-fourth, Captain Emilio in command advanced twelve men to draw the enemy's fire, which was done without casualty. Later two companies of the Fifty-fourth New York moved out, skirmishing, and being met by a strong fire from the enemy's pickets commanded by Captain Lewis, Thirty-second Georgia, retired with the loss of two killed and six wounded. Our naval vessels shelled the enemy whenever discovered, and soon forced them to cover. After our force fell back, we could see a man of the Fifty-fourth New York lying on the open ground between the lines. He was alive, for he would occasionally raise himself. The enemy would not permit him to be brought in. A gallant officer of the staff essayed the dangerous task, but was fired upon. Our officers and men of the Fifty-fourth Massachusetts were exasperated at this firing on men engaged in a humane act, and sharply replied to the enemy for an hour. At dark a field-piece was brought near, and under cover of grape, a party of eight men from Company E with a stretcher went out to bring the poor fellow in. He was found dead. It was impossible to secure his body, as the enemy was rapidly advancing with a company. Capt. Gustav Blau and his men of the Fifty-fourth New York relieved our force at 9 P.M.

Admiral Dahlgren records that on the 4th, with General Foster, he reconnoitred the enemy's position from a point on John's Island across the Stono, "right opposite Pringle, in full view seventeen or eighteen hundred yards off." He recommended that a heavy battery be there established to enfilade the James Island lines; but it was not done. Our naval vessels fired slowly all that night.

General Hatch, on the 4th, moved on the road toward the Stono, making but six miles. He rested at a plantation where the road from Legareville came into the one that he was following. It was a terribly hot forenoon; little water could be found, and scores of men were sunstruck or fainted from fatigue and thirst. At this halting-place the force from General Schimmelfennig joined General Hatch. As it was feared many musket-charges had been spoiled by the rain of the previous day, all the regiments on James Island were marched to the front at 9 A.M., on the 5th, and discharged their pieces at the enemy. There was some light skirmishing. A few shells came over the line from Secessionville without damage. Our foe was busy erecting an earthwork and extending his trenches, seriously interfered with by the huge eleven and fifteen-inch shells of the navy and the fire of twelve-pounders from the decks of the monitors.

On the 5th the position of the Fifty-fourth was changed to the centre of General Schimmelfennig's line, which it held with the Thirty-third United States Colored Troops, both regiments under Lieutenant-Colonel Hooper's command.

General Hatch on the 5th moved forward some miles and took post at the "Huts." He occupied a good defensive line behind a creek, crossed at one point by a bridge. The failure to push on to the head of John's Island that day, before the enemy had concentrated there, was unfortunate, for they posted several guns of the Marion Artillery on a hill supported by infantry, and on the 6th shelled Hatch's lines.

All the day-hours of the 6th the Fifty-fourth was resting in bivouac. At 8 P.M., a picket of four officers and 132 men under Captain Bridge went out in front of the right. The weather was more comfortable. It was very apparent that the enemy was stronger. The succeeding day, on the lines, only an occasional shell from the enemy disturbed the quietness. A mail came in the afternoon. Supplies were more abundant; and from sutlers at Cole's Island some additions to the army fare were procured. In the morning the naval vessels shelled Pringle and the woods until later, when they concentrated upon the battery. During the ensuing evening Colonel Montgomery with Birney's brigade was sent to join General Hatch. General Birney had returned to Florida.

At John's Island on the 7th, Colonel Silliman, with his regiment, the Twenty-sixth United States Colored Troops, supported by Lieutenant Wildt's section of Battery B, Third New York, made a gallant but unsuccessful attempt to capture the enemy's field-guns on the hill beyond the lines. Some ninety-seven men were killed and wounded. General Jones was considerably reinforced by this date from Atlanta and Wilmington. He also stripped Sullivan's Island of troops to confront us.

Quietness reigned at James Island on the 8th during the early hours, after a night disturbed only by the slow firing of the navy. As the day advanced, however, our vessels opened a terrific fire on Fort Pringle and Battery Tynes, which was continued for several hours, our fire overpowering that of the enemy and so exhausting the garrison of Pringle as to require its relief. There was a conference that afternoon between Generals Foster and Hatch and

Admiral Dahlgren, when it was decided that the enemy's force, in connection with their works, was "too large to render further serious efforts profitable," and that General Hatch should withdraw from John's Island on the night of the 9th. The admiral records, "I am utterly disgusted," and in another place, speaking of General Foster, "The general remarked that he had done all he intended."

In the afternoon a fire broke out in the hamlet of Legareville on John's Island. Lieutenant Spear, who came in a rowboat from Black Island, visited the regiment, and informed us that mortars were being planted there to fire upon James Island. At 7 P.M. Captain Emilio was placed in charge of a fatigue detail of two hundred men from the Fifty-fourth and Fifty-fifth Massachusetts and Thirty-third United States Colored Troops, and began work on a road from the left of our line toward a point of woods in our front, designed to facilitate the advance of infantry and artillery in the event of an assault.

Early on the morning of the 8th at John's Island, there was an artillery duel between our field-pieces and those of the enemy on the hill. From the tree-tops our lookouts there saw reinforcements crossing the Ashley River to join the enemy. An attack was fully expected the next day; and the troops slept in position on their arms that night, their rest being broken by shells from Battery Tynes.

Gen. B. H. Robertson, the Confederate commander on John's Island, with four regiments, a battalion of Georgians, and two field batteries was ordered to attack General Hatch in his threatening position. Colonel Harrison led the advance at 4 A.M., on the 9th, covered by a fog, and surprised the One Hundred and Forty-fourth New York on picket beyond the bridge, driving it back. But the troops defending the lines received the enemy with a hot fire of musketry and canister, which forced them to a sheltered position and strewed the ground with dead and wounded. Bringing up artillery, the enemy made another attempt to carry the bridge at 6.30 A.M., with a similar result, after which their main body withdrew. This engagement is known as "Bloody Bridge." We lost some eighty-two killed and wounded, the enemy some seventeen killed and ninety-three wounded, according to their own account. That night, in pursuance of the prearranged plan, General Hatch withdrew from John's Island upon transports without molestation, Montgomery's brigade returning to James Island.

About daylight our troops on James Island heard the sounds of battle across the Stono. The day was close and sultry. There occurred the usual bombardment of Pringle, Tynes, and the enemy's lines. Replies from a Brook gun and a ten-inch Columbiad in Pringle were effective against our gunboats, but the monitors stood their ground. Late that day it was seen that we were to abandon James Island. A fatigue party of the Fifty-fourth was engaged constructing another bridge to Cole's Island; all the surplus stores were conveyed away, and the wharf repaired. When it was dark the troops began to move over the bridges, the Fifty-fourth marching with other regiments, all in silence. Companies G and K were detailed to burn a house, the lookout, and one of the bridges. Our pickets were supported by the Seventy-fourth Pennsylvania until all the other troops were withdrawn, when they crossed to Cole's Island. Colonel Hartwell conducted the retreat and put out a picket line on Cole's Island. Our naval vessels kept up the usual night-shelling until daylight, when they got under way and ran down the river.

After a scanty breakfast the Fifty-fourth, at 9 A.M., marched to Stono, accomplishing the three miles in as many hours, for the day was hot and the men much exhausted. There a sutler was found, from whom some supplies were obtained. The regiment crossed the inlet on the steamer "Golden Gate," whose captain kindly furnished refreshments for the officers. Our march to Lighthouse Inlet was equally severe, for the temperature was at 98°. Thence the companies repaired to their several stations, and welcomed the opportunity for rest, baths in the surf, and clean clothes.

Thus the combined movements, admirably planned, against a weaker enemy came to naught, for want of concerted action and persistence in attack. At every point we largely outnumbered the enemy. General Hatch's force, had it not been so delayed, might have found no enemy in its front capable of withstanding its advance. Many thought at the time that had Hatch's force been sent against the repulsed enemy after the action at Bloody Bridge, John's Island might have been swept of them, and the James Island lines thus flanked, Charleston would have fallen. Our total of losses in all the forces engaged was perhaps three hundred men, including the one hundred and forty captured with Colonel Hoyt, and eighteen drowned by the capsizing of a boat in the Stono. That of the enemy must have equalled ours. Their accounts of our losses, exaggerated as usual, gave the number as seven hundred.

CHAPTER XI

SIEGE OF CHARLESTON

U PON RETURNING to their several stations, the Fifty-fourth companies reassumed the old duties. The first noteworthy incident occurred on July 13, when, at noon, six shells passing over the Third Rhode Island Artillery camp, fell into ours, one of which, exploding in a tent, killed Private John Tanner and Musician Samuel Suffhay, both of Company B. We had supposed the location safe from any shell firing. These missiles came from Sullivan's Island, clear across the harbor. A lookout posted on the sand-bluff near by gave warning thereafter when this gun opened, which it did at intervals until the last of August. At such times, day or night, we were obliged to leave the camp for the sea beach. No further casualties occurred, however.

Another example of dislike to colored troops took place on the 15th. Lieut. John S. Marcy, Fifty-second Pennsylvania, when directed to join the Fifty-fourth detail for duty at the Left Batteries, with some of his men, the whole force to be under one of our officers, refused to do so, saying, "I will not do duty with colored troops." He was arrested and court-martialled, and, by General Foster's order, dishonorably dismissed. Colonel Hallowell returned on the 16th, bringing assurances that the men would soon be paid. With him came as visitors Mr. and Mrs. Lewis, relatives of Quartermaster Ritchie.

During the heated term, which began with the month and seemed interminable, we went about arrayed in as few clothes as possible. The blazing sun heated the sand beneath our feet, and reflected from land and sea, dazzled the eyes. No relief came until nightfall, when the sea breeze sprang up. On the 21st a change of weather brought cooler temperature for some days. Mr. Hoadly, the efficient agent of the Sanitary Commission on Morris Island, was supplying the troops with stores. Ice was still scarce.

For some weeks Sumter had been bombarded with unusual vigor, as during our season of quietness the enemy had constructed two large bombproofs there, and mounted five guns on the channel face. It was estimated that one hundred of the garrison were killed or wounded during this latest bombardment. Captain Mitchel, its commander, was killed, July 19, by a mortar-shell, and was succeeded by Capt. T. A. Huguenin, First South Carolina (regulars), who continued in charge until its final abandonment.

A special exchange of the fifty Confederate officers for the same number of ours in Charleston was effected on August 3. The released officers were received with cheers and a display of flags from the vessels. From Edward R. Henderson, steward of the truce boat "Cosmopolitan," Quartermaster Ritchie received a list containing forty names of Fifty-fourth prisoners captured July 16 and 18, 1863, which was smuggled out by an exchanged officer.

Maj.-Gen. Daniel Sickles, who was on a tour of inspection, landed on Morris Island on the 3d, accompanied by General Foster, and was received with a salute of thirteen guns. During the succeeding night two officers of the One Hundred and Third Ohio came to our lines, having escaped from Charleston, and, with the assistance of negroes, procured a boat in which to cross the harbor. The enemy's fire on Cumming's Point on the night of the 6th wounded five men of a colored regiment. A large propeller was discovered aground toward Sullivan's Island on the morning of the 8th, whereupon our guns opened from land and sea, soon destroying her. We gave our fire sometimes from the great guns in volleys,—their united explosions shaking the whole island and covering the batteries with a white pall of smoke. Peaceful intervals came, when the strange stillness of the ordnance seemed like stopped heart-beats of the siege. Then the soft rush of the surf and the chirp of small birds in the scant foliage could be heard.

Major Appleton, who had been in hospital since the movement to James Island, departed North on the 7th, and never returned. His loss was a great one to the regiment, for he was a devoted patriot, a kind-hearted man, and an exceedingly brave soldier. Captain Emilio came to camp with Company E from Fort Green, on the 8th, when relieved by Lieutenant Newell with Company B. Captain Tucker and Company H reported from Black Island on the 20th, and Lieutenant Duren and Company D were relieved at Fort Shaw on the 23d. Captain Pope succeeded Captain Homans in the command of Black Island on the 24th. Our details for grand guard were increased after the 16th, when the Thirty-second United States Colored Troops was ordered to Hilton Head.

Salutes in honor of Admiral Farragut's victory at Mobile were fired on the 25th. On the 28th, and again on September 1, the navy sent torpedoes, heavily charged, to float and explode near Fort Sumter, in the hope of shattering the structure; but they caused no damage.

In Congress the third Conference Committee reported, on June 10, that the House recede from the amendments reducing the bounty, and that all persons of color who were free on April 19, 1861, should, from the time of entering service, be entitled to the pay, bounty, and clothing allowed by the laws existing at the time of their enlistment. The Attorney-General was to determine any law question, and the Secretary of War make the necessary regulations for the pay department. After discussion this unjust compromise was accepted by both branches of Congress. Over two months, however, passed, until, on August 18, the War Department issued Circular No. 60, providing that officers commanding colored organizations should make an investigation to ascertain who of their men enlisted prior to January 1, 1864, were free April 19, 1861. The fact of freedom was to be settled by the sworn statement of the soldier, and entered against the man's name on the muster-rolls.

August 29, Sergeant Cross and a few men of the Fifty-fourth returned from Beaufort, where they had received full pay from enlistment in accordance with the foregoing regulations. Colonel Hallowell made the first effective muster for pay of the regiment on the 31st. As no particular form of oath had been prescribed, he administered the following:—

"You do solemnly swear that you owed no man unrequited labor on or before the 19th day of April, 1861. So help you God."

This form had been the subject of much thought, and was known in the regiment as the "Quaker Oath." Some of our men were held as slaves April 19, 1861, but they took the oath as freemen, by God's higher law, if not by their country's. A more pitiful story of broken faith, with attendant want and misery upon dependent ones, than this deprivation of pay for many months cannot be told. If ever men were seemingly driven to desperation and overt acts, they were. How they bore it all, daily exposing their lives for the cause and the flag they loved, has been feebly told. That they were compelled to take this or any oath at the last was an insult crowning the injury.

There was another meeting of truce steamers in the harbor on the 3d, when a release without equivalent was made by the enemy of thirty persons,—chaplains, surgeons, and some women. General Schimmelfennig, who had removed district headquarters from Folly to Morris Island August 2, on September 4 departed North, when General Saxton took command. The next day the Fifty-sixth and One Hundred and Fifty-seventh New York arrived; and Col. Charles H. Van Wyck of the Fifty-sixth assumed command of Morris Island, relieving Colonel Gurney.

Captain Homans, with Company A, having reported from Black Island to camp about September 1, there were the following companies with the colors; namely, A, D, E, G, H, and K, a larger number than for some months. On the 6th, several boxes of canned goods were received for the regiment,—the gift of Count Leo B. Schwabe, of Boston. This gentleman belonged to a noble family, and was born at Castle Schaumberg on the Weser. Before the war he lived in South Carolina, where he owned slaves and plantations. The slaves he freed as the war broke out. His means were lavishly given for building chapels and hospitals, establishing camp libraries, besides donations of money and provisions for Union soldiers. He died but recently; and it is sad to record that his last days were passed in reduced circumstances.

September 1, several hundred Confederate officers, sent to be confined under fire in retaliation for a similar hardship suffered by our officers in Charleston, arrived off Morris Island on the steamer "Crescent." An enclosed camp was made for them just north of Wagner, in full view of the enemy and exposed to his fire. The enclosure was 228 by 304 feet, and formed of palisading of pine posts, ten feet above ground, supporting a platform from which sentinels could watch the prisoners. The "dead line," marked by a rope stretched on posts, was twenty feet inside the palisading. Good A tents, each to hold four men, were pitched and arranged, forming eight streets. The ground was clean, dry, quartz sand.

Several days before, the Fifty-fourth was assigned to guard this prison camp. On September 7, Colonel Hallowell, with Companies D, E, G, and K marched to the landing, where the steamer "Cossack" soon arrived with the Confederates. The escort was composed entirely of colored soldiers. First came three companies of the Twenty-first United States Colored Troops in column, then the prisoners, flanked on either side by two companies of the Fifty-fourth, the rear closed by two companies of the Twenty-first in column. In this order the Confederates were taken to the camp.

This body of five hundred and sixty officers thus placed in our charge was a singular-looking set of soldiers. There were among them tall, lank mountaineers, some typical Southerners of the books,—dark, long-haired, and fierce of aspect,—and a lesser number of city men of jauntier appearance. The major part were common-looking, evidently of the poorer class of Southerners, with a sprinkling of foreigners,—principally Germans and Irish. Hardly any two were dressed alike. There were suits of blue jeans, homespuns, of butternut, and a few in costumes of gray more or less trimmed. Upon their heads were all sorts of coverings,—straw and slouch hats, and forage caps of gray, blue, or red, decorated with braid. Cavalry boots, shoes, and bootees in all stages of wear were on their feet. Their effects were wrapped in rubber sheets, pieces of carpet, or parts of quilts and comforts. Some had hand-sacks of ancient make. Haversacks of waterproof cloth or cotton hung from their shoulders. Their physical condition was good; but they made a poor showing for chosen leaders of the enemy. It did seem that men of their evident mental and intellectual calibre—with some exceptions—might be supporters of any cause, however wild or hopeless. They were of all grades, from colonels down in rank.

At the camp the prisoners were divided into eight detachments, with a non-commissioned officer of the Fifty-fourth, detailed from the guard, in charge of each, as warden. Clean straw was provided for the tents, and a good blanket given each officer. The regulations, so far as they related to the prisoners, were read to them. Our six companies of the Fifty-fourth were formed into three reliefs; namely, A and H, D and G, and E and K, each relief furnishing one hundred men, with proper officers, for duty at the stockade from 6 P.M. until the same hour the following day. When relieved, the detachment went into Wagner for the succeeding night, returning to camp the next morning. At the gate of the stockade was posted a Requa rifled battery in charge of the reserve, and a section of Battery B, Third Rhode Island Heavy Artillery, reported there each day.

Three times a day the roll was called by the wardens, and every man accounted for to the officer of the day. Policing of the streets was done by the prisoners. Sick call was attended to by a surgeon, who removed the severe cases to hospitals outside. Barrel-sinks were provided and cared for by the prisoners. At night the camp and vicinity were made bright as moonlight by means of a calcium light on Wagner's parapet. Oil lanterns were also used inside the stockade when required. After taps sounded, no light was allowed the prisoners, and they were not permitted to enter the streets except to go to the barrel-sinks. During the day they had free range of the camp; but groups of more than ten prisoners were warned to disperse under penalty of being fired upon if the order was disregarded. Our charges were allowed to purchase writing materials, pipes, tobacco, and necessary clothing. Letters could be sent after inspection. Their rations were cooked by men of the guard. The nearness of the enemy necessitated the utmost vigilance. It was a tempting opportunity for some bold rescue, and a boat attack was not improbable. At first there was thought to be some danger from stray shells, as Cumming's Point was the focus of the enemy's fire. But as time passed, this seeming danger to friend and foe was not realized.

Everything was done to care for and protect these unfortunate officers whom the fortunes of war placed in our hands except in two particulars,—they were kept in a place within reach of the enemy's fire, and their rations were reduced to conform in quantity to those furnished our officers in Charleston, at first to one half the army ration, and after some time still less. Food and cooking was the same otherwise as furnished the Fifty-fourth. Of these inflictions in retaliation the enemy was duly informed as the result of their own uncivilized acts, which would be discontinued whenever they ceased to practise the same.

September 9, Wagner fired a salute of shotted guns in honor of the capture of Atlanta, Ga. The next day a reconnoissance was made in small force by the army and navy about Bull's Bay. Our shells caused a large fire in Charleston on the 17th, plainly seen from Cumming's Point, by which twenty-five buildings were destroyed. Another, the next day, burned two mansions at the corner of Trade and Meeting Streets. With increased elevations our shells fell a distance of two blocks beyond Calhoun Street. A prisoner of war in Charleston thus graphically describes the firing:—

"Every fifteen or twenty minutes we could see the smoke and hear the explosions of 'Foster's messengers,'—two hundred-pound shells. They told us of the untiring perseverance of our forces on Morris Island. So correct was their aim, so well did the gunners know our whereabouts, that shells burst all around, in front, and often fell, screeching, overhead, without injury to us. When the distant rumbling of the Swamp Angel was heard, and the cry, 'Here it comes,' resounded through the prison-house, there was a general stir: sleepers sprang to their feet; conversation was hushed; and all started to see where the messengers would fall.... The sight at night was truly beautiful. We traced through the sky a slight stream of fire similar to the tail of a comet, followed its course, until 'whiz! whiz!' came the little pieces like grape-shot."

Charleston papers gave us information that yellow fever was prevalent and increasing, not only among the prisoners, but the citizens, and especially the Germans.

At the stockade the captives gave no trouble, and readily conformed to the rules. The wardens took great pride in

First Lieutenant Stephen A. Swails
Massachusetts Commandery Military Order of the Loyal Legion and the U.S.
Army Military History Institute

their office. At roll-calls they accurately dressed the lines, and doubtless imparted some useful hints to the Confederate officers. From Major McDonald, Fifty-first North Carolina, who was present in Wagner during the assault of July 18, 1863, very interesting particulars of the affair were obtained. He confirmed the story of Colonel Shaw's death and manner of burial.

After a few days' experience the prisoners lost all fear of being struck by stray shells thrown by their friends; but they watched the bombardment always with interest, so far as they were able. When Wagner opened, the heavy Parrott projectiles passed directly over the camp, but high in air. Our charges lounged about during the day, visiting friends, or played cards, smoked, and read. There were ingenious fellows who passed much time making chains, crosses, rings, and other ornaments from bone or guttapercha buttons. Our officers found a number of most agreeable gentlemen among them, who seemed to appreciate such attentions and politenesses as could be extended within the scope of our regulations.

Sudden orders came on September 21, at 10 A.M., to remove the prisoners to Lighthouse Inlet. This was done by the Fifty-fourth, and they were placed on two schooners. The reason for this temporary change is not known. Possibly some fear of a rescue under cover of the exchange which was to take place may have occasioned it. On the 23d, after the truce had expired, the Fifty-fourth escorted the prisoners back to the camp. When the rolls were called, it was discovered that six officers were missing. Without a moment's delay, Lieutenant-Colonel Hooper and Quartermaster Ritchie rode to Lighthouse Inlet, and with guards, searched all the vessels there. Five officers were recaptured just as they came from the hold of a vessel with no clothes on, prepared to swim in an attempt to escape. Lieutenant-Colonel Hooper himself searched every part of a steamer previously examined, and at last found his missing man concealed in the paddle-box. The recaptured officers were doubtless surprised when the lieutenant-colonel took them to his tent, offered stimulants, told them they were blameless, and gave them permission to try again, before sending them to join their comrades.

Among the prisoners were some rabid Secessionists who would receive no favors at our hands. It is pleasant to record, that, on the 27th, Capt. Henry A. Buist, Twenty-seventh South Carolina (now a prominent lawyer of Charleston), about to be exchanged, politely expressed his thanks to our officers for kindnesses received.

September 28 was a red-letter day for the Fifty-fourth. Paymaster Lockwood, on that date and the 29th, paid the men from enlistment. They were wild with joy that their only trouble was over. An officer wrote:—

"We had been eighteen months waiting, and the kaleidoscope was turned,—nine hundred men received their money; nine hundred stories rested on the faces of those men, as they passed in at one door and out of the other. Wagner stared Readville in the face! There was use in waiting! Two days have changed the face of things, and now a petty carnival prevails. The fiddle and other music long neglected enlivens the tents day and night. Songs burst out everywhere; dancing is incessant; boisterous shouts are heard, mimicry, burlesque, and carnival; pompous salutations are heard on all sides. Here a crowd and a preacher; there a crowd and two boxers; yonder, feasting and jubilee. In brief, they have awakened 'the pert and nimble spirit of mirth, and turned melancholy forth to funerals.' "

It required $170,000 to pay the Fifty-fourth. Over $53,000 was sent home by Adams' Express; and the sum ultimately forwarded reached $100,000. There was for a time lavish and foolish expenditure of money on the part of some.

October came in with clear, warm mornings and soft breezes in the afternoon. During a truce on the 3d some prisoners were exchanged, and two thousand suits of clothing and many packages were sent to our prisoners. We received clothing and tobacco for the Confederate officers from Charleston people. Brig.-Gen. E. P. Scammon on the 4th relieved General Saxton of the district command, and reviewed the Morris Island troops on the 6th. We had twenty-four officers and seven hundred and twenty-six enlisted men of the regiment present for duty at the several posts on this date.

For some time the freedmen had been contributing to a Shaw monument fund to which the Fifty-fourth added liberally. The following letters relate thereto:—

> HEADQUARTERS FIFTY-FOURTH MASS. VOLS.,
> MORRIS ISLAND, S.C., Oct. 7, 1864.

BRIG.-GEN. R. SAXTON.

DEAR GENERAL,—In behalf of the enlisted men of the Fifty-fourth Massachusetts Volunteer Infantry, I respectfully request you to receive the enclosed sum of money to be added to the sum subscribed by the freedmen of the Department for the purpose of erecting a monument to the memory of Col. Robert G. Shaw and those who died with him.

Thanking you for the interest you have always manifested in the cause which is so dear to us, and for the trouble you have taken to do honor to those who so nobly died in its support, I have the honor to be, General, very respectfully,

Your obedient servant,
E. N. HALLOWELL,
Colonel Commanding Regiment.

HEADQUARTERS U.S. FORCES,
DISTRICT OF BEAUFORT, Oct. 17, 1864.
MY DEAR COLONEL,—I have received your letter of the 7th, forwarding $1,545, as a contribution from the enlisted men of your regiment to the monument soon to be erected in memory of their former colonel, Robert Gould Shaw, and those who fell with him in the assault on Fort Wagner. Please inform the donors that their generous contribution with that contributed by the freedmen in this Department makes the fund now about $3,000. It is safely invested in Massachusetts interest-bearing bonds. The glorious work which our armies in the field and patriots at home are now doing means that the day is not far distant when a granite shaft shall stand unmolested on South Carolina soil, to mark the spot where brave men died, not, as recent developments have shown, alone as soldiers, but as martyrs in the cause of Freedom. When for a month under my command, your brave regiment guarded so vigilantly and so soldierly six hundred Rebel officers near the spot where their colonel and comrades were massacred, it required but little faith to believe that the scales of justice were turning toward the right, and that it was time to commence the monument.

I am, Colonel, with great respect, yours sincerely,
R. SAXTON,
Brig.-Gen. Volunteers.

To COL. E. N. HALLOWELL,
Commanding Fifty-fourth Mass. Infantry.

Further sums were subsequently sent by the Fifty-fourth, until, on the last of October, the total contributed by them was $2,832. A much larger amount would have been given had it been proposed to erect the monument elsewhere than near Fort Wagner. It was then seen that what has since occurred would take place,—the sea was gradually washing away Morris Island at that point. Besides, there was no confidence that a monument erected on South Carolina soil would be respected when the Union forces were withdrawn. Ultimately the project was given up and the money used to aid in establishing a free school for colored children in Charleston, bearing Colonel Shaw's name. Efforts were made in the North to erect some memorial to our colonel. One fund at least exists. To this day no object stands in public place to point the lesson of Shaw's life and glorious death. Nevertheless he lives in memory, and his work renders his name immortal.

A large steamer on the night of October 5, in attempting to run into Charleston, struck a wreck and sank, showing only her masts above water when daylight came. On the 8th the weather suddenly grew colder, with lower temperature the next day, when a chilling northwest wind blew. We received forty-seven recruits on the 11th, who had looked forward to joining the regiment of their choice. As our rolls were full, they were transferred to the Fifty-fifth Massachusetts on Folly Island. Our musicians were made happy by the receipt of twelve brass drums. Still another change of post commander occurred on the 19th, when Colonel Hallowell relieved Colonel Van Wyck, who went North temporarily.

General Foster, when informed that the Union officers under fire in Charleston were removed elsewhere, ordered the Confederates on Morris Island to be conveyed to Fort Pulaski. Accordingly, on the 21st, Captain Emilio, with a battalion of the Fifty-fourth composed of Companies D, E,

G, and K, escorted the prisoners to the landing and turned them over to Col. P. P. Brown and his One Hundred and Fifty-seventh New York. During the time they were in our charge not one had been injured by the artillery firing; there was no disturbance, no complaint of ill usage or lack of medical attention. None had escaped. Only two cases of shooting by the guard occurred. In one instance two quarrelsome men engaged in a fight, and when warned by a sentinel to desist, failed to do so, were fired upon, and both were slightly wounded. The other case occurred at night, when a light being discovered, a sentinel fired as instructed, wounding an innocent man. In both instances it was a clear disregard of orders, involving a penalty known to the offenders and their comrades. The following official letter was received at headquarters and read as ordered, fitly closing the record of the duty.

> HEADQUARTERS NORTHERN DISTRICT,
> DEPARTMENT OF THE SOUTH,
> MORRIS ISLAND, Nov. 2, 1864.
> COL. E. N. HALLOWELL, Fifty-fourth Mass. Vols.
>   COLONEL,—The brigadier-general commanding desires me, in the name of the major-general commanding the Department, to tender you his sincere thanks for the prompt and efficient manner in which you and the officers and men of your command discharged their duties while guarding the Rebel prisoners-of-war. Your close observance of orders and vigilance have attracted the attention of the major-general commanding. This letter will be read to your command on dress parade. I have the honor to be, Very respectfully, your obedient servant,
>   THOMAS J. ROBINSON,
> *First Lieutenant Twenty-First U.S.C.T. and A.A.A. Gen'l.*

Nearly every night about this period escaped prisoners came into our lines at various points about Charleston.

Each had a new and thrilling story to tell of trial and peril on the way; but all united in acknowledging the kindness and assistance of their only friends, the negroes. Besides the departure of the One Hundred and Fifty-seventh New York, on the 21st, the Morris Island garrison was further reduced by the transfer of the One Hundred and Twenty-seventh New York to Beaufort. This necessitated the detail the next day of Lieutenant Leonard and Company K as provost guard, and Company A joined in that duty shortly after. At a meeting of the officers on the 24th the Rev. James Lynch, a colored man, was elected chaplain of the Fifty-fourth. He was subsequently commissioned, but not mustered. Sergeant Cezar, of Company D, was appointed acting sergeant-major, and Wm. J. Netson, principal musician.

With a diminished garrison the duties bore heavily on the remaining troops. The Fifty-fourth began furnishing grand-guard details when relieved of the prisoners. It was nearly two miles from the camp to Gregg. Reliefs going beyond Wagner were exposed to the enemy's fire. On this service, after the pickets were established on posts about the works, and along the water-fronts, the reserves were held inside the forts, sheltered in the damp and vermin-infested bombproofs. The officers were generally the guests of the permanent officers in charge, and occupied tents. There were also the ceaseless calls for fatigue details to land ordnance and other stores at the wharf, drag guns to the front, and return disabled pieces to the depot, besides constant work repairing the batteries damaged by the enemy's fire or the elements.

A large sidewheel steamer with smokestacks painted red and lead-color, called the "Flore," was chased ashore on Sullivan's Island during the night of the 22d, and was destroyed the next day by our guns. On or about the 29th, Brig.-Gen. Edward E. Potter assumed command of the district, relieving General Scammon. About this period our fire upon the city was stronger than for some time. November 5, a small vessel was discovered ashore in front of Fort Moultrie. She seemed to be loaded with cotton and turpentine, for our shells soon set her on fire, and she burned until after dark. Colonel Mulford, our commissioner of exchange, had arrived at Hilton Head with 3,200 Confederate prisoners. He met Captain Black, the Confederate agent, on the 11th, in the Savannah River, and arranged for exchanges at that point which took place soon afterward. With November came colder and more stormy days, rendering it bleak and cheerless on Morris Island, exposed to the chilling winds and damp atmosphere. News of the re-election of President Lincoln was received with enthusiasm as a guarantee that the war would be vigorously prosecuted. Brigadier-General Hatch relieved General Potter on the 17th of the district command.

Some changes had taken place among the officers since the return from James Island. Lieut. Frederick H. Webster reported for duty July 16, and Asst.-Surg. Louis D. Radzinsky, August 16. Captain Jones departed North sick, July 29, and never returned. Lieutenant-Colonel Hooper, Adjutant Howard, Quartermaster Ritchie, and Captains Emilio and Tucker received leave of absence for short periods. Lieutenant Swails was furloughed to prosecute his claims for muster in the North. Captain Bridge was in command of the regiment during Lieutenant-Colonel Hooper's absence; and Lieut. David Reid acted as quartermaster while Lieutenant Ritchie was away.

Thanksgiving Day, November 24, Colonel Hallowell assembled the regiment and conducted proper services. Afterward there were foot and sack races on the beach, "Spanish horse," and various sports. In the evening the Shaw Glee Club gave a musical performance in the storehouse of the post quartermaster.

Orders were received on the 24th for the Fifty-fourth to be prepared for moving at short notice. When the departure took place, Colonel Hallowell remained in command of Morris Island with Captain Walton and Lieutenant Duren on his staff. Captain Bridge with Company F at Battery Purviance, Lieutenant Newell with Company B at Fort Green, and Lieutenant Edmands with part of Company F at Black Island remained at their posts. Companies C and I at Black Island were relieved by two companies of the Fifty-second Pennsylvania, under Capt. John B. Fisk, and reported at camp to proceed with the regiment. Lieutenant Littlefield was ordered to remain in charge of the camp and sick on Morris Island. Owing to the scarcity of transportation, the Fifty-fourth departed in detachments. Acting Major Pope, with Companies A, D, I, and K, crossed to Folly Island on the evening of the 26th, made a night march, and arrived at Stono about midnight. At dark the next day this force embarked with the Fifty-sixth New York and General Hatch and staff on the "Cosmopolitan," reaching Hilton Head on the 28th. Lieutenant-Colonel Hooper, with Companies C, E, G, and H, left Morris Island on the steamer "General Hooker" on the 27th, arriving at Hilton Head about 3 A.M. the next day. This departure from Morris Island was the final one for these eight companies and their officers. The companies of the regiment that remained held their several stations until Charleston fell into our hands.

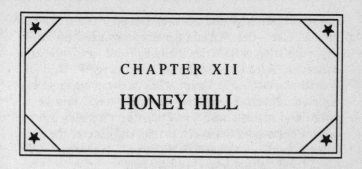

CHAPTER XII

HONEY HILL

Our arrival with other troops at Hilton Head was in consequence of General Foster's orders to co-operate with General Sherman in his "march to the sea," for the latter had telegraphed General Halleck from Kingston, Ga., November 11,—

> "I would like to have Foster break the Charleston and Savannah Railroad about Pocotaligo about the 1st of December."

A force of some five thousand men was gathered at Port Royal and organized as the "Coast Division," under command of General Hatch. Gen. E. E. Potter's First Brigade was composed of the Fifty-sixth, One Hundred and Twenty-seventh, One Hundred and Forty-fourth and One Hundred and Fifty-seventh New York, Twenty-fifth Ohio, Thirty-second, Thirty-fourth, and Thirty-fifth United States Colored Troops; Col. A. S. Hartwell's Second Brigade, of the Fifty-fourth and Fifty-fifth Massachusetts, Twenty-sixth and One Hundred and Second United States Colored Troops. Lieut.-Col. William Ames commanded the artillery, consisting of Batteries B and F, Third New York, and Battery A, Third Rhode Island. Capt. George P. Hurlbut, Fourth Massachusetts Cavalry, had a detachment of his regiment. Admiral Dahlgren formed a naval brigade of sailors and marines with some howitzers for duty ashore under Commander George H. Preble, and ordered the gunboats "Pawnee," "Mingoe," "Pontiac," "Sonoma," "Winona," and "Wissahickon" to take part.

Our regiment started on this expedition in light marching order, with Lieutenant-Colonel Hooper, commanding, Acting Major Pope, Surgeon Briggs, Assistant-Surgeon Radzinsky, Adjutant Howard, Quartermaster Ritchie; Company C, Captain Homans and Lieutenants Bridgham and Spear; Company E, Lieutenant Chipman, commanding, and Lieutenant Cousens; Company G, Lieut. David Reid, commanding, and Lieutenant Webster; Company H, Captain Tucker and Lieutenant Stevens; Company A, Lieutenant Knowles; Company D, Lieutenant Emerson, commanding, and Lieutenant Hallett; Company I, Lieut. Lewis Reed; Company K, Lieutenant Leonard, commanding, and Lieut. Charles Jewett,—a force of twenty-one officers and 540 men. Captains T. L. Appleton and R. H. L. Jewett were on staff duty with General Hatch.

A large fleet was ready at Port Royal, the decks of the transports crowded with troops; and the pier at Hilton Head was full of stores and men awaiting transportation. During the 28th Captain Pope's companies were transferred to the steamer "Golden Gate," on which was Colonel Hartwell. After Companies C and E under Captain Homans were taken upon the steamer "Fraser," General Hatch made the "General Hooker" his flagship.

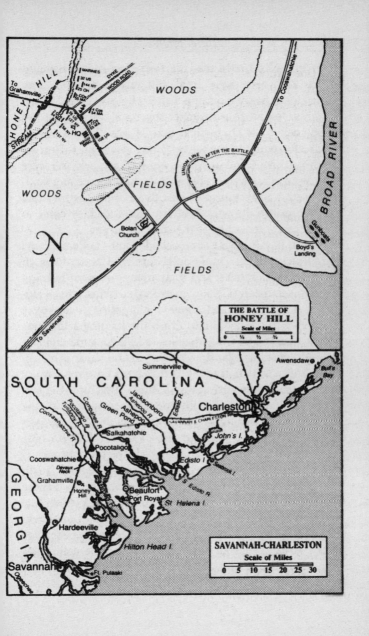

THE BATTLE OF
HONEY HILL
Scale of Miles
0   ¼   ½   ¾   1

To Grahamville
HONEY HILL
MARINES
32 US
144 NY
25 OH
HONEY STREAM
WOOD ROAD
DYKE
WOODS
F Co
55 US
56 NY
127 NY
NAVY HQ
102 US
NAVY BRIG
Bolan Church
UNION LINE AFTER THE BATTLE
WOODS
FIELDS
N
FIELDS
To Savannah
BROAD RIVER
To Coosawhatchie
Gunboats
Boyd's Landing

SAVANNAH–CHARLESTON
Scale of Miles
0   5   10   15   20   25   30

SOUTH CAROLINA
Summerville
Awensdaw
Bull's Bay
Jacksonboro
Ashepoo R.
Edisto R.
Charleston
Green Pond
Pocotaligo R.
Combahee R.
Tullifiny R.
Coosawhatchie R.
Salkahatchie
Pocotaligo
SAVANNAH & CHARLESTON RR
John's I.
Cooswahatchie
Devaux Neck
Edisto I.
Grahamville
Honey Hill
Beaufort
Port Royal
S. Edisto R.
St. Helena I.
GEORGIA
Hardeeville
Hilton Head I.
Savannah
Ft. Pulaski
Ogeechee

Orders were issued that the fleet start before daylight on the 29th at a signal light; but just as anchors were hauled up, a heavy fog came drifting in, preventing much progress. Owing to a mistake, the naval vessels did not move until 4 A.M., but which hour it was clear overhead, but the fog clung to the water below. However, they crept up Broad River, and at 8 A.M. entered a creek and were soon at Boyd's, where a dilapidated wharf served as a landing; not an army transport was to be seen, for they had either run into the wrong estuary, grounded, or come to anchor in consequence of the thick weather.

As the naval vessels approached, loud "holloas" came from a picket of the Third South Carolina Cavalry through the misty atmosphere; and their fires were seen burning in front of some huts. Soon uncultivated fields, stock grazing, and fine woodland about a plantation house were discovered as the fog lifted. From the landing a tortuous wagon-road led to Grahamville,—a village some eight or ten miles distant, near the Charleston and Savannah Railroad. Only a squadron of the Third South Carolina Cavalry and one field-piece were in the vicinity at this time. General Foster had selected this line of advance instead of the fortified roads leading to Coosawhatchie and Pocotaligo.

General Hatch's flagboat, the "Fraser," flying a blue pennant with a single star, on which were Companies G and H, was the first army vessel to arrive. The Fifty-fourth men, headed by Lieutenant-Colonel Hooper, sprang ashore eagerly, and were the first troops to land. A skirmish line was formed, and advanced without opposition, though several of the enemy's cavalrymen were seen along the edge of the stream. Moving about half a mile, the companies were then halted and disposed to watch the enemy and resist attack. The Naval Brigade landed and advanced to the first cross-road, pushing a small force farther to the right, which met a few of the enemy. It then moved to a second cross-road and halted. The Thirty-second United States Colored Troops, one of the first regiments to arrive, was sent to support the blue jackets.

Our companies on the "Golden Gate" started at the signal; but about daylight the pilot admitted that he was lost. When the fog lifted and land was seen near by, a boat was sent ashore to obtain information. At last the proper course was ascertained, and the craft made Boyd's Landing, the fourth transport to arrive. Captain Pope landed his men on the rude wharf one at time, and then joined Lieutenant-Colonel Hooper up the road. Captain Homans's companies on the "Fraser" moved on time, but the steamer grounded. After a while she floated, and this detachment also disembarked at the landing and joined the regiment.

In the afternoon the creek was crowded with craft. General Foster was there at 2 P.M., and General Potter at 3.30. The latter infused new life into affairs. Small boats were employed to put men ashore. General Potter moved out with the larger part of his brigade about 4 P.M. At the cross-road the general and Commander Preble had a consultation. Concluding that the map furnished was incorrect, and that the Naval Brigade was on the wrong road, General Potter moved the whole force back to the Coosawhatchie cross-road. There the Naval Brigade remained; and Potter's troops, continuing on to Bolan's church two miles distant, marched to the left in the direction of Savannah, when they should have turned to the right at the church to reach Grahamville. It is said that the guide employed was either ignorant or faithless. Potter continued the march on the wrong road until after midnight, when he retraced his steps, going into bivouac about 2

A.M., on the 30th, at Bolan's church. About this rude structure painted white, the troops rested without fires, the pickets disturbed by occasional shots on the Grahamville road during the night.

Our failure to seize the railroad on the 29th or very early the next morning was fatal to success, for the enemy took prompt and effective measures to oppose us. Their small cavalry force in the vicinity was collected; word was sent in every direction of our landing, and that reinforcements must arrive the next morning or the positions would be given up. General Hardee could spare no troops from Savannah, but ordered two regiments from Charleston to Grahamville. But fortune favored the enemy by the opportune arrival at Savannah at 2 A.M., November 30, of Gen. Gustavus W. Smith with a force of Georgia militia brought from Macon by a roundabout way. Governor Brown had refused to allow his State troops to serve elsewhere than in Georgia; but General Smith permitted himself to execute the instructions of General Hardee, and the cars holding the Georgians were shunted from the rails of the Gulf to those of the Charleston and Savannah Railroad; the leading brigade arriving at Grahamville about 8 A.M., on the 30th. With Smith's and the local force it was hoped to protect the railroad until the arrival of other troops later in the day.

Col. C. J. Colcock, the district commander, who was temporarily absent, arrived at Grahamville at 7 A.M. It was arranged that General Smith should advance about two miles to Honey Hill, which was already fortified for defence, and that Colonel Colcock should take some cavalry and one field-piece, and move in advance of that point to support his pickets and contest our advance.

Colonel Hartwell at the landing made his headquarters

at Boyd's house, and saw to the disposition of the troops as they arrived. The regiments were bivouacked in the fields; and the troops, not knowing how moments necessary for success were being lost, were in fine spirits.

Before daybreak on November 30, the regiments of Potter's brigade at the landing moved to join him, followed by Colonel Hartwell, with the Fifty-fifth Massachusetts and the remaining artillery. The Twenty-sixth and One Hundred and Second United States Colored Troops had not arrived at that hour. At about 7 A.M. our cavalry beyond Bolan's church reported the enemy advancing down the Grahamville road. General Hatch moved his column at 7.30 A.M., preceded by the One Hundred and Twenty-seventh New York, skirmishing. For half a mile the road was bounded by dense woods, then a cotton-field, beyond which were thick woods reaching to a creek crossed by a causeway. Across this field our skirmishers at 8.15 A.M. met the enemy's light troops, who retired slowly.

Our advance had crossed the field, when, at 8.30 A.M., the first cannon-shot was heard, coming from the enemy. General Hatch formed line of battle, and Lieut. E. A. Wildt's section, Battery B, Third New York, shelled the Confederates. Then our skirmishers entered the woods, and Col. George W. Baird's Thirty-second United States Colored Troops, moving along the causeway by the flank at the double-quick, through a severe fire which wounded Lieut.-Col. Edward C. Geary and killed or wounded a number of men, cleared the head of the causeway. Before this retirement the enemy set fire to the dead grass and stubble of an old field beyond the swamp which delayed our progress as intended, and they continued to annoy our advance with occasional shots. Over part of the way still farther onward the troops were confined to the narrow road in column by woods and swamps, while the skirmishers and flankers struggled through vines and underbrush. At a point where the road turned to the left, Colcock made his last stand before seeking his works at Honey Hill; and in the artillery firing that ensued the brave Lieutenant Wildt received a mortal wound.

General Smith was in position, protected by the earthworks at Honey Hill. In his front was a swamp thick with underbrush and grass, through which flowed a sluggish stream. This stream was about one hundred and fifty yards in front of the earthwork, and was crossed by a bridge, the planks of which were torn up. Bushes and trees covered the slight elevation occupied by the enemy. Their left reached into pine lands; the right along a fence skirting the swamp. The enemy's position and the bridge were concealed from our troops, coming up the road to the turn, by a point of woods. Just before the turn was reached, as one came from Bolan's church, a wood-road ran from the main road to the right, with an old dam between it and the creek.

General Smith's force engaged in the battle is given as about fourteen hundred effectives, and consisted of the First Brigade of Georgia Militia, the State Line Brigade of Georgia, Thirty-second and Forty-seventh Georgia Volunteers, Athens Battalion, Augusta Battalion, detachments from four companies Third South Carolina Cavalry, and two guns each of the Beaufort Artillery and De Pass's Battery, and three guns of the Lafayette Artillery. It is believed, however, that this force exceeded the total as given. General Smith posted his main body at the earthwork supporting the guns in position, a heavy line of skirmishers on either flank and a small reserve, giving Colonel Colcock the executive command.

Our skirmishers, on turning the bend of the road, were at once met by a heavy fire which drove them to cover. General Hatch, perceiving that the enemy held a strong position, directed General Potter to put his troops into line, and the One Hundred and Twenty-seventh New York formed on the left of the road, then the Fifty-sixth New York and the One Hundred and Fifty-seventh New York on the extreme left. To the right of the road he sent the One Hundred and Forty-fourth New York and Twenty-fifth Ohio. Lieut. George H. Crocker, with the section of Battery B, Third New York, was ordered into battery at the turn. Although it is difficult to establish the relative time of events, it is believed that these dispositions having been made, the Thirty-fifth United States Colored Troops, Col. James C. Beecher, charged up the road. It went forward with a cheer, but receiving a terrible fire, after severe loss, was forced to retire and form in support of the artillery.

Colonel Hartwell, commanding the Second Brigade, with eight companies of the Fifty-fifth Massachusetts under Lieut.-Col. Charles B. Fox, hearing volley firing breaking the pervading stillness, moved rapidly to the front. There the leaders filing along the wood-road, three companies became separated from the regiment when Colonel Hartwell ordered a charge in double column. Twice forced to fall back by the enemy's fire, their brave colonel giving the command, "Follow your colors!" and himself leading on horseback, the Fifty-fifth turned the bend, rushed up the road, and in the face of a deadly fire advanced to the creek. But it was fruitless, for the pitiless shot and shell so decimated the ranks that the survivors retired after losing over one hundred men in five minutes, including Color Sergeant King, killed, and Sergeant-Major Trotter, Sergeant Shorter, and Sergeant Mitchell, wounded. Colonel Hartwell, wounded and pinned to the ground by his dead horse, was rescued and dragged to the wood by the gallant Lieut. Thomas F. Ellsworth of his regiment. Captains Crane and Boynton were both killed after displaying fearless gallantry. The One Hundred and Twenty-seventh New York supported this charge by an advance, but after the repulse retired also. On the right the Twenty-fifth Ohio and Thirty-second United States Colored Troops, swinging to the left, moved from the wood-road, forcing the enemy's left back to their works, but being met by a murderous fire, were brought to a stand, sustaining their position with great tenacity under severe losses for a considerable time. To this line the Battalion of Marines from the Naval Brigade was brought up later, forming on the right of the Thirty-second; and the three companies of the Fifty-fifth Massachusetts under Maj. William Nutt, which had separated from their regiment, formed to the left of the Twenty-fifth, while the One Hundred and Forty-fourth New York remained in support.

General Smith, on the part of the Confederates, was obliged to put his reserve into action when the full force of our attack was made. A Confederate officer wrote, when the action was at its height:—

> "The noise of the battle at this time was terrific,—the artillery crashing away in the centre, while volley after volley of musketry ran down both lines and were reverberated from the surrounding forests."

It was 5 A.M. when reveille sounded for the Fifty-fourth, and two hours after, the regiment moved from bivouac. It was the rear-guard, and was directed to secure the communications for the division. The regiment marched rap-

idly over good roads with a bright sun overhead, making
the morning hours delightful. Not a hostile sound reached
their ears as the men moved at route step, with only the
tinkle, tinkle, of pans and cups striking the bayonets, for
music. After marching about two and a half miles, we came
to the Coosawhatchie cross-road unprotected even by a
picket. Lieutenant-Colonel Hooper, deeming it imperative
that this important point should be covered, detached Captain Pope with Companies C, D, G, and K to remain there
until relieved. He then moved on with the other companies
to Bolan's church, where Companies A and I under Lieut.
Lewis Reed were left to picket the road beyond.

Pushing forward again over a road clear of troops, Lieutenant-Colonel Hooper proceeded with only Companies E
and H. Nearing the front, from which came sounds of
battle, some stragglers and soldiers were encountered sit-
ting on or about the fences at the sides of the road. As we
approached, they took off their hats, and after hurrahing,
shouted, "Here's the Fifty-fourth!" Farther on the sailors
were found halted. They were in good spirits, calling out,
"Go in, boys! No loading in nine times there!" Still farther
onward at about noon Lieutenant-Colonel Hooper was met
by Col. William T. Bennett, the chief of General Hatch's
staff, to whom application was made for orders. Bennett
seemed excited, according to the lieutenant-colonel's account, and said but little else than "Charge! charge!" pointing to the front. Lieutenant-Colonel Hooper naturally
asked, "Where?" but received no other reply than
"Charge!" Desirous to render service, but realizing the folly
of attempting to carry out such orders with but two companies when there was no concerted movement, and the
artillery just at that time not being served, Lieutenant-
Colonel Hooper moved his men to the left of the road and

attempted to enter the wood by company front. Vines and underbrush, however, offered so great obstructions that at last, pushing on ahead, the men followed him as best they could. He formed line not far from the road on wooded ground sloping to the creek, through the middle of which ran a fence. There the men were ordered to lie down, to avoid the enemy's fire, which at times was sharp, and to which they were directed not to reply, but husband their ammunition. Firing came in their direction too from the rear, and as it was found to proceed from the One Hundred and Twenty-seventh New York, stationed behind and some-what to the left, Lieutenant-Colonel Hooper sent word of our position, and it was discontinued. Hugging the ground, although the firing in front swelled out at times into volleys, we suffered comparatively little. The whole left was paralyzed, in the position occupied, throughout the action. Such was the nature of the ground that it could have easily been held with a smaller force, and a part of the troops been spared for more enterprising work on the flanks.

Meanwhile at the Coosawhatchie cross-road the wisdom of having that point guarded was demonstrated. Captain Pope's account is,—

"I immediately threw out one company (K) under Leonard on the Coosawhatchie road as skirmishers, and with the others threw up a barricade across the road. Soon Leonard reported a body of cavalry coming down the road, and at the same time a naval ensign with two boat howitzers manned by sailors reported to me, sent back by Hatch from the main force. I was very glad to see them, and at once sent word to Leonard to fall back as fast as the Rebel cavalry advanced. This he did; and when within easy range I ordered the ensign to fire. He gave them shrapnel with good aim, and they were apparently surprised, as they had seen nothing of artillery."

After this repulse and some time had elapsed, Captain Pope was relieved by the Thirty-second United States Colored Troops, and moved on. Halting at the church for dinner, just as fires were lighted, heavy volleys were heard, and he again moved forward at the double-quick. Nearing General Hatch and staff, the enthusiastic Capt. T. L. Appleton of "ours" flung up his cap, shouting, "Hurrah! here comes the old Fifty-fourth!" The road was found blocked with ambulances, caissons, and wagons causing the men to be strung out. It was about 1.30 P.M. Captain Pope continues, saying,—

"I saw General Hatch speak to Colonel Bennett, chief of staff, who at once rode to me and said, 'Follow me.' I replied, 'I would like a moment to close my men up, Colonel,' when he said in a most excited manner, 'General Hatch's orders are for you to follow me.' . . . Well, after Bennett's remark I had only to follow, which I did. Arriving near the section of artillery posted at the intersection of the roads, he halted, and said, 'Go to the rear of that battery, file to the left, and charge.' I obeyed orders, all but charging. Arriving on the right of the battery, I looked round for the first time and found only Lieut. David Reid and eight men. How the shot tore down that hill and up the road! I could see where the Fifty-fifth had charged, and their dead lying there. I went back, and only two men followed me."

Lieutenant Reid and Corp. R. M. Foster of Company C were there killed. Captain Pope joined Colonel Beecher, Thirty-fifth United States Colored Troops, in the front battleline, and after nearly an hour, hearing a familiar cheer on the right of the Thirty-fifth, found his companies there. Captain Homans's account is that the four companies were following Captain Pope, when, owing to the blockaded road

and the passage of a light battery at full gallop, few were
able to cross the road and they lost their leader. In consequence, the column halted, uncertain where to go. Homans took command and led to the right along the wood-
road and formed on the right of the Thirty-fifth United
States Colored Troops. Adjutant Howard, the colors, and
guard, owing to a mistaken order, did not follow Lieutenant-Colonel Hooper's companies, but joined the four companies when they came up. In the position taken, Homans
ordered the men to lie down. Color Sergeant Lenox, writing of that time, says,—

> "We were hurried up and went into the woods on the right
> side of the road, and took our position near where there
> were, I think, three pieces of artillery. The gunners had a
> hard time of it. I believe two of the cannon were disabled.
> I saw two of the horses struck by shells, and an officer
> pitching out cartridges with his sword, and in a few min-
> utes the caisson blew up. The woods were so thick in front
> that the movements of most of the force could not be seen.
> ... Wagner always seemed to me the most terrible of our
> battles, but the musketry at Honey Hill was something
> fearful. The so-called 'Rebel yell' was more prominent than
> I ever heard it."

It is probable that the battery at full gallop which Captain Homans refers to was Battery F, Third New York
Artillery, relieving Battery B, which Lieutenant Crocker
had fought long and gallantly, although wounded.

Our last regiment to reach the field was Col. H. S.
Chipman's One Hundred and Second United States Colored
Troops. That officer took command of the Second Brigade.
After a severe contest our right fell back to the line of the
old dam. Reconnoissances made from this force to the
right front found no enemy. As the afternoon wore on, the

sounds of battle sometimes stilled down to scattering shots, to rise again into crashes of musketry and cannon discharges. After a while the musket ammunition ran low; and as the supply received was small, it was sparingly used to repel attack. It was reported to General Hatch by deserters that the enemy was receiving reinforcements by railroad; and indeed Gen. B. H. Robertson arrived with the Thirty-second Georgia, a battery, and a company of artillery.

Our Fifty-fourth companies on the wood-road held an angle of the line much exposed to the enemy's fire. They at times blazed away into the woods they fronted. Lieutenant Emerson was severely wounded in the face; and Lieutenant Hallett in the left thigh. Captain Homans received a severe contusion on the inside of the left leg, a pocket-book with greenbacks therein saving him from a mortal wound. Besides the officers, one enlisted man was killed, twenty-one wounded, and three missing. Sergeant-Major Wilson states that sometime in the afternoon, with Sergt. H. J. Carter, Corp. John Barker, and Privates J. Anderson, Thomas Clark, and Peter J. Anderson, all of Company G, he went out from Captain Homans's position, and brought back Lieutenant Reid's and Corporal Foster's bodies. The former was killed by a grape-shot.

Meanwhile Lieutenant-Colonel Hooper with Companies E and H maintained their line unchanged on the left of the main road. During the afternoon Lieutenant-Colonel Hooper made a personal reconnoissance of the ground in front, and returning, sent two notes to General Hatch, saying that with two regiments the enemy's right could be flanked. His suggestion was not acted upon. Lieutenant Chipman was wounded in the left arm, and thirteen enlisted men wounded. At one time that day Colonel Beecher,

Thirty-fifth United States Colored Troops, who was wounded, came along in rear of our line acting in a dazed sort of way. Fearing he would be killed, Lieutenant-Colonel Hooper sent two men to assist him to the rear.

At about 3.40 P.M., Battery F's section was relieved by two of the heaviest naval howitzers under Lieutenant-Commander Matthews. In hauling back the army guns by hand, the One Hundred and Second United States Colored Troops lost a number of officers and men. When the naval guns began firing, the sailors worked their pieces in a lively manner on their hands and knees. The enemy's fire slackened at 3.30 P.M. They made no serious attempt to advance at any time; neither did we make further aggressive movement. Preparations were made for retirement at dark by General Potter, who bore himself with conspicuous gallantry at the front throughout. He caused a reserve of two regiments supported by artillery to be first posted half a mile in rear; and when darkness covered the field, the retreat began and was executed by means of successive lines. One section of the naval howitzers fired until the ground was abandoned about 7.30 P.M. The retirement was effected without alarm or loss.

When the order came for the Fifty-fourth to move, Captain Pope filed off, meeting Lieutenant-Colonel Hooper's companies, which were coming into the road from the left. Our few ambulances, crowded with sufferers, had departed; and as many wounded remained, the Fifty-fourth and Fifty-fifth were broken into squads to remove them. Stretchers were improvised from muskets, shelter tents, and blankets, by which means and bodily help the Fifty-fourth alone carried one hundred and fifty wounded from the field. When we came to Bolan's church, the whole vicinity was weirdly lighted by great fires of fence-rails and brushwood.

A confused turmoil of sounds pervaded the night air, from the rumbling of artillery, the creaking wagons of the train, and the shouts of drivers urging on their animals. The church, cleared of seats, afforded resting-places for the wounded, whom Surgeon Briggs of the Fifty-fourth and his assistants were attending there or outside. Stores of every description were strewn about to make room in the vehicles for their further conveyance to the landing. General Potter arrived at Bolan's church about midnight. Having disposed troops to cover it, he addressed himself to the task of further retirement, and did not cease therefrom until 3 A.M., December 1.

After moving back to the church, the Fifty-fourth took a large number of wounded onward, many men making more than one trip. Our regiment bivouacked on the ground occupied the night before. General Hatch's front line was kept at the Coosawhatchie cross-road, where the guns were placed in position, supported by the Naval Brigade and the Thirty-fourth and Thirty-fifth United States Colored Troops.

Regarding this battle, General Potter reports of the troops: "Nothing but the formidable character of the obstacles they encountered prevented them from achieving success." Capt. Charles C. Soule, Fifty-fifth Massachusetts, a participator, in his admirable account of the battle in the Philadelphia "Weekly Times," says: "The generalship displayed was not equal to the soldierly qualities of the troops engaged. There appears to have been a lack of foresight in the preparations." He gives our loss, from official sources, as eighty-eight killed, six hundred and twenty-three wounded (of which one hundred and forty were slight cases), and forty-three missing: a total of seven hundred and fifty-four. Of the Fifty-fourth (with six companies engaged, numbering sixteen officers and three hundred men), the loss was one officer killed and three wounded; and of enlisted men, one killed, thirty-five wounded, and four missing: a total of forty-four. Lieutenant Reid, who was killed, fully expected his fate. He gave last injunctions regarding his family before leaving Morris Island to a brother officer. At Hilton Head he purchased an emblem of the ⸱reemasons, with which order he was affiliated. Lieutenant Chipman wrote:—

"I can remember poor Reid that morning before we broke camp at the landing. He was blue enough, and said to me that it was his last day on earth; that he should be killed in the fight. Lieutenant Reid was a faithful, experienced, and brave officer, and met his death in the forefront of battle, his body lying in advance of the artillery pieces until brought back."

The Confederates fought steadily and gallantly. But their position more than counterbalanced our preponderance of numbers. It is doubtful, however, if we had more than thirty-five hundred men engaged. Lieut.-Col. C. C. Jones, Jr., in his "Siege of Savannah," gives their loss as four killed and forty wounded. But the Savannah "Republican" of Dec. 1, 1864, stated, "Our loss was between eighty and one hundred killed and wounded." Our defeat lost us results which are thus summarized by Lieutenant-Colonel Jones: "The victory at Honey Hill released the city of Savannah from an impending danger, which, had it not thus been averted, would have necessitated its immediate evacuation."

As Sherman's army on November 29 was about Louisville, Ga., threatening Augusta, it would seem now that if our movements had been delayed a week, when Sherman was near Savannah, Hardee's whole army might have been captured, as the enemy then would not have dared to detach against Foster, and our force could have cut the railroad, thus preventing escape of the Confederates by the only available route.

It would seem with the light of the present that our position was as strong for us to hold as was the enemy's. This granted, the natural criticism is, Would not the battle have been better fought to have held the position with a portion of our troops and pushed out the main body well on one flank or the other, drawing the enemy from his work to fight us and preserve his communications?

CHAPTER XIII

OPERATIONS ABOUT POCOTALIGO

About Boyd's Landing on the morning of December 1, the wounded were being gathered for conveyance to Hilton Head. In the forenoon the division moved out to the cross-road, where with the other troops, the Fifty-fourth maintained a line of battle for some time. It was formed in the woods, a small stream and swamp covering a portion of the front. The Twenty-sixth United States Colored Troops having arrived, its colonel, William Silliman, assumed command of our Second Brigade. During the day Companies A and I with Captain Homans as brigade officer of the day went out on the skirmish line. A few of the enemy were seen, but they made no demonstration, though reinforced since the battle by Brig.-Gen. James Chestnut, with three hundred and fifty South Carolina Reserves and Baker's brigade of two thousand men. Their Georgia State troops returned to Savannah that day.

A quiet night followed; but at 7 A.M. on the 2d the enemy

opened with field-pieces, forcing the skirmishers back and then shelling the centre of our line, to which our guns replied. An intrenchment was ordered constructed covering the cross-road, and the Fifty-fourth completed its allotted work rapidly. Trees were cut and laid to form a foundation for the parapet. As the ground was wet in places, large areas of the surface had to be taken to procure sufficient earth. Rations were not procurable; but our quartermaster borrowed hard bread from the naval force, and secured three head of cattle. Good weather prevailed on the 3d, when the Fifty-fourth moved to the right for work on a prolongation of the fortifications. In the afternoon the Thirty-second and One Hundred and Second United States Colored Troops and part of the Fifty-fifth Massachusetts and two guns went toward Bolan's church, and after light skirmishing returned with but one casualty. That night there was much wild picket firing by men of new colored regiments; and Capt. Alonzo B. Whitney, Twenty-sixth United States Colored Troops, was mortally wounded by our own people.

Except occasional shots from the outposts and gun discharges from the naval howitzers on the left to try the range, the forenoon of the 4th passed quietly. Later, a reconnoissance was made by the Thirty-fourth and Thirty-fifth United States Colored Troops, the One Hundred and Forty-fourth New York, and some artillery four miles toward Coosawhatchie, driving the enemy's skirmishers to a battery, with which cannon-shots were exchanged. That day the Twenty-fifth Ohio went by water to Blair's Landing, advanced on the Beaufort road, and flanking a work of the enemy, compelled its abandonment and captured two guns, one of which was brought away, and the other spiked.

Our naval vessels were daily reconnoitring up the rivers and shelling hostile works when discovered.

From the cross-road on the 5th two reconnoitring parties went out,—the Fifty-fifth Massachusetts and two naval howitzers to the left as a diversion, while General Potter, with part of his brigade, moved upon the battery found the previous day, which was again cannonaded. Important information was received from a "galvanized Yankee," who deserted from the Forty-seventh Georgia to Potter's force. His regiment had a considerable number of men like himself,—Union soldiers who enlisted to escape starvation when prisoners-of-war,—numbers of whom deserted to us subsequently. That evening the outposts were drawn closer in, and dispositions made to hold the line with the Second Brigade only, as the remainder of our force, with a part of the artillery, moved at midnight to the landing. Just as daylight broke on the 6th the Fifty-fourth marched to the extreme right of the intrenchments near Merceraux's Battery B, Third New York Artillery. That day the cavalry made a short reconnoissance; and at sunset our guns shelled the woods vigorously.

Potter's and the Naval Brigade landed on the 6th at Devaux's Neck, and with the howitzers pushed toward the railroad, which, crossing to the Neck by means of a bridge over the Coosawhatchie, ran over the peninsula and left it by another bridge spanning the Tullifinny River. Potter, leading his skirmishers, forced back the enemy's light troops, making a few captures. Brig.-Gen. L. H. Gartrell, the Confederate district commander, sent the Fifth Georgia, supported by a body of Georgia Reserves and a battery, to oppose us. They took position in the woods along the State road, between us and the railroad, and delivered a sharp musketry fire as we advanced. After some preliminary movements, a charge of the Fifty-sixth and One Hundred and Twenty-seventh New York was made, which nearly enveloped the Fifth Georgia, and secured some prisoners and its flag. The enemy, on retiring, left twenty killed and wounded, and partially destroyed the Coosawhatchie Bridge. Our loss was about twelve killed, and perhaps one hundred wounded. Potter, first destroying Mason's Bridge on the State road, over the Tullifinny, and throwing out a skirmish line, intrenched, awaiting reinforcements.

December 7, orders came for the abandonment of the cross-road at Boyd's Neck. General Hatch directed the Fifty-fifth Massachusetts, the cavalry, and some artillery to remain and hold the landing covered by the gunboat "Pontiac." About midnight the pickets were drawn in by Captain Emilio, brigade officer of the day, and joined the Fifty-fourth, which had marched to the landing. From its arrival until nearly daylight, the regiment was embarking amid a heavy rain-storm on the steamer "Mayflower," on which were General Hatch and Colonel Silliman. Our transport started out of the creek when day dawned, ran up Broad River, and into the Tullifinny, where she grounded. Small craft were brought, and the command was ferried to the lower landing, while rain still poured down. Lieutenant-Colonel Hooper without delay, soon after 2 P.M., marched to the front, where the regiment formed division column and bivouacked.

General Jones, upon receiving news of our invasion of Devaux's Neck, gathered a force to attack us. Col. A. C. Edwards, Forty-seventh Georgia, with his regiment, a battalion of the Thirty-second Georgia, Major White's battalion of South Carolina Cadets, and the German Artillery (four guns), was to move from the Tullifinny trestle-bridge, and give battle. General Gartrell, with the Coosawhatchie force, was ordered against our left. At 7 A.M. on the 7th, covered in their advance to within sixty yards of our front, by a heavy growth of timber and foggy weather, the enemy moved to surprise us. He first struck the Thirty-second United States Colored Troops, causing severe losses; but the regiment repulsed the foe. The attempt was renewed, but we were then better prepared, and our infantry and artillery beat them back with loss. Our left was then assailed by Gartrell's force, when the same result followed. After an action lasting about three hours the enemy called back his troops, with a loss which we estimated at one hundred; ours was about eighty. That day a detachment from the Coast Division landed at Mackay's Point across the Tullifinny, marched up, and took post opposite Gregory's plantation, where it intrenched. Gregory's was made the landing-place on Devaux's Neck for all our supplies and stores.

So near were the troops to the railroad that the rumbling of trains and whistling of locomotives could be heard. The position was in an open space surrounded by woods, the main body well intrenched, with pickets in the forest confronted by those of the enemy. Our attempts to reach the railroad on the Neck having failed, the purpose now was to destroy or command it with artillery. It was also important to keep as many of the foe in our front and from Sherman's as possible, for the coming of the Western army was daily looked for. No change occurred in the position of the Fifty-fourth from that first taken up until 6 P.M. on the 8th, when, carrying boards for intrenching, it moved to slightly higher ground in rear of the right of our line, and worked all night by reliefs.

Brig.-Gen. B. H. Robertson on the 8th assumed command of the enemy in our front, comprising some fifty-five hundred effectives.

It was determined to cut an opening through the woods before our right, to better cannonade the railroad. Accordingly, on the 9th, Colonel Silliman led forward with the One Hundred and Twenty-seventh and One Hundred and Fifty-seventh New York, skirmishing. General Potter followed with the Fifty-sixth and One Hundred and Forty-fourth New York and One Hundred and Second United States Colored Troops, constituting the main line; then came the Twenty-fifth Ohio with axes to execute the work, and a reserve of the Thirty-second, Thirty -fourth, and Thirty-fifth United States Colored Troops. The Naval Brigade also took part. In this order, on that cold, raw morning, the troops having formed at 8.45 o'clock, ten pieces of artillery opened fire for fifteen minutes to clear the woods in front. Colonel Silliman advanced the skirmishers about half a mile and became engaged just before 10 A.M., the enemy replying briskly. General Potter supporting with the main line, the woodsmen from the West followed, felling the trees. This novel operation of war caused the familiar sound of battle to be allied on this occasion with that of falling timber crashing down to earth. The path of the forest reapers, twenty yards wide, could be plainly seen from the rear as the axemen advanced.

Our skirmishers moved to within six hundred yards of the railroad. General Potter was at the extreme front. Capt. W. C. Manning of his staff, ascending a tall tree to make a sketch of the ground, could see the railroad, and a Rebel battery firing, to the left. It was 3 P.M. when the lane, five hundred yards long, was cut through the belt of wood to an opening beyond. Suddenly, as we were about to withdraw, the enemy became bolder, and a regiment out of cartridges fell back, exposing the woodsmen of the Twenty-fifth Ohio. Lieutenant-Colonel Haughton of that regiment ordered muskets unslung, and as the foe came on with their mobbish scream, gave them a costly repulse. All attacks along our whole line were successfully met; but when driven back, the enemy still maintained a brisk response. From the reserve, late in the afternoon, the Thirty-second United States Colored Troops relieved the One Hundred and Forty-fourth New York and Twenty-fifth Ohio, when their ammunition was expended. Our artillery, supplemented by Hamner's Third Rhode Island Battery, toward the close, was ably handled. At dark the enemy fell back, when our troops retired to their fortified camp. The enemy's loss was about one hundred in all, including General Gartrell wounded. Ours was about two hundred. Colonel Silliman, after displaying marked gallantry, was mortally wounded. His aid, Lieut. Edwin R. Hill, Fifty-fifth Massachusetts, an able soldier of experience and valor, was also mortally wounded.

In this action the Fifty-fourth was in reserve, and throughout the day continued working upon the rifle trench, and a battery for guns to command the opening cut in the forest. All was in readiness for a call to the front, but the demand was not made. At 5 P.M. that day Colonel Hallowell arrived with five hundred men of the Fifty-fourth New York and Thirty-third United States Colored Troops. He took command of our Second Brigade, retaining Lieut. Geo. F. McKay, Fifty-fifth Massachusetts, as acting assistant adjutant-general. At night Lieutenant Knowles was wounded on picket, and went to the rear.

Though foiled in further advance, we held on, not knowing where Sherman might strike the coast. Deserters reported his near approach. We were within good range of the railroad. Another battery was constructed in the swamp on our left, mainly to command a culvert on the railroad. From that point four half-moons of the enemy could be seen near Coosawhatchie. General Hatch made his headquarters under canvas, while General Potter occupied Talbird's house.

From our camp of shelter tents pitched in an open field, details for picket and work on the intrenchments went out daily. Damp, rainy weather prevailed, causing considerable sickness, but it cleared, with sunny outbursts, on the 11th. The Seventy-fifth and One Hundred and Seventh Ohio joined the division on the 10th. Our brigade the next day was increased by the transfer to it of the Thirty-fourth United States Colored Troops. We were shelling the railroad through the cut whenever trains were heard, and also at intervals after nightfall. Firing in the direction of Savannah occurred on the 11th, and, as we hoped, proved to be Sherman's guns. On the 12th, Captain Duncan, Third Illinois Cavalry, and two men, drifted down past the enemy's batteries at Savannah in a boat, and brought a despatch that the Western army was confronting that city.

Frosty nights were now the rule, and the troops, lightly sheltered, thinly clothed, and in many cases without blankets, suffered. Supplies came regularly, and fresh beef in limited quantity was issued. The Sanitary Commission at Devaux's Neck did much for the sick and well. It was now a daily occurrence to hear Sherman's guns. Companies D and I, on the 14th, were detailed as guard at brigade headquarters. We had present at Devaux's Neck about four hundred and ninety enlisted men. News came on the evening of the 14th that Fort McAllister was taken, and Sherman and Foster in communication. As the news spread through the camps the men turned out, giving repeated cheers, while the only band present played the "Star Spangled Banner." These noisy demonstrations aroused the Johnnies, who set up the usual yelling. Captain Emilio, in command of the pickets, on the 17th made a reconnoissance with a few men to a point near the enemy's line on the Tullifinny.

In a letter from General Sherman to General Foster dated December 18, the former expressed his desire to have the railroad cut. As an alternative he suggested, "or it may be that you could diminish that force and use the balance in a small handy detachment east of Tullifinny over about old Pocotaligo."

December 19, at 11 P.M., the Fifty-fourth and Thirty-third United States Colored Troops moved to Gregory's Landing, whence the Thirty-third first crossed on the "General Hooker." The Fifty-fourth followed at 3 A.M. on the 20th, upon the same steamer. We ran up the river a short distance, and disembarked at Graham's Neck. Rain was falling, as was usual, seemingly, when the regiment moved. Marching about two miles to higher ground included in the "Mike" Jenkins plantation, arms were stacked, and we rested. Near by were the Twenty-sixth and Thirty-third United States Colored Troops, which, with the Fifty-fourth, constituted the force under Colonel Hallowell. We perhaps made up the "small, handy detachment" Sherman had suggested, as old Pocotaligo was in our front.

When morning came, preparations were made for an advance. About 4 P.M. the Thirty-third made a reconnoissance, and Companies H and I of the Fifty-fourth moved in support. The Thirty-third met some of the enemy's light troops after a march of two miles or more, drove them, and then returned to camp. It is probable that Colonel Hallowell's force would have been called upon for an attempt against the enemy's works about old Pocotaligo had not Savannah fallen on the night of the 20th. Hardee evacuated the city after abandoning or burning immense stores and many guns, retiring to Hardeeville, S.C., across the river.

Graham's Neck, occupied by our brigade, is the point of land between the Tullifinny and Pocotaligo rivers. Along its length farther inland than our position was a road from Mackay's Point on the Broad to the State road, which crossed Graham's as well as Devaux's Neck. In our vicinity were the abandoned plantations known to us as the Dr. Hutson, Mason, Steuart, and Howard places. To our right front was an open country as far as Framton Creek; but in our immediate front bordering the Tullifinny were creeks, swamps, and heavy woods.

During the night of the 21st, the pickets of the Twenty-sixth United States Colored Troops captured three cavalrymen. In retaliation, the next morning the enemy attacked their line, killing one man and wounding another, forcing them back. Major Pope, with Companies C, E, H, and K, relieved the Twenty-sixth men later that morning, taking up the same badly run and dangerous line, which was given up for a better position the same evening.

Our brigade expected an attack the succeeding day, as Colonel Hallowell was warned to be on the alert. At night news came of the occupation of Savannah, causing great enthusiasm. Early each morning the brigade moved to and occupied an intrenched line beyond the Fifty-fourth camp. Daily scouting parties were sent out. Quartermaster Ritchie drew rations at Gregory's, ferried them over in pontoons, and brought them to camp with details of men, as there were no teams. A commissary was established at Gregory's, but no sutler was with the troops.

Christmas was a cloudy day, and brought no festivities for the regiment. Some "Quaker" guns were made and mounted to deceive the enemy, as we had no artillery. On the 26th a party of five deserters came in, bringing a false report that Wilmington was captured. Across the river on Devaux's Neck little was going on besides shelling the railroad. Such portions of Hardee's army as passed, did so on foot, but cars laden with guns and ammunition ran the gauntlet of our fire over the rails. General Beauregard expected that Sherman would make an immediate advance, and directed Hardee to oppose his progress behind the large streams, and secretly to prepare for evacuating Charleston. Governor Magrath of South Carolina and the newspapers were frantically but fruitlessly calling upon all men to arm and defend the State.

From Devaux's Neck, on the 28th, the Naval Brigade departed for Port Royal, where it disbanded two days later. A family of ten contrabands came in to us at Graham's on the 29th, reporting but few Confederates in our immediate front, and that they were taking up the railroad iron. Captain Tucker, the next day, with twenty men, went out on a scout, and exchanged shots with the enemy. The last day of the year was warm and springlike; but after sundown the temperature fell, ice formed, and large fires were found necessary for warmth. The chilly nights drove the officers to make huts of logs or slabs, first covered with straw and then with earth. Though cave-like, they proved warm.

By this date the troops on Devaux's Neck were reduced by the departure of some regiments. January 3, at night, the Twenty-sixth United States Colored Troops left Graham's for Beaufort, and the Fifty-fourth the next morning took position at the former regiment's old camp close behind the intrenchment. With the shanties there, and boards brought from a plantation, the command found better shelter. Lieutenant-Colonel Hooper, with four officers and 125 men, reconnoitred that day toward Pocotaligo, returning at dark, having seen a few mounted men only.

Sherman was now transferring his right wing from Thunderbolt to Beaufort; his left wing was ordered to Robertsville. There seemed to be some uncertainty regarding the movements of the Fifty-fourth about this time, for it was rumored at Morris Island that we were to return there, and on the 5th our horses were ordered to Hilton Head. A deserter from the Fiftieth North Carolina came in on the 10th, reporting ten regiments in our front,—making a total force of two thousand men.

January 14, Lieutenant-Colonel Hooper at 10 A.M., with four officers and 125 men, went out to the Steuart house, seeing but a picket of the enemy. Colonel Hallowell, about 4 P.M., with 225 men and officers of the Fifty-fourth and about the same number of the Thirty-third, marched out under instructions to find and engage any hostile force. We fully expected a fight, but at the Steuart house orders came from General Hatch postponing the attack. That evening there were cannon-shots in our front, and at Devaux's Neck the sound of moving wagons and artillery was heard. Those of the Fifty-fourth on picket very early on the 15th were first mystified and then elated by hearing drums and fifes far to our right and front, sounding reveille and playing national airs. Captain Emilio, in charge of the line, at once sent word to brigade headquarters that a part of Sherman's army was near. Colonel Hallowell, at 11 A.M., with the Fifty-fourth and Thirty-third, moved to the Steuart house, and coming to the Mackay Point and Pocotaligo road, turned into it. Captain Tucker, with Companies A, G, H, and I, preceded the column, skirmishing. It was a fine bright day, and we moved on over high rolling land on the route pursued by Gen. J. M. Brannan's force, when, in October, 1862, he attacked the enemy at Pocotaligo. Remains of fires and the debris of picket posts were seen as we advanced. Coming near lower ground, we could see a strong line of works beyond a swamp with heavy woods in rear, the road running along the front of the low ground bordering Framton Creek. It had been fortified since Brannan's attack, and could have been held by a small force against an army. Halting our column on the higher ground, Colonel Hallowell sent the skirmishers forward, and they soon occupied the abandoned works. Moving onward past the intrenchment, we at last gained the State road, coming in from the left. A mile and a half farther on we arrived near a bridge and Pocotaligo, where the strong works were found in possession of a division of the Seventeenth Corps; near there we halted. The Fifty-fourth had formed a junction with Sherman's army, the first body of Eastern troops in the field to meet the stalwart Westerners.

On the morning of January 14, the larger part of the Seventeenth Corps, under Maj.-Gen. Frank Blair, crossed from Port Royal Island to the main on a pontoon bridge, and moved toward Pocotaligo, twenty-five miles from Beaufort. They encountered Colonel Colcock, our old friend of Honey Hill, at Gardner's Corners, and drove him with loss to the works mounting twelve guns, at Pocotaligo, before which they bivouacked, intending to assault in the morning; but the enemy under Gen. L. McLaws during the night abandoned this and all his positions along our front, and retired behind the Combahee. Thus fell a stronghold before which the troops of the Department of the South met repeated repulses. It was the most important position between Charleston and Savannah, for there, over the Pocotaligo River, was a trestle of a mile in length, crossing a swamp over which the railroad ran. This trestle the enemy attempted to destroy; but it was only partially damaged. After resting, at 3.30 P.M. the brigade took up the return march for camp, where the regiment arrived, well tired out. At Devaux's Neck that morning the usual pickets of the enemy in front of the railroad were not seen, and our men soon discovered that their works were abandoned; several regiments at once occupied them.

It was a welcome change to be freed from the anxiety of the enemy's proximity and thus enabled to sleep until daylight, and relieved from all picket duty. With rest, supplies and drills the regiment was speedily brought into fine condition once more. It soon became manifest that we were to assist in refitting Sherman's troops. Pocotaligo was thoroughly strengthened as a base. Gen. O. O. Howard, commanding that wing, was directed not to demonstrate up the peninsula, but toward the Salkehatchie, as if preparing to advance directly on Charleston; and as early as the 15th he made such movements. Dense smoke-clouds over the railroad indicated its destruction along our whole front.

South Carolina was already feeling the mailed hand her temper had invoked. Her sons made frantic efforts to convince others that the success of the Confederates depended upon meeting Sherman there even at the expense of Richmond. The newspapers also assailed their chosen leaders. The Charleston "Mercury" said on January 12:

"Let old things pass away. We want no more Jeff. Davis foolery.... North Carolina, Georgia, and South Carolina are in no mood for trifling. . . . South Carolina don't intend to be conquered. She don't intend to be hampered or turned over to the enemy. When she is thus dealt with, there will be reckoning,—a reckoning where there will be no respecter of persons."

By orders from the War Department received January 17, Lieutenant Swails was permitted to muster, thus ending a struggle waged in his behalf for nearly a year by Colonel Hallowell and Governor Andrew. He was one of the earliest if not the first colored officer mustered; and this decision, persistently solicited and finally granted, must rank high with the moral victories wrung from the general government by the regiment and its founders.

On the 18th the steamer "Wyoming" landed the first supplies for Sherman's army at our wharf. That day news was received of the capture of Fort Fisher, North Carolina, by our old commander, Gen. A. H. Terry, causing great rejoicing. Our horses were returned from Hilton Head on the 19th. Rainy weather seriously interfered with bringing up supplies. Daily details from the Fifty-fourth were sent out repairing roads or to the wharf unloading stores. All the enlisted men and eight officers were employed on the 21st making a corduroy road from the landing. Innumerable wagons of Sherman's army came and went over the roads, carrying supplies from various landings on the Tullifinny and Pocotaligo rivers to the camp.

January 24 was cold but clear, after several days of rain. In accordance with orders received to move when favorable weather came, Colonel Hallowell that day transferred his command to Devaux's Neck. The Fifty-fourth moved at 8.30 A.M., and crossing the river on lighters, camp was established in a large field near the hospital. While in this location the regiment received clothing and camp supplies, long sadly needed.

Sherman was now ready for his "great next," and Hatch's Coast Division was ordered to Pocotaligo to relieve Gen. Giles S. Smith's division of the Seventeenth Corps. With the Second Brigade the Fifty-fourth moved at 8 A.M., on the 28th, through the old intrenchments to the State road, and along it to Pocotaligo. We passed through the Rebel fort there, and by the Seventeenth Corps, noting the immense train of wagons, ambulances, and pontoons parked thereabout. Keeping on to the extreme right front, after a march of some ten miles we halted at a point a mile and a quarter from Salkehatchie Creek. Brigade line was formed with the Fifty-fourth, Thirty-third, Thirty-fourth, and One Hundred and Second United States Colored Troops and the artillery, in the near vicinity of some of Sherman's men. In a good position with low ground in front, the Fifty-fourth being in the woods, a rifle trench was made, shelters were pitched, and we camped.

Here we had a brief opportunity of seeing the Western troops. They were a seasoned, hardy set of men. They wore the army hat, instead of the forage-caps affected by most of our regiments. Their line-officers were generally clad in government clothes, with only shoulder-straps and swords to distinguish them. Altogether they impressed us with their individual hardiness, powers of endurance, and earnestness of purpose, and as an army, powerful, full of resources and with staying qualities unsurpassed.

In letters to General Foster dated January 28 and 29, General Sherman expressed his wish that Hatch's force should not be reduced or moved until Foster ascertained the effect of his (Sherman's) appearance west of Branchville, upon the Charleston garrison. He said,—

"My movement to the rear of Charleston is the principal, and all others should be accessory, merely to take advantage of any 'let go.'"

He did not wish the railroad broken until the latter part of the succeeding week. Should the enemy retire beyond the Edisto, then Foster was to cut the railroad on our side anywhere. Admiral Dahlgren should make demonstrations on February 1 and 2 in the Edisto and Stono, and the troops on Morris Island effect a lodgement, if possible, on James Island.

Colonel Van Wyck's brigade, of Hatch's division, came to our vicinity on the 29th. Sherman's men near us moved on the morning of the 30th, to get into proper position for advancing. When they departed, our men visited the deserted camps, finding much corn and rice, besides many useful articles. Four cannon-shots were heard in the distance that morning. The Salkehatchie Bridge had been burned by the enemy; and the high water which overflowed the banks made it difficult to reach the stream itself.

By General Sherman's order General Hatch sent the Twenty-fifth Ohio, on the 30th, to the forks of the wagon-road and railroad, from where a reconnoissance was pushed to the stream, and shots were exchanged. Strong works were seen on the farther bank. Again the camp of the Fifty-fourth was changed, for on the 31st, we marched along the railroad track back to Pocotaligo. Passing around the fort there, we camped near the railroad station, on the extreme left of our line, upon ground formerly occupied by Sherman's men. From the debris strewn about and log foundations for shelter tents, we soon made this resting-place comfortable. Brigade headquarters were located at

John A. Cuthbert's house, the mansion of a fine rice plantation previously occupied by Gen. Frank Blair.

There the writer first saw the famous William T. Sherman. He was riding unattended upon a steady-going horse, and was instantly recognized from his portraits. His figure, tall and slender, sat the horse closely, but slightly bowed. Upon his head was a tall army hat covering a face long and thin, bristling with a closely cropped sandy beard and mustache. His bright keen eyes seemed to take in everything about at a glance. There was hardly a sign of his rank noticeable, and his apparel bore evidence of much service. He was on his way to General Hatch's headquarters. Captain Appleton relates what occurred there. He and others of the staff were playing cards when the door opened and a middle-aged officer asked for General Hatch. Without ceasing their card-playing, the young officers informed the stranger of the general's absence. Imagine their consternation when their visitor quietly said, "Please say to him that General Sherman called." They started up, ashamed and apologizing, but the general softly departed as he came. The next day he took the field with the Fifteenth Corps.

February 1, a report came that the enemy had crossed to our side of the Combahee River and intrenched. At noon, Colonel Hallowell with the Fifty-fourth and two guns moved to Gardner's Corners, whence, with the One Hundred and Seventh Ohio also, he proceeded. We arrived at Combahee Ferry about 6 P.M., where observations were purposely made quietly, after dark. Abandoned works were found on our side, and a foot-bridge crossing the stream. On the farther bank were posts of the enemy and their camp.

After Sherman departed, we picketed the front again.

Our camp was near Daniel B. Heyward's plantation, in a rice country. It was rainy weather, with mud everywhere under foot. At this time Lieutenant-Colonel Hooper wrote,—

> "Sherman destroys everything that stands in his line of march,—rice-mills, houses, fences. All through this country, as far as it can be seen, pillars of black smoke rise. . . . The saying is that 'when Sherman gets through South Carolina, a crow can't fly across the country unless he carries rations with him.'"

The Western army had crossed the Salkehatchie and compelled McLaws to fall back upon Branchville. In the action at Rivers's Bridge, Brig.-Gen. Wager Swayne lost a leg, and with other wounded was brought back to Pocotaligo. Foster, on the 3d, made demonstrations with the Fifty-fifth Massachusetts and One Hundred and Forty-fourth New York in the South Edisto, and with the Thirty-second United States Colored Troops on Edisto Island. On the 4th, the Twenty-fifth Ohio crossed at Combahee Ferry, and after unsuccessful attempts to flank works beyond the rice-fields, recrossed with small loss.

News came of Lieutenant Webster's death, at Beaufort, January 25, of fever. This faithful young officer was the only one the Fifty-fourth lost by disease. On the 5th a force went to a cross-road three miles in advance, from whence the enemy retired over a branch of the Salkehatchie, rendering the bridge spanning it impassable. We lost three men wounded in an attempt to cross.

February 7, at 8 A.M., Colonel Hallowell with the Fifty-fourth and One Hundred and Second United States Colored Troops marched in a rain-storm over the destroyed railroad to Salkehatchie. The enemy had abandoned his extensive works on the farther side of the burned trestle-bridge there. We were joined there by two guns of the Third New York Artillery and two companies of the Fourth Massachusetts Cavalry. An advance was then made simultaneously along both the railroad and turnpike. Crossing the river, the Fifty-fourth moved on the turnpike, Captain Emilio, with Companies E, H, and I, preceding the column skirmishing. Rain was falling, and continued nearly all day, drenching us to the skin, and making the road a quagmire. Soon the enemy, supposed to be of Cobb's Georgia Legion, was discovered in small force, mounted, with a piece of artillery. They halted on every bit of rising ground, or on the farther side of swamps, to throw up barricades of fence-rails against a rush of our cavalrymen, and delayed our advance by shelling us with their field-piece. But our skirmishers moved on steadily through water, swamp, and heavy undergrowth, until their flanks were threatened, when, after exchanging shots, they would retire to new positions. About noon, the enemy were driven out of their camp in haste; and after a rest, the column moved on again. At dark, orders came for Colonel Hallowell to retire about a mile, to a cross-road, five miles from Pocotaligo, where his force halted and intrenched.

Maj. Newcomb Clark, One Hundred and Second United States Colored Troops, on the 8th, with four companies of his regiment, made a reconnoissance toward Cuckwold Creek, and after light skirmishing, destroyed a part of the railroad. Our force at the cross-road was joined by the Twenty-fifth Ohio and two guns. Lieut. P. McLaughlin, quartermaster of the One Hundred and Second United States Colored Troops, was killed by guerillas on that date. February 9, the One Hundred and Twenty-seventh New York and Twenty-fifth Ohio advanced with some artillery and cavalry, driving the enemy from positions about the rice plantations, and damaging the railroad. The Fifty-fourth was now divided up and stationed on picket at several points.

General Gillmore had returned and relieved General Foster, whose old wound required attention. This change gave great dissatisfaction to Admiral Dahlgren, who disliked Gillmore, and he asked to be relieved. Our naval vessels were engaging the enemy's batteries in the Edisto. General Schimmelfennig on the 10th landed the Fifty-fifth Massachusetts, One Hundred and Forty-fourth New York, and Thirty-second and Thirty-third United States Colored Troops on James Island, and drove the enemy from some advanced works, effecting captures. He withdrew his force on the succeeding day. General Hatch, on the 10th, with a portion of the division, attempted to pass Cuckwold Creek, but desisted after finding the bridge burned and the enemy in strong position. This force bivouacked ten miles from Salkehatchie that night, and retired the next day.

February 12, Captain Homans had a man wounded, while foraging. A scouting party of the One Hundred and Seventh Ohio was fired into that morning, having one man wounded and another missing. Guerillas, or small parties of the enemy, were about, and Captain Emilio with Company E and Lieutenant Reed with Company G scoured the region for them without success. At dark the Fifty-fourth, except Companies E and G, left on picket, moved back from the cross-road in company with the Twenty-fifth Ohio, our regiment bivouacking inside the fort at Salkehatchie.

On the evening of the 12th, word was received that the enemy had abandoned Combahee Ferry. The Twenty-fifth Ohio, by a night's march, crossed the river the next day, and took station at Lownde's plantation. The effect of Sherman's advance was being felt in our front, for the Western army was across the North Edisto near Orangeburg. Gen. A. R. Wright retired from Ashepoo across the Edisto, and McLaws from Branchville to Four Hole Swamp. Hardee was also concerned for Charleston, as General Potter, with the Fifty-fifth Massachusetts, One Hundred and Forty-fourth New York, and Thirty-second United States Colored Troops entered Bull's Bay on the 12th, shelled the enemy's batteries at Owendaw Creek, and landing on the 16th, intrenched. General Schimmelfennig was again making demonstrations on James Island.

We received early news of this retirement, for on the 13th a party of thirteen contrabands arrived and reported, "De Rebs clean gone to Ashepoo." During the night Company H joined the others on picket, and two escaped Union prisoners came in, one of whom, unfortunately, our pickets wounded. General Hatch pushed the One Hundred and Second United States Colored Troops along the railroad, and the Twenty-fifth Ohio through Green Pond, to Ashepoo, on the 14th, where the bridges were found burned. A force crossed the river in boats, and drove a few of the enemy away.

Meanwhile, during our field service, the following changes had occurred in the Fifty-fourth: Lieutenant Duren, having broken a leg by falling from his horse at Morris Island, went North, and never returned. Lieutenant Littlefield resigned, and Lieutenant Hallett took charge of the camp. Lieutenant Rogers re-joined the regiment from there. Lieutenant James, recommissioned, reported; but his old wound soon forced him to return to Hilton Head.

Captain Pope was made major, Lieutenant Howard captain of Company I, and Second Lieutenants Stevens and Charles Jewett, Jr., were promoted first lieutenants. Lieutenants Charles F. Joy and William L. Whitney, Jr., newly appointed, joined.

CHAPTER XIV

CHARLESTON AND SAVANNAH

ALL THE STRONG POSITIONS along the railroad having been abandoned by the enemy, the road to Charleston was now open to the Coast Division for an advance without opposition. Colonel Hallowell, on February 15, was ordered with the Fifty-fourth, One Hundred and Twenty-seventh New York, some artillery, and a small force of cavalry to proceed to Ashepoo by way of a road above the railroad leading through Blue House. We moved at noon of a bright, warm day, the companies on picket joining the regiment as it passed. From recent rain the road was heavy with clayey mud, making marching most wearisome. There was constant delay passing through overflowed places, or while bridges were being repaired. We reached Blue House and a mile beyond at 8 P.M., making but six miles. Three bridges had been rebuilt, and two more were reported just in front. Colonel Hallowell, finding it impossible to longer pursue that route, then moved back. We were on a causeway, and in turning around, a wagon stalled and was abandoned. The Fifty-fourth secured from it one hundred and thirty pairs of trousers and three hundred pairs of shoes, free of government charges. After one of the hardest marches the Fifty-fourth ever made, we reached Salkehatchie fort at 3 A.M. on the 16th. Our advance troops were, on the 15th, at the junction of the roads to Jacksonboro and Parker's Ferry.

February 16, Colonel Hallowell was directed to move forward again by way of Combahee Ferry; and at 9 A.M. the Fifty-fourth proceeded, with the usual rests, over a rough country. Much standing water was found in places, and at times the wading was knee-deep. In the afternoon we came to a higher point, where a view of the region bordering the river was obtained. Spread below us was the finest tract we saw in the South,—a cultivated country, thickly spotted with plantations. It was the famous and fertile valley of the Combahee, devoted to rice culture. The negro quarters and mills had been burned by our advance. After crossing a bridge over the river, we moved on a mile and rested after a march of twelve miles.

With fine weather again, on the 17th the Fifty-fourth marched at 9 A.M. toward Ashepoo, which being only eight miles distant and the road excellent, we reached at 1 P.M. There we camped near the railroad bridge on the plantation of Col. Charles Warley. The mansion of this gentleman of wealth and prominence had been plundered by the first comers; and fine books, furniture, and household effects were strewn about, making a sad scene of wastage and pitiless destruction.

Reveille was sounded by the Fifty-fourth bugles at sunrise on the 18th. Foraging parties brought in immense quantities of corn, poultry, sweet potatoes, and honey.

Many of the field-hands were found on the plantations, and our coming was welcomed with joyful demonstrations. A Dr. Dehon and his son were brought in and entertained by the brigade staff that night. Refugees and contrabands were coming into our camps in considerable numbers.

Having repaired the bridge over the Ashepoo, the First Brigade crossed on the 19th, and marched for the South Edisto. Our Second Brigade remained. Dr. Dehon had been sent to General Hatch, but returned that afternoon. Lieutenant Ritchie relates the following particulars of this gentleman's troubles:—

"While gone, his 'chattels' had been helping themselves and carrying furniture off by whole boat-loads. Dehon brings an order from General Hatch that his 'slaves' shall be permitted to choose for themselves whether to go back to the plantation with him or not. Dehon got us to back this up, and as a consequence, loses all his slaves, young and old."

Just at dark, we received the great news that Charleston was evacuated by the enemy. Cheer after cheer rang out; bonfires were lighted; and the soldiers yelled long and frantically. Far into the night nothing else was talked about around the camp-fires.

Our Third Brigade having arrived at Ashepoo on the 20th, at 1 P.M., the Second Brigade moved for Jacksonboro and the Edisto, where our advance had crossed that day in boats. The Fifty-fourth arrived at the Edisto by 5 P.M., going into bivouac in a pine grove but thirty miles from Charleston. We were detained there by repairs upon the burnt bridges over the river until noon of the 21st, when the march was resumed. Just beyond, we passed a Rebel work mounting four guns. Proceeding three miles, the

Second Brigade turned to the right into a road running
nearly parallel with the main route, and four miles farther
brought us to Adam's Run. This was a small hamlet with
numerous rough barracks,—an old and important camp
of the Confederates. Beyond, some four miles, we camped
at a cross-road about 6 P.M., where the One Hundred and
Second United States Colored Troops joined us at 9 P.M.
During that day the country was thoroughly scouted as
the division advanced by the different roads.

February 22 we resumed the onward march at 9 A.M.,
the Fifty-fourth in rear, and passed through woods nearly
the whole day, with here and there a plantation and cultivated fields. By orders everything along the road was
burned. Foraging parties brought in all kinds of provisions
which they loaded into every description of vehicle; wagons, carts, and even antiquated family coaches were used,
drawn by horses, mules, and bullocks, which, with the
contrabands, made our train a curious spectacle. Some
twelve miles from the Ashley River we passed an abandoned
battery of three guns commanding Rantowle's Ferry; another was found on the right at Wallace's. The Fifty-fourth
camped at dark ten miles from Charleston. Our bivouac
was a festive one, for supplies of chickens, turkeys, ducks,
geese, honey, rice, meal, sheep, and beef, were in profu-
sion. Only a few armed but ununiformed men had been
seen, who, when we followed, escaped, and were thought
to be guerillas.

A move was made early on the 23d, our Second Brigade
in advance, the Third Brigade following. The First Brigade
remained to secure abandoned guns, for the whole region
was thickly studded with works. We marched rapidly over
good roads, arriving at the Ashley at 1 P.M. There, across
the river, we saw Charleston, long the Mecca of our hopes;

but the bridges were burned, so we camped with our long train, impatiently awaiting orders to cross. Captain Emilio was made acting assistant provost-marshal of the division, with Company E and a company of the One Hundred and Second as the guard. While there, the weather was rainy and chilly. On the 25th orders came for the First Brigade to report to General Potter, our Second Brigade to take post on Charleston Neck and the Third Brigade to remain. At 6 P.M. we marched to a wharf, but as transportation was not furnished, returned again to camp. With this day the Fifty-fourth completed its longest term of field service.

General Hardee in command of Charleston, disregarding General Beauregard's orders, deferred abandoning the city until the last moment. For some days previous to February 17, trains loaded with army supplies and citizens with their effects were being sent away. At the last the place was largely deserted by its people, the streets littered with refuse and the books and papers of the merchants, and stores and residences showed few signs of occupancy. From James and Sullivan's Islands the Confederates moved to the city on the 17th, thence taking the road to Cheraw, their ranks depleted by desertion as they marched. Detachments were left in the city until the 18th with orders to burn every building holding cotton. They fired a large shed at the Savannah railroad wharf and another on Lucas Street. Lucas's mill and Walker's warehouse were destroyed. The bridge over the Ashley was burned. A terrific explosion occurred at the Northeastern Railroad Depot, filled with ordnance stores, causing great loss of life and communicating the flames to several adjoining blocks.

Not only on land but on the water was this fell work carried out. The gunboats "Palmetto State," "Chicora," and "Charleston" were fired, and blew up with deafening reports; and vessels in the shipyards, torpedo-boats, and blockade-runners, were scuttled or burned. Over 450 pieces of ordnance in the city and vicinity were abandoned, besides immense stores of provisions and army supplies. That the whole city was not obliterated in consequence of these acts of General Beauregard and his subordinates, can only be attributed to the exertions of our soldiery and the negro inhabitants.

Our companies at Morris Island passed the winter months with little of moment to disturb the quiet of garrison life. At about 1 A.M., on February 18, the bridge over the Ashley River was discovered burning, fires were seen in various parts of Charleston, and the storeship "John Ravenel" was a mass of flames lighting up the harbor. At 6 A.M. the magazine of Battery Bee blew up. When day dawned, a heavy fog covered the waters, but at 7.45 A.M. it lifted. With powerful glasses no enemy could be seen at Sumter, James, or Sullivan's Island, although Rebel flags were over the works.

Lieut.-Col. A. G. Bennett, Twenty-First United States Colored Troops, commanding Morris Island, gave orders for his force to gather at Cumming's Point, and had boats prepared to transport the troops. Major Hennessy, Fifty-second Pennsylvania, was sent to Sumter, and Lieut. John Hackett, Third Rhode Island Artillery, to Moultrie, and the navy despatched Acting Ensign Anson to Moultrie, and Acting Master Gifford to Mt. Pleasant. At all these points, about 9.30 A.M., the Rebel flags gave place to the stars and stripes planted by these officers.

Lieutenant-Colonel Bennett, with Lieut. J. F. Haviland, One Hundred and Twenty-seventh New York, joined on the way by other boats containing a few officers and men of the Fifty-second Pennsylvania and Twenty-first United

States Colored Troops, reached Mills's wharf on the city front at 10 A.M., after hoisting the United States flag over Castle Pinckney and Fort Ripley. There they were welcomed by a gathering of colored people, who cheered them and the national symbol. Soon George W. Williams, Dr. Albert G. Mackey, and other citizens appeared, and representing that the Rebel rear-guard was still in the place, begged protection, and assistance in quelling the flames, which threatened the total destruction of the city. Major Hennessy was despatched to the arsenal, and Lieutenant-Colonel Bennett with the remainder of his force, which had been increased by the arrival of some of the Third Rhode Island Artillery, moved to the Citadel. Guards were soon sent to public buildings, storehouses, and important points, and the abandoned fire apparatus, manned by negroes, firemen, and soldiers, was put into use, checking the fires.

Captain Walton and Lieutenant Newell with Company B, and Captain Bridge with Company F, on the 18th, proceeding from Morris Island in rowboats, reached Charleston after the advance troops under Lieutenant-Colonel Bennett. Being the first considerable body of colored soldiers to arrive, their march through the streets saw a continual welcome from crowds of their people of both sexes. Upon reaching the Citadel, officers and men were placed on provost duty. Lieutenant Edmands and his Fifty-fourth men at Black Island, with the Fifty-second Pennsylvania companies there, rowed to Fort Johnson, where they remained until the 19th and then joined Company F in Charleston.

General Schimmelfennig, with a force from Cole's Island, crossed to James Island on the night of the 17th. He early discovered the evacuation, and at 1 P.M., on the 18th, entered Charleston after crossing the Ashley. General Potter learned of the abandonment on the 19th, and moved from Bull's Bay through the Christ Church lines to Mt. Pleasant on the 20th. Potter, on the 22d, with a force, followed Hardee's track to St. Stephen's depot, but as the latter had burned the Santee River Bridge, he returned.

Into the war-ravaged city of Charleston, with its shattered buildings, disrupted grass-grown streets, deserted wharves, and scuttled hulks, the Fifty-fourth entered at 9 A.M., on the 27th, having crossed the river on the steamer "Croton." We could not but be exultant, for by day and night, in sunshine and storm, through close combat and far-reaching cannonade, the city and its defences were the special objects of our endeavor for many months. Moving up Meeting and King streets, through the margin of the "burnt district," we saw all those fearful evidences of fire and shell. Many colored people were there to welcome the regiment, as the one whose prisoners were so long confined in their midst. Passing the Mills House, Charleston Hotel, and the Citadel, the Fifty-fourth proceeded over the plank road one and a half miles to the Neck, where the Confederate intrenchments extended clear across the peninsula. Turning to the right, we entered Magnolia Cemetery, through which the line of works ran, and camped along it among the graves. It was the extreme right of the fortifications, fronting Belvedere Creek. The One Hundred and Second took post on our left. Brigade headquarters were at the Cary house near by. Companies B and F, relieved in the city, re-joined the regiment that day.

Our camp among the tombstones seemed a desecration of the beautiful grounds which should have been sacred to the dead; but our foes were responsible for constructing the lines there. Lieutenant Cousens, on the 28th, was sent for our camp effects at Morris Island, and as a portion was brought in small boats, some damage by water resulted to company books and officers' baggage. Major Pope, on March 1, with Companies C, E, H, and I, visited the Benjamin Whaley place thirteen miles distant, moving over the plank road and fording Nine-Mile Run on the way. At the plantation the detachment rested for the night, receiving abundant supplies from the negroes. Some fifty hands were found there, and the next day returned to Charleston with our force.

There was bad weather the first week of March; then warm and springlike days came. We received a large number of men who had been detailed, detached, or were sick when the Fifty-fourth left Morris Island. Details were furnished for picket duty, generally along the plank road. Headquarters for the line were at the Four-Mile House, which had been a tavern, but was then occupied by a hospitable Irishman—Lawler by name—and his wife. Opportunities were given officers and men to visit the city, where they wandered about, deeply interested in sightseeing. Several Fifty-fourth officers were detailed there, and always entertained visiting associates. The most interesting building to us of the Fifty-fourth was the jail,—a brick structure surmounted by a tower and enclosed with a high wall, where the prisoners of the regiment were confined many months with black and white criminals as well as other Union soldiers.

Of the townspeople but some ten thousand remained, largely blacks, all mainly dependent upon our bounty. The whole banking capital of Charleston was lost. A loyal edition of the "Courier" newspaper was being issued; the "Mercury" had decamped to Cheraw. Schools were opened, and market-wharves designated. The post-office was established at the southwest corner of King and George streets, the headquarters of the commandant at the northwest corner of Meeting and George streets, and General Hatch, the district commander, was at No. 13 King Street. Applicants thronged the provost-marshal's office to take the oath of allegiance, and the recruiting of colored troops was going on rapidly.

Regimental orders, on the 8th, directed the line to be formed as below, with Company F on the right,—

E G D A H B I K C F

The brigade having been ordered to Savannah, on the 12th, Lieutenant-Colonel Hooper marched the right wing to the city and embarked on the steamer "W. W. Coit," which in the afternoon ran down the harbor past the now silent batteries on either side, and arrived at Hilton Head about midnight. Proceeding in the morning, the steamer entered the Savannah River and tied up at the city front at noon. Disembarking, the wing moved out Bull Street and to the edge of the place, where on high ground it took possession of a fine camp of board shelters constructed by Sherman's men, near the One Hundred and Second United States Colored Troops, camped on our right. Major Pope, with the left wing, left Charleston March 13 on the steamer "Chas. Houghton," arriving at Hilton Head about midnight. There the men disembarked on the pier, while the vessel went elsewhere to coal. At 3 P.M., on the 14th, this wing proceeded by way of Shell Creek and the inside channel, arriving at Savannah four hours later.

Upon the 14th also the Thirty-third United States Colored Troops arrived, and with the Fifty-fourth and One Hundred and Second United States Colored Troops, made up the colored brigade under Colonel Hallowell, who occupied No. 109 Broad Street, procured for him by Lieutenant Ritchie at the same rent as the Jacksonville houses. Bvt. Maj.-Gen. Cuvier Grover commanded the district, and his division of the Nineteenth Corps held the posts. Bvt. Brig.-Gen. E. L. Moleneux commanded the defences.

Savannah was a most attractive city, with wide, shaded streets, numerous parks, and many good buildings, and elegant residences. All the approaches to it had been well fortified by the enemy, for there were heavy works on the river and a line of fortifications from the Savannah to the Little Ogeechee River. Beyond, facing this land defence, were the works thrown up by the besiegers. On every side were the deserted camps of Sherman's and Hardee's armies, marked by debris, rough shanties, cleared spaces, and approaching roads. When captured, the population was estimated as twenty thousand, of whom thousands were supported upon army supplies or those sent from the generous North by ship-loads. The most attractive spot was the beautiful cemetery of Bonaventure, with its majestic live-oaks and wooded paths. Savannah had fallen by siege in every war; to the British in 1788 and 1812, and to the Federal troops in 1864.

It was a busy time, our short stay there, for returns were in arrears, and the books had to be written up. Clothing was issued and drills resumed. The regiment furnished picket details in proper turn for the brigade. It was delightful weather, the gardens already blooming with camellias, japonicas, and Cape jessamine. On the 18th, the Fifty-fourth with the whole division was inspected by Brig.-Gen. Seth Williams, U.S.A. Our regiment was in excellent condition, and the colored brigade made a good appearance, numbering twenty-three hundred men.

It seemed that the government, having paid us once in

the two years' service, was allowing that to suffice, for six months' pay was due at this time. The officers were penniless, and had to send North for money or borrow it to subsist upon. Sherman's victorious progress, Sheridan's brilliant successes, Lee's inability to hold back Grant, and the whole seaboard fallen, made it manifest that the war was virtually over. The Fifty-fourth then expected but a brief period of garrison duty, followed by a homeward voyage, without again hearing a hostile shot; but a new field of service was before them, for after a review of the troops on the 25th by General Grover at "The Plain," orders came for the Fifty-fourth and One Hundred and Second United States Colored Troops to proceed to Georgetown, S.C.

The following changes took place among the officers at Savannah,—Lieutenant Emerson re-joined; Lieutenant Knowles resigned at the North; Captains Emilio and Homans were mustered out at the expiration of their personal terms of service; Lieutenant Chipman was promoted captain of Company D; Lieutenant Duren, still at the North, was appointed adjutant.

On the 27th Lieutenant-Colonel Hooper embarked with the right wing on the steamer "W. W. Coit," accompanied by Colonel Hallowell. The same day Major Pope with the left wing boarded the steamer "Canonicus." After getting to sea, both transports touched at Hilton Head and then went on to Charleston, where Colonel Hallowell was directed to report to General Hatch. Bad weather and the want of coal prevented sailing thence until the morning of the 31st, when the voyage was resumed.

CHAPTER XV

POTTER'S RAID

WHILE AT COLUMBIA, S.C., General Sherman sent and destroyed the railroad to Kingsville and the Wateree Bridge. From Cheraw he broke the railroad trestles toward Florence as far as Darlington, and the enemy burned the railroad bridge over the Pedee. Between Florence and Sumterville was a vast amount of rolling-stock thus hemmed in. Sherman, considering that this should be destroyed before the roads could be repaired, and that the food supplies in that section should be exhausted, wrote General Gillmore from Fayetteville, N.C., directing him to execute this work. He suggested that Gillmore's force be twenty-five hundred men, lightly equipped, to move from Georgetown or the Santee Bridge, that the troops be taken from Charleston or Savannah, and added,—

> "I don't feel disposed to be over-generous, and should not hesitate to burn Charleston, Savannah, and Wilmington, or either of them, if the garrisons were needed....Those cars and locomotives should be destroyed if to do it costs you five hundred men."

301

These instructions caused the concentration of a selected force at Georgetown, of which the Fifty-fourth formed a part. The resultant movement, called "Potter's Raid," during which almost the last encounters of the Rebellion occurred, is little known, as it took place when momentous military events were taking place elsewhere.

Georgetown was the port of one of the richest regions in the South, and until our vessels were stationed off its entrance, a resort of blockade-runners. There were decayed wharves, regular streets, some fine residences, public buildings, and the hall of the Winyaw Indigo Society in the place. Up the Waccamaw some fifteen miles was "The Oaks," the plantation of Governor Alston, whose wife, the beautiful and accomplished Theodosia, only daughter of Aaron Burr, was lost at sea on the pilot-boat "Patriot," with all on board.

Major Pope and the left wing of the Fifty-fourth on the "Canonicus" entered Winyaw Bay, ran up the river some eleven miles past Battery White and other works, and disembarked on March 31, the first troops to arrive. The wing marched to the outskirts and camped in a field where the right wing soon joined. Most of the troops for the expedition having arrived, on April 2, General Gillmore reviewed them in a large ploughed field. The "Provisional Division," under Gen. Edward E. Potter, was organized, composed of the First Brigade, commanded by Col. P. P. Brown, One Hundred and Fifty-seventh New York, of the One Hundred and Fifty-seventh New York, a detachment of the Fifty-sixth New York, and the Twenty-fifth and One Hundred and Seventh Ohio; and the Second Brigade under Colonel Hallowell, composed of the Fifty-fourth Massachusetts, eight companies of the Thirty-second United States Colored Troops, and five companies of the One

Hundred and Second United States Colored Troops. There were also detachments of the First New York Engineers and Fourth Massachusetts Cavalry, and two guns of Battery B, Third New York Artillery. It was a total force of about twenty-five hundred men.

Our regiment marched with six hundred and seventy-five enlisted men and the following officers: Lieutenant-Colonel Hooper, Major Pope, Surgeon Briggs, Acting Adjutant Whitney, and Acting Quartermaster Bridgham; Company F, Captain Bridge; Company C, Lieutenant Spear; Company B, Lieutenant Hallett; Company H, Captain Tucker and Lieutenant Stevens; Company A, Lieutenant Rogers; Company D, Captain Chipman and Lieutenant Swails; Company G, Captain Appleton; Company E, Lieutenant Emerson, commanding, and Lieutenant Cousens; Company I, Captain Howard; Company K, Lieutenant Reed. Lieutenants Newell and Joy took part on Colonel Hallowell's staff. Lieutenant Leonard was directed to remain in charge of the camp. A pioneer corps of twenty men was placed under Sergeant Wilkins of Company D for this field service.

April 5, at 8 A.M., Potter's force moved from Georgetown, the First Brigade in advance, over the centre or Sampit road for three miles, when the column took another to the right leading to Kingstree. Marching through a heavily timbered country and encountering no hostiles, the division compassed nineteen miles, camping at nightfall near Johnson's Swamp. Hallowell's brigade had the advance on the 6th, preceded by the cavalry, the close, warm day causing some exhaustion and straggling. The column entered a better region with rolling ground, where foraging parties found good supplies and draught animals. Major Webster of the cavalry encountered a few of the

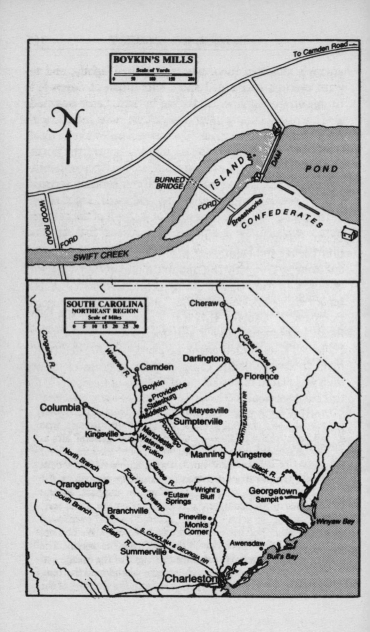

BOYKIN'S MILLS
Scale of Yards
0   50   100   150   200

N

To Camden Road

POND

BURNED BRIDGE

ISLAND

FORD

DAM

Breastworks

CONFEDERATES

WOOD ROAD

FORD

SWIFT CREEK

SOUTH CAROLINA
NORTHEAST REGION
Scale of Miles
0 5 10 15 20 25 30

Cheraw

Congaree R.

Wateree R.

Camden

Darlington

Great Pedee R.

Florence

Boykin
Providence
Statesburg
Middleton

Columbia

Mayesville

Sumpterville

Manchester
Wateree
Fulton

Kingsville

Poccotaligo

NORTHEASTERN RR

Manning

Kingstree

Black R.

North Branch

South Branch

Orangeburg

Four Hole Swamp

Santee R.

Eutaw Springs

Wright's Bluff

Georgetown

Sampit

Winyaw Bay

Branchville

Pineville
Monks Corner

Edisto R.

S. CAROLINA & GEORGIA RR

Summerville

Awensdaw

Bull's Bay

Charleston

enemy's mounted men, who skirmished lightly, and toward evening exchanged shots with them at Seven-Mile Bridge on the right, which the foe burned. Camp was made at Thorntree Swamp after a nineteen-mile march, with Kingstree across the Black River, seven miles to our right.

An early start was made on the 7th toward the northwest, through a more open and settled country, containing still more abundant supplies, which our foragers secured, but, by orders, burned all cotton and mills. Light troops of the enemy, easily dislodged, kept in front of the column. Potter reached the Northeastern Railroad that day and broke the track for several miles, and the One Hundred and Second United States Colored Troops, sent to the right, destroyed the Kingstree Bridge across the Black River, exchanging shots with a small force.

Captain Tucker, with Companies A and H of the Fifty-fourth, was sent to Eppes's Bridge on the Black River at about 3 P.M. That officer furnishes the following account of what befell him:—

"Leaving the main column, we filed to the right, marching by that flank nearly or quite a mile. I had previously mounted old Cyclops [a horse of Lieutenant Ritchie's, who was not on the raid], and put on as many 'general' airs as my general health and anatomy would endure. Great clouds of smoke were now coming up over the woods directly in our front. Stevens deployed one platoon on the left of the road, holding the other for support. Rogers disposed of his company on the right in the same way. Advancing, we soon found the ground low and overflowed with water. The men were wading knee-deep. We had not gone far before we received the fire from the enemy. The fire was returned. We advanced in sight of the bridge and easy musket-range, when the enemy abandoned the temporary works they had improvised from the flooring of the

bridge on the opposite side of the river, making quick their
retreat and leaving behind the heavy timbering of the work
in flames. During the interchange of shots Rogers and two
men of his company were wounded. We did not or could
not cross the river. I remember well of being sufficiently
near to give them a bit of my Yankee eloquence and calling
attention to their nervousness in not being able to shoot
even old 'Cyclops.' Our object being accomplished, we
started for and joined the regiment at Mill Branch about
two o'clock next morning. My impression is that the force
opposed to me was a company, or part of a company, of
dismounted cavalry."

Privates J. C. Johnson and J. H. White, of Company H,
were the men wounded. When Lieutenant Rogers was disabled, Lieutenant Stevens took command of Company A,
which he retained until his death. After a march of fifteen
miles the Fifty-fourth camped at Mill Branch.

April 8, the column moved over fair roads through a
wooded country, with a bright sky overhead, our advance
sighting the enemy now and then on the flanks and front.
For four miles the course was westerly; then, in consequence of a false report that a bridge in front near Ox
Swamp was burned, to the left five miles, on a road running
toward the Santee. Then turning again to the right north-
westerly until the road of the morning was again entered,
it was pursued toward Manning. On the edge of that town
our cavalry had a slight skirmish, driving out a small force.
Manning, a town of a few hundred inhabitants, was occupied at dark, after an eighteen-mile march that day.
General Potter established himself at Dr. Hagen's house.
Major Culp, Twenty-fifth Ohio, Colonel Cooper, One
Hundred and Seventh Ohio, and some soldier-printers took
possession of "The Clarendon Banner" newspaper office,
and changing the title to read "The Clarendon Banner of

Freedom," issued an edition which was distributed. In the evening Colonel Hallowell, receiving orders to build a bridge across Pocotaligo Swamp, moved his force to the river of that name, and prosecuted the work to completion by midnight.

At 1.30 A.M. on the 9th the Second Brigade broke camp, marched to and crossed the Pocotaligo Bridge, and advanced two miles, where it bivouacked in readiness for attack. At daybreak on a rainy morning the troops moved toward Sumterville, through a fine region with numerous plantations, from which the negroes flocked to the force by hundreds. The train had grown to a formidable array of vehicles, augmented every hour. During the morning the enemy's light troops fell back readily after exchanging shots. Information was received that the enemy was to dispute our progress at Dingle's mill on Turkey Creek four miles from Sumterville, with five hundred men, chiefly militia, and three guns. A mile from Dingle's the division halted, and a reconnoissance was made. Hallowell's brigade was then sent to the left and rear of the enemy's position; but the guide furnished proving incompetent, the brigade returned to the main force, arriving after the action was over. At 2 P.M. the skirmishers of the First Brigade pushed toward the swamp, the enemy holding earthworks beyond a burned bridge, and opening with artillery as we came in range. The Twenty-fifth and One Hundred and Seventh Ohio, on either side of the road, moved forward to a dike on the border of the swamp, from which a musketry fire was maintained. At the same time Potter sent the One Hundred and Fifty-seventh and Fifty-sixth New York to turn the enemy's left, which was done, the Rebels retiring, leaving their dead, wounded, and some prisoners, besides the three guns, in our hands.

Our force then crossed the creek, the Twenty-fifth Ohio forcing the enemy into the woods, where they made another stand along a fence skirting the timber. Upon the arrival of the One Hundred and Seventh Ohio, the force advanced and the enemy fled, closing the action, in which our loss was small. The division then moved to Sumterville, arriving at dark, after a march of eighteen miles that day.

Sumterville, on the Manchester and Wilmington Railroad, boasted some good dwellings, two female seminaries, and the usual public buildings. Here the soldier-printers issued a loyal edition of the "Sumter Watchman." Every one was in fine spirits at having gained the railroad without serious opposition, for the rolling-stock was known to be below on the Camden Branch. Another cause of exultation was the news that Richmond, Mobile, and Selma were in our hands, in honor of which a salute of thirteen shots was fired from the captured guns. During the 10th, the Thirty-Second United States Colored Troops moved along the railroad to Maysville, where some seven cars and a bridge were destroyed. The One Hundred and Second United States Colored Troops went at the same time toward Manchester about three miles, burning a long covered railroad-bridge, four cars, two hundred bales of cotton, a gin-house, and a mill filled with corn. Our regiment, from its bivouac in the town, sent details which destroyed three locomotives, fifteen cars, and the large and thoroughly equipped railroad machine-shop in the place.

Gen. A. S. Hartwell with the Fifty-fifth Massachusetts, Fifty-fourth New York, and two guns of the Third New York Artillery, from Charleston, reached Eutaw Springs on April 10, by way of Monk's Corner and Pineville, to cooperate with General Potter. An effort was made to open communication from there by Maj. William Nutt, Fifty-fifth Massachusetts, with two companies of his regiment, which was unsuccessful, for Potter was thirty miles distant. Hartwell's force returned to Charleston on the 12th, with over one thousand negroes and many wagons and draught animals.

Potter resumed the march April 11, leaving the Twenty-fifth Ohio as a covering force for the division, the large number of contrabands, and the immense train. The Fifty-fourth passed through Sumterville singing John Brown's hymn in chorus, and with the brigade, reached Manchester after a march of twelve miles. A mile and a half beyond that town the other regiments of the brigade bivouacked toward evening on the Statesburg road; the First Brigade moved on a mile or so farther, camping in a fine grove on the Singleton plantation.

At Manchester the Fifty-fourth was detached, moving along the railroad about six miles and to a point near Wateree Junction. A reconnoissance made by Lieutenant-Colonel Hooper resulted in the discovery at the junction of cars, water-tanks, and several locomotives,—one of which had steam up. It was not known whether there was any armed force there or not; and it was important to seize the locomotive before it could be reversed and the rolling-stock run back. Night had set in. Some sharpshooters were posted to cover an advance and disable any train-men. Then our column, led by Lieutenant Swails, First Sergeant Welch, of Company F, and eighteen picked men, rushed over an intervening trestle for the junction. Swails was the first man of all, and jumped into the engine-cab where, while waving his hat in triumph, he received a shot in his right arm from our sharpshooters, who in the darkness probably mistook him for the engineer. The train-hands, some fifteen in number, fled down the railroad embankment into the swamp.

There were five engines and thirteen cars, besides tanks, a turn-table, and a large quantity of finished timber found at Wateree Junction. Learning from a contraband that there was more rolling-stock to the westward, after first burning the trestle-bridge on the Camden Branch, so that the enemy could not interfere suddenly, Captain Tucker with two companies was sent in search of it. Shortly after, Lieutenant-Colonel Hooper started on the return, leaving Major Pope with a detachment at the junction. Later the One Hundred and Seventh Ohio came there from the direction of Camden along the railroad.

Captain Tucker proceeded some three miles, and secured three locomotives and thirty-five cars without opposition. Steam being up in one engine, to return more rapidly he embarked his men, and himself acting as engineer, ran back until he came in sight of the trestle, which we had fired, supposing he would march back. Captain Tucker thus narrates the sequel:—

> "Knowing that any delay would be dangerous, and that life and death hung in the balance, I crowded on all steam, and we crossed the bridge through flame and smoke in safety, but with not a moment to spare, for scarcely had we accomplished the passage when it tottered and fell, a heap of blazing ruins."

While coupling cars, Sergeant-Major Wilson and Private George Jarvis of Company K were injured. Lieutenant Swails, with his wounded arm in a sling, assisted by Lieutenant Whitney, took charge of the leading engine and train and proceeded slowly away. The Fifty-fourth men and One Hundred and Seventh Ohio embarked on the cars brought in, Major Pope helping Captain Tucker with his engine. The destruction of all property at the junction was effected, and then the trestle leading toward Manchester was burned after crossing it. As progress was slow with the heavy second train, to lighten it cars were dropped from time to time and destroyed, until at last the engine alone proceeded with the injured men, while the troops marched. Lieutenant-Colonel Hooper's force was joined on the roadside. It was the hope to run the engines and remaining cars to Manchester; but a flue had blown out of Lieutenant Swails's locomotive, so they like the others were burned with the army supplies in them, estimated at a total value of $300,000.

When this was completed, and rest taken, the Fifty-fourth moved on, re-joining the Second Brigade at 7 A.M. on the 12th, after marching twenty-five miles and working all night. Sergeant Wilkins of Company D, relieved from charge of the pioneers by Sergeant Dorsey, of Company I, was appointed acting sergeant-major on the 12th. At 11 A.M. the regiment with the brigade moved forward and joined the First Brigade at Singleton's plantation. From there, on that day, Capt. Frank Goodwin of Potter's staff, accompanied by Lieutenant Newell of Hallowell's, with the Thirty-second United States Colored Troops as escort, took the wounded, several thousand contrabands, and the long train to Wright's Bluff on the Santee, twenty-five miles distant. They found some of our light draught vessels in the river, on which the wounded and the women and children were placed. Captain Goodwin distributed some two hundred captured muskets to the men and sent them overland to Georgetown.

From Singleton's on the 13th the One Hundred and

Fifty-seventh New York went to Statesburg, thirteen miles distant, where it destroyed some stores.

The next day the Twenty-fifth Ohio was sent to gain the rear of the enemy on the Statesburg road. Throughout the 13th and 14th the remainder of the division was stationary. Toward evening of the 14th some twenty of the enemy made demonstrations against our Fifty-fourth pickets, and later, Lieutenant-Colonel Hooper, with the right wing of the regiment, reconnoitred for two miles toward States-burg, but found no enemy, and returned.

Everything was ready for an early advance on the 15th, but it was not made until 3 P.M., when the Thirty-second United States Colored Troops having returned from Wright's Bluff, the division moved from Singleton's. It rained in the afternoon and evening. That morning the Twenty-fifth Ohio, ordered to Statesburg to await the division, encountered the enemy and drove them to Round Hill, where they made a stand, causing the Twenty-fifth some loss in repulsing them from there. Potter coming up with the main force, the One Hundred and Seventh Ohio was sent with six companies of the Twenty-fifth to engage the enemy as a demonstration, while the rest of the division, taking a road five miles from Singleton's, leading to the right, moved to flank the enemy collected on the main road. Potter marched until midnight, making twelve miles, and bivouacked near Jenning's Swamp and Providence Post-Office. The force on the main road after dark withdrew, joining the main column.

April 16, the march was resumed, the colored brigade leading, and Providence Post-Office was left on the right hand. With good weather the route was through a hilly and rolling country sparsely settled with poor whites. A halt was made for dinner at Bradford Springs; and when the column again proceeded, the enemy's skirmishers were encountered, who gave way readily, but kept up a running fight all the afternoon. Private Lewis Clark, of Company C, was killed, and Private Levi Jackson, of the same company wounded that day while foraging. The skirmishers of the Thirty-second United States Colored Troops killed one Rebel and captured another. By sunset the colored brigade had advanced sixteen miles and camped at Spring Hill.

On the 17th the last forward march of the division was made. It moved at 6.30 A.M. toward Camden, the First Brigade leading, the foe yielding until we came to swampy ground, where works were discovered. There the First Brigade fronted the enemy; and a part of the Twenty-fifth Ohio flanked the position, when the Rebels retired. The Second Brigade was also sent to the left for the same purpose, but its aid was not required. No further opposition was made; and Potter's force entered Camden, the Second Brigade following the First, coming in at dark. Camden was historic ground, for there Gates was defeated by Cornwallis in 1780, and Greene by Lord Rawdon at Hobkirk's Hill near by in 1781. Sherman's Fifteenth Corps entered the town Feb. 24, 1865, after some resistance, when the railroad bridge, depot, and much cotton and tobacco were destroyed. It was ascertained that the rolling-stock had been sent below during our advance from Singleton's, making success assured, though fighting was expected.

Potter turned back from Camden toward Statesburg at 7 A.M. on the 18th. Our main body moved along the pike; the One Hundred and Seventh Ohio on the railroad with only slight resistance until we came to Swift Creek, after marching some seven miles. There the enemy held earthworks running through a swamp and over the higher ground beyond the creek. Gen. P. M. B. Young commanded the Confederates, his force consisting of four hundred men of Lewis's Tennessee, and three hundred and fifty of Hannon's Alabama brigades of mounted men, and Hamilton's field battery.

General Potter, demonstrating with his main body along Swift Creek in front, sent the Fifty-fourth, One Hundred and Second United States Colored Troops, and One Hundred and Seventh Ohio to attempt crossings down the stream to the right, under the guidance of a native. In this flanking movement Lieutenant-Colonel Hooper led the Fifty-fourth along the creek over ploughed fields bordering the wood of the swamp, with Company F, under Captain Bridge, skirmishing. From contrabands it was learned that the swamp was impassable nearer than Boykin's Mills, some two miles from the road. When in the vicinity of the mills, the enemy's scouts were seen falling back.

Leading from a small clearing, a road was found apparently running in the proper direction, and our skirmishers were again ordered forward. Just then Warren Morehouse, of Company E, who had been scouting in the woods to the left, came to Major Pope, saying, "Major, there's a lot of Rebs through there in a barn." The regiment was moving on; and deeming quick action essential, Major Pope faced the left company about and led it toward the point indicated through the woods; and as we approached, the enemy retired across the stream. This company was left at that point temporarily, and the major hastened to rejoin the regiment.

Captain Bridge pushed forward his skirmishers through the wood bordering the road until the mills were in view. It was found that the stream was there dammed by a dike, the water above it forming a pond. At each end of the dike were sluice-gates, controlling the water, which served to run a grist-mill at one extremity and a saw-mill at the other. The divided waters passed away in two streams, forming a sort of island; but the two branches united farther on. The road discovered ran to the first stream, where the water, seven feet deep, was crossed by a bridge, which had been burned, only a stringer remaining, thence over the island to the second stream, where was a ford through water waist-deep. Some fifteen yards beyond the ford up a slight ascent, the enemy held breastworks of cotton-bales. It was found that the dike and the road were one hundred and fifty yards apart on our side of the creek; but as the stream made a bend there, they met on the enemy's bank.

Captain Bridge's skirmishers, moving rapidly over the road, came to the ruined bridge. The leaders at once attempted to cross over the stringer, but received a volley which killed Corp. James P. Johnson, mortally wounded Corp. Andrew Miller, and wounded Sergeant Bennett and Privates Harding, Postley, and Sylvia, all of Company F. Thus checked, Captain Bridge retired to cover of the ground, keeping up a return fire. Lieutenant-Colonel Hooper, seeing that the position was strong and well defended against an attack in front, determined to make a diversion a quarter of a mile farther down the stream, where a ford was reported to be. He therefore sent Acting Adjutant Whitney to Major Pope with instructions to take the left wing and essay the task under the guidance of an old white-headed negro.

As the left company was already detached, Major Pope took only Companies A, D, G, and I, proceeding by a détour through the woods and swamps, with Company A under Lieutenant Stevens skirmishing; after pursuing a road fringed with heavy timber and underbrush, this force arrived near the point indicated. The enemy was there, for Major Pope and Lieutenant Stevens in crossing the wood-road drew several shots. To feel the strength of the opposing force opposite, Company A, which was in the brush along the bank of the creek, was directed to fire a volley. As if acting under the same impulse, at the very moment this order was executed, the enemy also fired a volley, one shot striking Lieutenant Stevens in the head, killing him instantly. He fell partially into the stream. It was a dangerous duty to remove him; but two men were selected from volunteers, who, crawling forward, brought back his body. As the orders were to entail no unnecessary risk of life, word was sent to Lieutenant-Colonel Hooper of the situation. Captain Chipman with Company D relieved Company A on the skirmish line.

While awaiting the result of Major Pope's flanking movement, Lieutenant-Colonel Hooper caused a musketry fire to be kept up from about the mill and the bridge, which enfiladed the enemy's breastworks. He also caused the sluice-gates of the dam at the first stream to be broken to allow the water in the pond to flow off, that a crossing there might be facilitated should Major Pope's project not succeed. When word came of Major Pope's encounter, Lieutenant-Colonel Hooper sent a message to General Potter informing him that the stream could only be crossed with a considerable sacrifice; but that if a field-gun was sent him, the enemy might be driven out, or a charge covered. At the same time Major Pope was ordered to hold his position.

A gun having been brought, dispositions were made to charge over the log dike at the mill. Lieutenant Hallett with a force was directed to cross the dam to the island between the streams, and open a covering fire from there when all was ready. Then the gun having fired some half a dozen shells, the Fifty-fourth, led most gallantly by Lieutenant Reed, charged across the dike in single file, receiving the enemy's fire, but causing their precipitate retirement. In this charge Corp. Wm. H. Brown, of Company K, always conspicuous for bravery, was the first enlisted man to gain the farther bank. We sustained the loss of Privates Scott, Freeman, and Green, of Company H; Johnson and Jay, of Company B; and McCullar, of Company K,—all wounded.

This last fight of the Fifty-fourth, and also one of the very last of the war, was well managed by Lieutenant-Colonel Hooper, when less discretion would have resulted in a repulse and heavy loss. The charge was a plucky affair under exceptionally adverse conditions. Our total regimental loss that day was one officer killed, one enlisted man killed, one mortally wounded, and twelve wounded: a total of fifteen, the greatest number of casualties sustained by one regiment in any action during Potter's Raid.

It was about 4 P.M. when the position was carried. Simultaneously with our victorious cheers, the One Hundred and Second United States Colored Troops and One Hundred and Seventh Ohio on the creek above, as well as the troops on the main road, advanced, the enemy flying before them. Major Webster with the cavalry pursued for some distance. At the mills the Fifty-fourth destroyed fifty-four bales of cotton and three of corn fodder used in the breastworks, besides the grist and saw mill. Lieutenant Stevens's body was buried at Boykin's, as was that of Corporal Johnson. Their bodies and resting-places were marked. In July, 1885, through the information furnished by Lieutenant Whitney, secretary of the "Association of

Officers Fifty-fourth Massachusetts Volunteers," their bodies were removed to the National Cemetery at Florence, S. C. Lieutenant Stevens was a genial comrade and brave officer. He must have been the last officer, or one of the very last officers, killed in action during the Rebellion.

Leaving Boykin's by a cross-road, the Fifty-fourth marched to the pike and re-joined the division, which proceeded several miles and camped for the night, after making twelve miles that day. A thunder-storm prevailed, the rain continuing all night. At this camp Colonel Chipman, with the right wing of the One Hundred and Second United States Colored Troops, joined Potter's force, having left Charleston April 11, crossed the Santee at Wright's Bluff, and made a bold march, meeting the enemy and losing some men.

April 19, a start was made at 6 A.M., the First Brigade in the lead, the Second Brigade following with the Fifty-fourth as rear-guard. Hardly had the column left camp and passed from the woods into open country, when the enemy was found posted behind breastworks of rails, supported by a piece of artillery. The Twenty-fifth Ohio and One Hundred and Fifty-seventh New York on the road and flank soon drove him thence, and later, from another stand on higher ground, until he retired across Big Rafting Creek. Some forty or fifty of the enemy followed the Fifty-fourth in rear during the march, occasionally firing upon us. Reaching the creek, the main body engaged the attention of the foe, while the One Hundred and Second and a wing of the Thirty-Second went to flank him on the right; the other wing of the Thirty-second, and the One Hundred and Seventh Ohio, were ordered down the Camden Branch of the railroad. After a slight resistance the enemy fell back.

At noon the Fifty-fourth was relieved as rear-guard, and for the rest of the day was with the advance. It was showery in the afternoon. Our road was through an open hilly country. Near Statesburg at a swamp and creek the enemy again fronted the division; but our skirmishers pressed him over the creek and in spirited style up the rising ground beyond, in full view of the troops. Lieutenant Chickering, of the cavalry, was wounded. Beyond Statesburg the resistance was slight, the column proceeding until 10 P.M., when the Fifty-fourth reached its former camp at Singleton's, having marched eighteen miles.

Fighting was now over. The rolling-stock was ours, massed on the Camden Branch, whence it could not be taken, as the Fifty-fourth had destroyed the trestle at Wateree Junction, on the 11th. General Potter devoted the 20th to its destruction. That day the Fifty-fourth marched to Middleton Depot and with other regiments assisted in the work. About this place for a distance of some two miles were sixteen locomotives and 245 cars containing railway supplies, ordnance, commissary and quartermaster's stores. They were burned, those holding powder and shells during several hours blowing up with deafening explosions and scattering discharges, until property of immense value and quantity disappeared in smoke and flame. Locomotives were rendered useless before the torch was applied. The Fifty-fourth alone destroyed fifteen locomotives, one passenger, two box and two platform cars with the railway supplies they held. After completing this work, the regiment returned to Singleton's.

Every purpose of the movement having been accomplished, on April 21 the return to Georgetown was ordered. It was about one hundred miles distant by the proposed route through Manchester and Fulton Post-Office. Early

that morning three companies of the One Hundred and
Second United States Colored Troops on picket were attacked by two hundred of the enemy, whom they repulsed.
The column started at 6 A.M., the Second Brigade in advance, moving over the Santee River road southwesterly.
Our rear-guard was the Twenty-fifth Ohio, the enemy following and attacking near Manning's plantation, but they
were driven back.

John L. Manning, a former governor of South Carolina,
was at home. He was a distinguished man and one of the
leaders of the Union party in nullification times. After the
war he was elected United States Senator, but was not
allowed to take his seat. He died only recently. While we
were at his plantation, a Confederate officer came to the
outposts with a flag of truce, to notify General Potter that
an armistice had been concluded between Generals Sherman and Johnston. Hostilities were not to be renewed
without forty-eight hours' notice. This great news created
the most intense joy and excitement, for it seemed to end
the war, as the Rebels themselves acknowledged. Cheers
without number were given, and congratulations exchanged. Then the Fifty-fourth was brought to a field,
where the last shots loaded with hostile intent were fired
as a salute. Soon after, the march was resumed in sultry
weather with frequent showers. Ten miles from the Santee
the division bivouacked after completing a journey of
twenty miles.

On the 22d the troops continued on over the Santee
road. When opposite Wright's Bluff, the wounded, sick,
and about five hundred contrabands were sent to the river
for transportation by water. News was received of Lee's
surrender which, though not unexpected, caused great
rejoicing. General Potter turned over the command to Col.

P. P. Brown, One Hundred and Fifty-seventh New York, and departed for Charleston to convey news of the armistice. After marching twenty-three miles, the troops halted for the night. At 5:30 A.M., on the 23d, the Second Brigade led out for the day's march. Now that hostilities had ceased, the force was dependent upon such supplies as could be purchased. A very large number of contrabands were with the column, straggling, and obstructing the rapid progress it was desirable to make. The day was cool and pleasant; the route through a fine country mainly, but wooded and low in places. Intelligence of President Lincoln's assassination was received,—sad tidings which could hardly be credited. There was much bitter feeling indulged in by the soldiery for a time. The division accomplished twenty-three miles that day, bivouacking at Stagget's Mill.

April 24, the troops proceeded through a wooded region where no supplies could be obtained. As a substitute for rations two ears of corn were issued to each man. A journey of twenty-three miles was made. Our last bivouac in the field was broken on the morning of April 25th, when in good weather through a timbered country we completed the march. Major Pope and Acting Quartermaster Bridgham preceded the regiment into Georgetown to prepare camp and rations. The troops reached town at 5 P.M. after making twenty-two miles.

Potter's Raid occupied twenty-one days, during which the troops marched some three hundred miles. About three thousand negroes came into Georgetown with the division, while the whole number released was estimated at six thousand. Our train was very large, for besides innumerable vehicles, five hundred horses and mules were secured, of which number the Fifty-fourth turned in one hundred and sixty.

Having taken possession of the old camp, the regiment rested. By the 28th troops began to depart for other posts. A tragedy occurred in the Fifty-fourth, on the 30th, when Private Samuel J. Benton shot and killed Corp. Wm. Wilson, of Company A, in a private quarrel. Benton was tried and sentenced to imprisonment, serving time until December, 1865, when he was pardoned.

Orders came for the Fifty-fourth to report at Charleston, when transportation could be furnished. Captain Bridge, with Companies A, F, and H, embarked on the steamer "Island City," May 4, and sailed, accompanied by Colonel Hallowell, in the morning. Lieutenant-Colonel Hooper, with Companies D, E, G, and K, sailed on the same steamer, May 6th; and the next day Major Pope, with Companies B, C, and I, followed on the "Loyalist."

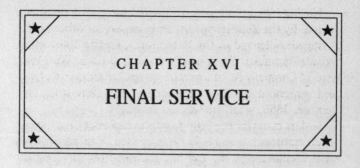

CHAPTER XVI

FINAL SERVICE

Upon the arrival of the several detachments of the Fifty-fourth at Charleston, Companies A, C, F, H, and K, comprising the right wing under Lieutenant-Colonel Hooper, located camp on the Neck in an open field to the right of the plank road, and nearer the city than Magnolia Cemetery. Major Pope, with the left wing, relieved the Fifty-fifth Massachusetts at St. Andrew's Parish, across the Ashley River, opposite the city, where they occupied high ground not far from the camp made just before first entering Charleston. From the Ashley to Wappoo Cut was an intrenched line with several redoubts made by the Confederates.

Colonel Hallowell was placed in charge of what was known as the "Defences of Charleston," comprising the intrenched line around the city, that at St. Andrew's Parish, and the James Island lines; Mount Pleasant was soon included in his command. The troops under him were the Fifty-fourth, One Hundred and Seventh Ohio, and Twenty-first United States Colored Troops. His headquarters were first at the Cary house, but on the 8th were removed to Nos. 6 and 8 Meeting Street, Charleston.

From camp on the Neck Lieutenant Reed, with Company A, was sent on the 8th as train guard over the South Carolina Railroad to Summerville, returning the next day. The One Hundred and Seventh Ohio arrived on the 8th and 9th, taking post at the intrenchments. The Twenty-first United States Colored Troops was stationed on James Island and Mount Pleasant. Orders being received for the right wing to join the left, on the 14th it marched from the Neck, crossed the river, and camped at St. Andrew's Parish, thus reuniting the regiment under Lieutenant-Colonel Hooper. He retained command until the 29th, when, having received leave of absence, he departed for the North, leaving Major Pope in charge of the regiment.

In accordance with Department orders issued May 29, Colonel Hallowell, Colonel Gurney, One Hundred and Twenty-seventh New York, and Major Willoughby, Twenty-first United States Colored Troops, were constituted a board for the examination of volunteer officers in the Northern District, with a view to their retention in the military service. All the officers of the Fifty-fourth appeared before this board.

Captain Tucker with twenty-five men, on June 2, was sent on a "tin-clad" steamer to the Santee River. On the 7th the men welcomed back to the regiment eleven of their comrades who had been prisoners of war. Two others had previously reported. These men were paroled near Wilmington, N.C., on March 4. Colonel Hallowell's command was broken up June 5; the Fifty-fourth was ordered to Charleston; the One Hundred and Seventh Ohio and Twenty-first United States Colored Troops remaining brigaded under Colonel Hallowell until the 10th. Our regiment was ordered to relieve the Thirty-fifth United States Colored Troops, forming part of the garrison. On the 8th four companies crossed the Ashley in small boats, taking post at the Citadel. They were joined by five other companies on the 10th, Company I remaining at St. Andrew's Parish. Colonel Hallowell took command of his regiment on the 10th.

Quartered in the Citadel, the Fifty-fourth entered upon the usual duties incident to guard and patrol service in the Upper District of the city. The event of each morning was guard mounting on Citadel Square, which always attracted numbers of colored people, young and old, to witness the evolutions and listen to the martial music. It was agreeable service for all. When off duty officers had the range of the city and its attractions. The men were allowed frequent passes outside the spacious Citadel grounds, making friends with the colored people, which in some cases resulted in a partnership for life.

Charleston at this time was slowly recovering from the effects of war and the siege. There was a growing trade in merchantable articles. The churches were turned over to their several congregations. The negroes who flocked in from the country greatly increased the population. This soon resulted in a heavy death-rate among this class, which at one time reached one hundred per week. Whites and blacks were closely watching the political developments, causing much friction. Dr. Mackey was the Collector of the Port, and Mr. Sawyer Inspector of Internal Revenue. Some arrests of prominent Secessionists were made,—notably that of George A. Trenholm, the Confederate Secretary of the Treasury. Prominent citizens were returning. Among them were Theodore D. Wagner, J. B. Campbell, James H. Taylor, William Gregg, Motte A. Pringle, and

Judge William Pringle. General Hatch was occupying the
fine mansion of the latter gentleman, situated on King
Street, as his headquarters. Some cotton was coming in,
and more was expected as soon as the railroads were repaired. Vegetables and fruits were becoming abundant in
the markets. Beef, mutton, and veal were ruling at thirty
cents per pound. Shipments were made North from the
large stores of rice in the city. From the paroled armies
of the defunct Confederacy came large numbers of soldiers
in dilapidated garments and emaciated physical condition.
They flocked to take the oath of allegiance and receive the
bounty of government. Such was their destitution that they
were glad to share the rations of our colored soldiers in
some instances. President Johnson's Amnesty Proclamation, when received, was variously regarded, according to
the status of the critic as a Secessionist Radical or Con-
servative.

Major P. E. Dye paid Companies A, B, and C of the Fifty-
fourth on the 17th, and the remaining companies on the
two succeeding days. This was only the second payment
of the enlisted men while in service. In Charleston the
Masonic Lodge organized on Morris Island, of which First
Sergeant Gray of Company C was the Master, met in the
third story of a house just across from the Citadel. Sergeants Vogelsang, Alexander Johnson, and Hemmingway
were among the members, who numbered some twenty-
five or thirty. It is thought that the charter of this lodge
was surrendered ultimately to Prince Hall Lodge of Boston,
whence it came.

Admiral Dahlgren departed for the North on the 17th,
after taking leave of his squadron in orders. On the 18th
an affray occurred on the Battery between a guard of the
One Hundred and Twenty-seventh New York and some of

the Thirty-fifth United States Colored Troops, when a few soldiers and civilians were wounded. A part of Jefferson Davis's and Beauregard's effects and correspondence brought into Jacksonville was turned over to Lieut. John W. Pollock, Assistant Provost-Marshal at Charleston, on the 24th. It included three handsome uniforms presented to Beauregard by the ladies of Columbia, Augusta, and Selma.

Independence Day was celebrated with great enthusiasm by the loyal citizens and soldiery. National salutes were fired from Sumter, Moultrie, Bee, Wagner, and Gregg, the harbor resounding with explosions, bringing to memory the days of siege. The troops paraded, the Declaration of Independence and the Emancipation Proclamation were read, and orators gave expression to patriotic sentiments doubly pointed by the great war which perfected the work of the fathers.

Captain Howard, with Company I, reported to the regiment from St. Andrew's Parish about July 1, but was soon sent to McClellansville, where this company remained until just before muster-out. On July 11 orders were received for the discharge of the Fifty-fourth. They emanated from General Gillmore, who afterward, finding that his authority was questionable, telegraphed to Washington for instructions. Meanwhile Capt. Thomas J. Robinson, Fifty-fourth New York, mustering officer, furnished necessary instructions for preparing the rolls. Naturally this order gave great satisfaction. At one time it was thought that the colored regiments would be retained until the expiration of their term of service.

Colonel Gurney's One Hundred and Twenty-seventh New York was mustered out on June 30, and the next day departed from Charleston. Brev. Brig.-Gen. William T.

Bennett, Thirty-third United States Colored Troops, succeeded to the command of the city. Lieutenant Whitney, with Company K, on July 31, was ordered to Fort Johnson to dismount guns on James Island for transportation elsewhere. This work was prosecuted until the company was relieved on August 16. Orders were received from General Gillmore directing that the commanding officers of the Fifty-fourth and Fifty-fifth Massachusetts, Twenty-sixth, Thirty-second, and One Hundred and Second United States Colored Troops, about to be mustered out, should nominate such officers of their regiments as were desirous of appointments in other colored organizations. No assurances were given of their receiving a higher grade than second lieutenancies. It is not known whether any nominations were made from the Fifty-fourth.

During the interval of time between the arrival of the regiment and its muster-out, many changes of rank and duties occurred. Commissions were received for Quartermaster-Sergeant Vogelsang and First Sergeant Welch, of Company F, as second lieutenants, May 22. Applications being made for their muster, they were returned "disapproved," and the commissions for some reason destroyed. Colonel Hallowell, determined that the precedent established in the case of Lieutenant Swails should be followed, appealed to higher authority, sending for new commissions. These colored men were finally mustered as officers, and ultimately promoted to first lieutenancies. Commissions were also issued to First Sergeant George E. Stephens, of Company B, and First Sergeant Albert D. Thompson, of Company D, but they were not mustered under them.

George Cranch, John H. Conant, and William McDermott, newly appointed, reported and ultimately became first lieutenants. Joshua B. Treadwell reported for duty as assistant-surgeon. Colonel Hallowell was brevetted brigadier-general. Major Pope was promoted lieutenant-colonel; and Captain Walton, major. Lieutenant Emerson became captain of Company E; Lieutenant James, captain of Company C; Lieutenant Reed, captain of Company K; and Lieutenant Newell, captain of Company B. Lieutenant Cousens, promoted first lieutenant, was afterward made captain of Company E. Lieutenant Joy, after taking the intermediate rank, became captain of Company F. Lieutenants Edmands, Swails, and Whitney were promoted first lieutenants. Assistant-Surgeon Radzinsky was made surgeon One Hundred and Fourth United States Colored Troops; and Lieutenants Leonard and Hallett, captains One Hundred and Third United States Colored Troops.

Those who resigned, or were mustered out at the expiration of their personal terms of service, were Lieutenant-Colonel Hooper, Adjutant Duren, Quartermaster Ritchie, Captains Bridge, Jewett, and Emerson, and Lieutenants Spear, Rogers, Bridgham, and Jewett. Lieutenant Edmands acted as quartermaster until June 21, when Lieutenant Vogelsang was made regimental-quartermaster. Lieutenant Joy relieved Lieutenant Whitney as acting adjutant until Lieutenant Swails relieved him July 1. The latter was then succeeded by Lieutenant Conant. Sergeant Wilkins, of Company D, was appointed acting sergeant-major, and Thomas E. Platner, of Company A, principal musician.

Preparatory to discharge the Fifty-fourth was relieved from garrison duty, and ordered to rendezvous at Mount Pleasant. Headquarters were located there on the 14th, and by the 17th the companies were all present. At this last camp the rolls and final papers were completed. Under the supervision of Capt. Thomas J. Robinson the Fifty-fourth was discharged August 20. The roster of officers at the time was as follows:—

Field and Staff,—Colonel and Brevet Brigadier-General, E. N. Hallowell; Lieutenant-Colonel, George Pope; Major, James M. Walton; Surgeon, Charles E. Briggs; Assistant Surgeon, Joshua B. Treadwell.

Captains,—James W. Grace (A), Thomas L. Appleton (G), Charles E. Tucker (H), Willard Howard (I), Charles G. Chipman (D), Garth W. James (C), Lewis Reed (K), Robert R. Newell (B), Joseph E. Cousens (E), Charles F. Joy (F).

First Lieutenants,—Benjamin B. Edmands, Stephen A. Swails, Peter Vogelsang (Regimental-Quartermaster), Frank M. Welch, George W. Cranch, William L. Whitney, Jr., John H. Conant, William McDermott.

Of the twenty-three officers, but eight were of those who left Massachusetts May 28, 1863, for the field.

August 21, at night, Brevet Brigadier-General Hallowell, with the right wing, embarked on the steamer "C. F. Thomas," sailed at 5 A.M. on the 22d, and reached Boston at noon of the 26th, where it disembarked at Gallop's Island. Lieutenant-Colonel Pope, with the left wing, left Charleston on the 23d upon the steamer "Ashland," completing the voyage on the 28th. Captain Grace did not return North with the regiment, and fifty-nine enlisted men were left behind sick in hospital. At Gallop's Island, in Boston harbor, the Fifty-fourth remained until September 2. There the stores pertaining to the quartermaster's department were turned over to the government officer, and the ordnance stores to Major C. P. Kingsbury. About two thirds of the men exercised the privilege of purchasing their arms, as mementos of service in the war. On September 1 final payment was made, accounts settled, and discharges given out.

A telegram from Charleston of the departure of the regiment was sent to the Adjutant-General of Massachusetts. Upon its receipt the friends of the officers and men arranged for their proper reception in Boston. The newspapers made announcement of the event, indicated the route, and requested the display of the national colors and that refreshments be served on the march.

September 2, the Fifty-fourth at 9 A.M. landed at Commercial Wharf from the tugs "Uncle Sam," "William H. Stroud," and another. There is was received by the Fourteenth Unattached Company Massachusetts Volunteer Militia (Shaw Guards, colored), Capt. Lewis Gaul; the Hallowell Union Association, A. M. Hewlett, marshal; a delegation from the Rev. William Grimes's Twelfth Baptist Society; and many citizens, accompanied by Gilmore's Band,—all under direction of J. J. Smith, chief marshal. The Boston Brigade Band was also provided for the Fifty-fourth.

After the regiment had landed and passed the escort, the column moved from Commercial to State Street. This thoroughfare was thronged with people, who greeted the veterans with repeated cheers. Great enthusiasm was displayed; and the passing of the colors was especially honored. As the Fifty-fourth moved through Washington, Franklin, Devonshire, Summer, and Winter Streets, similar plaudits greeted it from every side. Entering Tremont Street from Winter, an incident of the occasion was the display in the window of Childs and Jenks's establishment of a portrait of Lieutenant Webster, deceased, of the Fifty-fourth, draped in mourning. In passing, appropriate music was played, and the regiment gave a marching salute in honor of the deceased comrade.

From Tremont Street the column entered Park, thence to the State House, where from the steps Governor Andrew, accompanied by his staff and the Executive Council, reviewed the veterans as they passed. Proceeding down Beacon Street through Joy, Cambridge, West Cedar, Mount Vernon, Walnut, and Beacon to the Common, everywhere along the route cheers went up from admirers, and friends rushed to shake hands with relatives or acquaintances among the officers and men. Everywhere along the journey the public buildings, including the State House, and parks of the city floated the stars and stripes. Through the throng of citizens lining the curb, the Fifty-fourth marched, welcomed at every step, with the swing only acquired by long service in the field, and the bearing of seasoned soldiers.

Arriving upon the Common, the regiment halted. In the presence of a very large assemblage, including Mayor Lincoln, Colonel Kurtz, chief of police, Hon. Henry Wilson, and other gentlemen of prominence, the regiment was exercised for a few moments in the manual of arms. Forming from line into a hollow square, Brevet Brigadier-General Hallowell called his officers around him, thanked them for the efficient and manly way they had performed their service, their uniform kindness to him, and tendered his best wishes for their success and happiness through life. He then addressed the enlisted men, thanking them for the brave manner in which they had supported him in many trying times throughout their service. He said whenever a "forlorn hope" had been called for, the Fifty-fourth had been ready and prompt to respond. They had protected their colors and brought them home again,—there was little left of them, but enough to show how bravely they had been defended. They had proved good soldiers in the field; now he hoped they would become good citizens. When they left Massachusetts, it was the only State which recognized them as citizens. Now the whole country acknowledged their soldierly qualities. He hoped that by good behavior they would show their title to all the privileges of citizenship.

Continuing, he reminded them that their blood had enriched the soil of South Carolina, Georgia, and Florida; might the sweat of their brows now enrich the soil of Massachusetts. Might they show themselves to be men, without respect to color or former condition. He bade them good-by. He was glad to disband them, but he was sorry to part from them. Still, he knew they looked upon him as their friend, and felt sure that wherever he might go he would find friends among colored soldiers and colored men. In conclusion, he reminded them that having received large sums of money just paid to them, it should be kept. He hoped that all who had homes out of the city would return to them when disbanded.

Upon the conclusion of this address repeated cheers were given for General Hallowell. Then the square was reduced, and some manœuvres were executed by the regiment. It then marched to the Charles-street Mall, and there partook of a collation spread upon tables, which had been prepared by William Tufts at the order of friends of the Fifty-fourth. Then the regiment was disbanded.

Company C, recruited largely in New Bedford, was escorted to the cars by the Shaw Guards. At New Bedford, when the company arrived, a large number of citizens, a reception committee, and the Carney Guards (colored), with the New Bedford Band, were in waiting. With the escort, the veterans, some twenty-two in number, passed through crowded streets to the City Hall. There a meeting was held in their honor, which was called to order by W. H. Johnson, at which speeches were made by Henry F. Harrison and James B. Congdon. Afterward a collation was provided by the colored people for the company.

Before the officers of the Fifty-fourth parted, an invitation was extended to them for the succeeding Monday evening, to attend a reception at the residence of John Ritchie, Esq., their late quartermaster, at Chester Park.

The Boston "Evening Transcript" thus referred to the event of the day:—

"The Fifty-fourth Massachusetts Regiment, the pioneer State colored regiment of this country, recruited at a time when great prejudices existed against enlisting any but so-called white men in the army, when a colored soldiery was considered in the light of an experiment almost certain to fail, this command—which now returns crowned with laurels, and after two hundred thousand of their brethren, from one end of the traitorous South to the other, have fought themselves into public esteem—had such a reception to-day as befitted an organization the history of which is admitted to form so conspicuous a part of the annals of the country."

In the words of Von Moltke, "War is an element in the order of the world ordained by God. In it the noblest virtues of mankind are developed,—courage and the abnegation of self, faithfulness to duty and the spirit of sacrifice: the soldier gives his life." With the loyal volunteers who defended the Union of States these virtues were not only dominant, but were joined with the nobler one of patriotism, which nerved them to contend against national dissolution, brought on by Southern politicians to perpetuate their waning power, under the guise of a struggle for slavery and State rights.

It has been written that "the regiment is the family." To the soldier his true commander is a father; his superiors, elder brothers to be deferred to and obeyed; the recruits, his younger kinsmen whom he cares for and supports by example. He cherishes and proudly recounts the traditions of glorious deeds and dangerous enterprises.

The flag is the object of his sentimental devotion, which he has sworn to defend with his life. Every hole in the tattered silk or mark upon its staff tells of valorous strife in a just cause. Each legend inscribed upon its stripes is the brief story of regimental glory.

Such *esprit du corps* in its fullest perfection has served to carry men joyfully to death in the effort to win the imperishable renown secured by famous regiments. It earned for the Fifty-seventh Demi-Brigade before Mantua, in Napoleon's first Italian campaign, the name of "The Terrible;" for the Forty-second Royal Highlanders, whose black tartans shadowed many a battlefield, its undying reputation; and for the Zouaves of the Guard who led the assault upon the Malikoff, the plaudits of their countrymen. The gallant deeds of these foreign regiments were rivalled in our Civil War; but, unlike them, our organizations were of brief existence, and are of the past.

A recent writer upon our late war has said of the private soldier:—

> "He does not expect to see his own name on the titlepage of history, and is content with a proper recognition of the old command in which he fought; but he is jealous of the record of his regiment, and demands credit for every shot it faced and every grave it filled."

It is with a pride in the regiment which we trust others may deem pardonable, a painstaking endeavor to satisfy the natural expectations of the survivors who helped to acquire its honorable record and to preserve the traditions and recount the cheerful sacrifices of both the living and the dead, that this history has been written.

During a period of field-service covering twenty-six months almost every kind of military duty fell to the lot of the Fifty-fourth. Not only did it, in common with other infantry organizations, encounter the foe on advanced posts, in assault, and battle-line, but its services under fire as engineers and artillerymen were required during the siege operations in which it bore part.

Thrice was the regiment selected for desperate duty,— to lead the charge on Wagner, to advance the siege-works against the same stronghold when defeat confronted the troops, and to hold back the victorious enemy at Olustee until a new battle-line could be formed. Twice did it land upon hostile territory preceding all other regiments of the invading force, receiving the fire of the enemy or driving his light troops. The important task of guarding several hundred Confederate officers was also especially given to it.

But these services were not rendered without serious losses. How great they were was not even known to the author until after the history, except these closing lines, was in print, as the Roster which follows was not completed, and only from it could be gleaned the long list of those who died of wounds in hospital, home, and prison-pen. The mortality and casualty lists evidence the sacrifices made by the Fifty-fourth in the line of duty. With an aggregate enrolment of 1,354 officers and men, the regiment suffered a loss of 5 officers and 95 men known to have been killed or who died of their wounds. There were 106 men reported missing, 19 of whom are known to have died in prison, and 30 who lived to be released, leaving 57 missing in action. The casualty list is completed by the further loss of 20 officers and 274 men wounded, making a total loss of 500, which is 36.9 per cent of the enrolment. The death of 93 men out of an enrolment of 1,286, from disease and accident alone, gives a percentage of 7.2 against 15.9, which is said to be the rate for the total of colored troops enrolled. This evidences superior material or care on the part of the Fifty-fourth.

It has been shown how the regiment by its steadfast resolve, with the assistance of its friends, wrung justice and equal rights with white soldiers from the Government in the matter of pay and the muster of colored officers.

In connection with other colored organizations, the Fifty-fourth contributed to the establishment of a fact bearing strongly upon the military resources of our country then and now. We have read in the opening chapter that the United States only called the blacks to bear arms when disaster covered the land with discouragement and volunteering had ceased. It is also to be remembered that our enemy, having from the incipiency of the Rebellion employed this class as laborers for warlike purposes, at the last resolved upon enrolling them in their armies. This plan, however, was still-born, and was the final and wildest dream of Davis, Lee, and the crumbling Confederacy. But the courage and fidelity of the blacks, so unmistakably demonstrated during the Civil War, assures to us, in the event of future need, a class to recruit from now more available, intelligent, educated, and self-reliant, and more patriotic, devoted, and self-sacrificing, if such were possible, than thirty years ago.

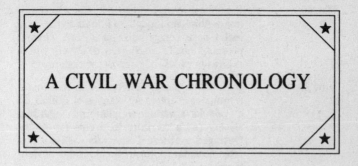

A CIVIL WAR CHRONOLOGY

1859

October 16 — John Brown, with sixteen whites and five blacks, captures the arsenal at Harpers Ferry in anticipation of fomenting a slave rebellion in Virginia. U.S. troops led by Lt. Col. Robert E. Lee storm the arsenal and capture Brown, on the morning of October 18th.

December 2 — John Brown is hanged for treason. Among his final words: "I, John Brown, am now quite certain that the crimes of this guilty land will never be purged away but with blood."

1860

May 3 — Democratic party, meeting in Charleston, South Carolina, adjourns unable to agree upon a candidate following the withdrawal of delegates from eight southern states.

May 9 — Constitutional Union party, meeting in Baltimore, nominates John Bell of Tennessee for president.

May 16 —	Republican party, meeting in Chicago, nominates Abraham Lincoln of Illinois on the third ballot as a compromise candidate. Lincoln promises not to interfere with slavery where it already exists, but opposes its extension.
June 23 —	Democratic party, reconvened in Baltimore, nominates Stephen A. Douglas of Illinois on a popular-sovereignty platform regarding slavery (each territory to decide for itself). Outraged southern Democrats walk out and later nominate John C. Breckinridge of Kentucky.
November 6 —	Lincoln wins the election. Though he has but 40 percent of the popular vote, his Electoral College count is 180, versus 72 for Breckinridge, 39 for Bell, and 12 for Douglas.
November 9 —	The state of South Carolina calls a secession convention.
December 20 —	South Carolina secedes from the Union.
December 26 —	Major Robert Anderson withdraws federal forces in Charleston to Fort Sumter. He has but eighty men.

1861

January 9—	South Carolina shore batteries open fire on the *Star of the West*, carrying supplies and reinforcements to Fort Sumter. The ship is forced out of Charleston Harbor. On the same day Mississippi secedes from the Union.
January 10 —	Florida secedes from the Union.
January 11 —	Alabama secedes from the Union.
January 19 —	Georgia secedes from the Union.
January 26 —	Louisiana secedes from the Union.

February 1 —   Texas secedes from the Union. Governor Sam Houston is removed from office for opposing secession.

February 4 —   A convention meets in Montgomery, Alabama to create a new government for the seceded states. It passes a constitution on the eighth and elects Jefferson Davis of Mississippi provisional president and Alexander Stephens of Georgia provisional vice-president on the ninth.

February 11 —   Lincoln departs from Springfield for Washington. "I now leave, not knowing when, or whether ever, I may return, with a task before me greater than that which rested upon Washington," he tells his friends and neighbors.

February 18 —   Davis is inaugurated at Montgomery, declaring that obstacles "can not long prevent the progress of a movement sanctified by its justice and sustained by a virtuous people."

February 23 —   Lincoln reaches Washington, entering the city secretly for fear of assassins.

March 4 —   Lincoln is inaugurated, declaring that "In your hands, my dissatisfied countrymen, and not in mine is the momentous issue of Civil War."

March 6 —   The Confederate States of America calls for 100,000 volunteers for its army.

April 4 —   Lincoln orders an expedition to relieve besieged Fort Sumter, and it departs from New York four days later.

April 12 —   At 4:30 A.M. General P. G. T. Beauregard orders his men to open fire on Fort Sumter. The commander of the fort had been his artillery instructor at West Point.

April 13 — Major Anderson surrenders after 34 hours of bombardment.

April 15 — Lincoln calls upon the states for 75,000 militia to suppress the insurrection in South Carolina.

April 17 — Virginia secedes from the Union.

April 19 — Lincoln orders a blockade of Confederate ports.

April 20 — Col. Robert E. Lee resigns from the U.S. Army. "Whatever may be the result of the contest," he writes a friend, "I foresee that the country will have to pass through a terrible ordeal, a necessary expiation for our national sins."

May 6 — Arkansas secedes from the Union.

May 6 — Tennessee secedes from the Union.

May 13 — Great Britain declares neutrality, in effect recognizing the Confederacy as a belligerent.

May 20 — North Carolina secedes from the Union.

May 21 — The Confederacy decides to move its capital to Richmond, Virginia.

May 23 — Virginia voters endorse secession.

June 3 — Union troops under Gen. George B. McClellan defeat Confederates at Philippi in western Virginia.

June 10 — France declares neutrality.

June 11 — Pro-Union counties in western Virginia disavow secession and are recognized by Lincoln as the loyal Virginia government. This soon evolves into the new state of West Virginia.

July 16 — Gen. Irvin McDowell, with 30,000 Union troops, advances toward Manassas Junction, Virginia.

July 21 — Battle of Bull Run ends in the defeat of Union forces, although the Rebels are too disorganized to follow up their victory. A strong stand by Thomas J. Jackson's Virginia brigade earns him the nickname "Stonewall." Each side suffers about 625 killed.

July 27 — McDowell is replaced by McClellan as commander of the troops around Washington.

August 6 — A Confiscation Act is passed which allows the seizure of all property used for insurrectionary purposes. This includes slaves.

August 10 — Confederates under Sterling Price and Ben McCulloch defeat a Union force under Gen. Nathaniel Lyon at Wilson's Creek, Missouri. Lyon is killed in action, and each side suffers about 1,300 casualties.

August 30 — Gen. John C. Fremont, in command of Union forces in the West, orders the confiscation of all property, including slaves, belonging to Missouri Confederates.

September 10 — Gen. Albert Sidney Johnston of Texas assumes command of Confederate forces in the West.

November 1 — McClellan replaces Gen. Winfield Scott as Union general in chief.

November 2 — Fremont is relieved of his command in the West, and is soon replaced by Gen. Henry W. Halleck.

November 8 — Capt. Charles Wilkes of the U.S. Navy stops the British mail steamer *Trent* and arrests Confederate envoys James Mason and John Slidell, setting off an international incident. They will be released on December 27 after British saber rattling.

1862

January 19 —   Union Gen. George Thomas, a Virginian loyal
                  to the Old Flag, defeats Rebel forces at Mill
                  Springs, Kentucky, securing federal control
                  of the eastern section of that state.

February 6 —   Gen. Ulysses S. Grant, with 15,000 troops and
                  several naval gunboats under Flag Officer An-
                  drew Foote, attacks Fort Henry on the Ten-
                  nessee River. The fort quickly falls to Foote's
                  naval forces, but most of its defenders escape
                  to Fort Donelson, a dozen miles away on the
                  Cumberland River.

February 7 —   Gen. Johnston orders his forces to retreat
                  from southwestern Kentucky.

February 13 —   Grant, with 40,000 troops, attacks Fort Do-
                  nelson, defended by 18,000 Confederates.

February 16 —   Gen. Simon Bolivar Buckner surrenders Fort
                  Donelson. Grant's terms, unconditional sur-
                  render, win him a nickname.

February 21 —   Confederate troops under Gen. Henry H. Sib-
                  ley defeat Union forces under Gen. Edward
                  Canby and Col. Kit Carson at Valverde, New
                  Mexico. Sibley is then able to occupy Albu-
                  querque and Santa Fe.

February 25 —   The Confederates are forced to abandon Nash-
                  ville.

March 3 —   Andrew Johnson is named military governor
                  of Tennessee by Lincoln.

March 8 —   Gen. Samuel Curtis defeats Gen. Earl Van
                  Dorn at Pea Ridge and Union control of Mis-
                  souri is secured.

March 8 —   The *Virginia*, a Rebel ironclad converted from
                  the captured Union warship the *Merrimac*,
                  destroys the Union wooden warships the *Con-
                  gress* and the *Cumberland* and drives the *Min-
                  nesota* aground at Hampton Roads, Virginia.

March 9 — ·   The *Monitor*, a Union iron-plated raft with a revolving gun turret built by John Ericsson, engages the *Virginia* (*Merrimac*) at Hampton Roads. They battle inconclusively all morning, but the *Virginia* withdraws and does not again threaten the Union blockade. A revolution in naval warfare has been wrought. The *Virginia* is burned to prevent its capture a month later. The *Monitor* sinks in a storm off Cape Hatteras on December 31, 1862.

March 11 —   Lincoln reorganizes the Union high command: Halleck takes charge of all troops west of the Appalachians while McClellan is reduced from general in chief to commander of the Army of the Potomac.

March 17 —   McClellan begins moving his forces by sea to Fort Monroe in anticipation of the Peninsular Campaign against Richmond.

March 23 —   Stonewall Jackson is defeated at Kernstown, Virginia, by a much stronger Union force. The battle raises fears in Washington of a Confederate attack, and troops are withheld from McClellan to defend the capital.

March 28 —   Union forces defeat the Confederate invaders at Glorieta Pass, New Mexico.

April 4 —   McClellan's forces on the peninsula advance toward Richmond.

April 6 —   Grant's 37,000 men at Shiloh Church and Pittsburg Landing, Tennessee, are surprised by A. S. Johnston's 42,000 Confederates and almost defeated. Johnston is killed and Beauregard assumes command.

April 7 —   Grant, reinforced by 25,000 fresh troops under Don Carlos Buell and Lew Wallace, attacks at Shiloh, recapturing all lost ground. Each side suffers 10,000 casualties. Beauregard retreats to Corinth, Mississippi.

April 8 — Gen. John Pope captures Island No. 10 in the Mississippi River, taking 5,000 Confederate prisoners.

April 12 — James J. Andrews leads fifteen men on a bold raid to seize a Western and Atlantic Railroad locomotive at Big Shanty, Georgia, and then race north in it burning all bridges on the line between Atlanta and Chattanooga. The raid fails after a wild eight-hour railway chase, and Andrews and seven of his men are eventually hanged.

April 16 — The Confederate Congress passes a conscription bill.

April 16 — Slavery is abolished in the District of Columbia.

April 25 — New Orleans is captured by Union naval forces under Flag Officer David C. Farragut.

May 1 — Union troops under Gen. Benjamin Butler begin the occupation of New Orleans.

May 3 — McClellan's army forces Gen. Joseph E. Johnston to retreat from Yorktown, Virginia.

May 8 — Stonewall Jackson's 10,000 men in the Shenandoah Valley defeat attacking Federals under Gen. Robert Schenk at McDowell, Virginia.

May 9 — Gen. David Hunter at Hilton Head, South Carolina, declares slaves in South Carolina, Georgia, and Florida to be free. His act is later repudiated by Lincoln.

May 9 — Confederate forces retreat from Norfolk.

May 10 — Union forces occupy Pensacola, Florida.

May 12 — Baton Rouge, Louisiana, is occupied by Union forces.

May 25 — Jackson crushes Gen. Nathaniel Banks's 8,000-man force at Winchester, Virginia.

June 1 — Robert E. Lee assumes command of Confederate forces defending Richmond after Joseph E. Johnston is wounded at the Battle of Fair Oaks.

June 8 — At the Battle of Cross Keys, Virginia, Union forces under Gen. John C. Frémont are defeated by Jackson's men.

June 9 — Jackson again defeats Union forces under Frémont and Gen. James Shields at Port Royal.

June 12 — Gen. James E. "Jeb" Stuart leads his Rebel cavalrymen on a bold four-day reconnaissance completely around McClellan's forces on the peninsula.

June 17 — Jackson's victorious army departs the Shenandoah to reinforce Lee.

June 19 — Slavery is abolished in all federal territories.

June 25 — The Seven Days' Battles begin as the forces of McClellan and Lee contend inconclusively.

July 1 — Lee's forces are defeated in their assault on the Army of the Potomac at Malvern Hill. He has lost 20,000 men. Nevertheless, the Seven Days' Battles conclude with the nervous McClellan retreating and Richmond secure.

July 4 — Confederate Col. John Hunt Morgan begins a daring raid into Kentucky.

July 11 — Halleck is named general in chief of Union forces.

July 17 — A second Confiscation Act is passed by Congress, freeing the slaves of those who are in rebellion against the government.

July 29 — The Rebel cruiser *Alabama* departs Liverpool, England, under the command of Captain Raphael Semmes. In the next two years it will capture or destroy sixty four merchant ships.

August 9 — Jackson defeats Union forces under Banks at Cedar Mountain, Virginia.

August 16 — McClellan moves north to unite with the Northern Army of Virginia under Gen. John Pope at Alexandria.

August 26 — Jackson captures the railroad line at Manassas Junction.

August 28 — Gen. Braxton Bragg leads his Rebel forces from Chattanooga to unite with Gen. Kirby Smith in Kentucky.

August 29 — The Second Battle of Bull Run begins as Pope attacks Jackson. The overly confident Pope sends a victory telegram to Washington.

August 30 — Confederate reinforcements under Gen. James Longstreet turn the tide at Second Bull Run and Pope's army is routed.

September 2 — McClellan is given command of Pope's army and the forces defending Washington.

September 5 — Lee leads 55,000 men into Maryland.

September 9 — Lee sends Jackson to capture the 12,000 Union troops at Harpers Ferry. Jackson is then to rejoin Lee for a movement against Harrisburg, Pennsylvania.

September 13 — Near Frederick, Maryland, two Union soldiers discover a copy of Lee's plans wrapped around three cigars lost by a Confederate officer.

September 14 — McClellan, who has 80,000 men and his opponent's plans, still waits eighteen hours before moving. This delay proves crucial in allowing Lee to regroup his army.

September 15 — Jackson captures Harpers Ferry.

September 16 — Jackson hurriedly rejoins Lee at Sharpsburg, Maryland. McClellan masses his forces a mile east across Antietam Creek.

September 17 — The Battle of Antietam becomes the single bloodiest day of the war as the two sides fight to a grisly standstill. 6,000 are killed and 17,000 are wounded.

September 18 — Lee escapes into Virginia.

September 22 — Lincoln decides to issue the Emancipation Proclamation freeing all slaves in states in rebellion as of January 1.

October 8 — Don Carlos Buell's Union forces defeat Gen. Bragg's Confederates at Perryville, Kentucky, repelling the Rebel invasion of Kentucky.

October 30 — Gen. William Rosecrans replaces Buell in command of the redesignated Army of the Cumberland.

November 2 — Grant moves against Vicksburg, Mississippi.

November 7 — McClellan is replaced as commander of the Army of the Potomac by Gen. Ambrose Burnside.

December 13 — Burnside is defeated by Lee at Fredericksburg, Virginia.

December 15 — The Army of the Potomac retreats.

December 31 — Bragg attacks Rosecrans at Stones River near Murfreesboro, Tennessee.

1863

January 1 — Lincoln signs the Emancipation Proclamation.

January 2 — Rosecrans wins the second day of heavy fighting at Stones River. Bragg retreats on January 3.

January 26 — Gen. Joseph Hooker replaces Burnside as commander of the Army of the Potomac.

March 3 — The U.S. Congress passes a conscription act that provides for a draft of all men between twenty and forty-five.

March 9 — Confederate partisan ranger John S. Mosby makes a daring raid behind Union lines and captures Brig. Gen. Edwin H. Stoughton. Lincoln, upon being informed that Mosby has taken Stoughton, thirty-two soldiers, and fifty-eight horses, responds: "Well, I'm sorry for that. I can make new brigadier generals, but I can't make horses."

April 16 — Admiral David Porter's Union gunboats make a daring run past the shore batteries at Vicksburg.

April 17 — Col. Benjamin Grierson leads 1,700 cavalrymen out of La Grange, Tennessee, and heads south. His goal is to disrupt Confederate communications and divert attention from Vicksburg.

April 30 — The Army of the Potomac, 115,000 strong, begins to concentrate at Chancellorsville. Lee faces them with but 60,000 men.

May 1 — Gen. Hooker's 70,000 infantry inconclusively engage Gen. Lee's forces at Chancellorsville. Hooker inexplicably pulls back after fighting in a forest called the Wilderness. That night Lee and Jackson plan a daring flanking attack on Hooker.

May 2 — Lee faces Hooker with but 15,000 men while Jackson leads 30,000 infantry on a flank march across the Union front. Jackson attacks at 5:15 p.m. and rolls up the Union right, but is mistakenly wounded by his own pickets that night while scouting.

May 2 — Grierson's cavalry reach Union lines at Baton Rouge after a daring 600-mile raid.

May 3 —   Gen. Stuart assumes command of Jackson's corps at Chancellorsville and continues to pound the faltering Federals.

May 4 —   Gen. John Sedgwick has no success against Lee's rear and retires to Fredericksburg.

May 6 —   Hooker retreats, and Lee achieves his greatest victory. Confederate forces suffer 13,000 casualties while Union losses are over 17,000.

May 10 —   Stonewall Jackson dies at Guiney's Station. "Let us cross over the river and rest under the shade of the trees," are his last words.

May 16 —   Grant, advancing on Vicksburg, defeats Gen. John C. Pemberton's forces at Champion's Hill.

May 18 —   Pemberton pulls his forces into the Vicksburg defenses.

May 19 —   Governor John Andrew of Massachusetts presents four flags to Col. Robert Gould Shaw and the 54th Massachusetts Regiment, the first black regiment raised in the Northeast. The regiment is ordered to join Gen. David Hunter at Hilton Head, South Carolina. Already with Hunter is Col. Thomas Wentworth Higginson's First Regiment of South Carolina Volunteers, made up of contrabands (liberated slaves).

May 19 —   Grant's forces assault Vicksburg but fail to breach the defenses.

May 22 —   Grant's second assault on Vicksburg is repulsed with heavy losses. He begins a siege.

May 27 —   Gen. Banks fails in his assaults on Port Hudson, Louisiana, and lays siege.

June 3 —   Lee departs Fredericksburg for a second invasion of the North. He has three infantry corps and six cavalry brigades—75,000 men.

June 9 — Gen. Alfred Pleasonton's 11,000 Union cavalry surprise Stuart's 10,000 horsemen at Brandy Station, and the greatest cavalry engagement of the war follows. Stuart holds his ground but Lee's advance is revealed.

June 15 — Gen. Richard S. Ewell captures Winchester in the Shenandoah.

June 20 — West Virginia is admitted to the Union.

June 25 — Stuart leads three cavalry brigades on a ride around Hooker's army. The raid causes great alarm in Washington, but Stuart's separation from the Army of Northern Virginia will prove costly.

June 28 — Gen. Jubal Early captures York, Pennsylvania.

June 28 — Gen. George Gordon Meade assumes command of the Army of the Potomac, replacing Hooker.

June 29 — Lee orders his forces to reunite near Gettysburg, Pennsylvania.

July 1 — Gen. A. P. Hill's infantry, in search of shoes in Gettysburg, clash with two brigades of Union cavalry under Gen. John Buford. Soldiers from both armies rush to the sound of the guns, and the Rebels soon sweep the Yankees in disorder through the town. Union forces dig in on Cemetery Ridge while the Confederates take up positions on Seminary Ridge.

July 2 — Lee sends Gen. James Longstreet against the Union left while Gen. Richard Ewell assaults the Union right. Both assaults fail. Stuart finally rejoins the army.

July 3 — After a terrific artillery barrage, Lee sends 14,000 men against the Union center in Pickett's Charge. Scarcely half return.

July 4 —   Gen. Pemberton surrenders his 30,000 men, and Vicksburg, to Grant.

July 8 —   Gen. John Hunt Morgan leads 2,500 men across the Ohio River into Indiana and toward Ohio.

July 9 —   Port Hudson surrenders to Gen. Banks. The Mississippi is again a Union river and the Confederacy is split.

July 13 —   Four days of antidraft rioting begins in New York City. Much of the violence is directed at blacks before troops suppress a mob estimated at 50,000.

July 18 —   Battery Wagner, defending the entrance to Charleston harbor, is assaulted by Union troops. Spearheading the attack are 600 men of the 54th Massachusetts. The position is impregnable, although the black soldiers of the 54th gain Wagner's parapets and hold them for an hour before falling back. Col. Robert Shaw is killed and the regiment suffers casualties of over 40 percent.

July 19 —   Over 800 of Morgan's raiders are killed or captured at Buffington, Ohio.

July 26 —   Gen. Morgan is captured at New Lisbon, Ohio.

August 21 — Col. William Clarke Quantrill's Confederate guerrillas sack Lawrence, Kansas.

September 9 — Gen. Rosecrans's Federal troops enter Chattanooga as Gen. Bragg's forces retire into northern Georgia.

September 19 — Gen. Bragg, reinforced by Longstreet's corps, attacks Gen. George Thomas's corps on the left of Rosecrans's army at Chickamauga Creek, Georgia.

September 20 — Longstreet routs the Union right, and the army is only saved by Thomas's bold stand; Thomas earns the nickname of "Rock of Chickamauga." Rosecrans's army retreats to Chattanooga, where it is besieged. Bragg occupies high ground at Lookout Mountain, south of the city, and along Missionary Ridge to the east. In the fighting each side has suffered 28-percent casualties.

October 15 — The Confederate submarine *Hunley* sinks during a practice run in Charleston harbor, drowning its inventor and seven crewmen.

October 17 — Grant is named commander of all Union forces west of the Appalachians.

October 19 — Thomas replaces Rosecrans as commander of the 35,000-man Army of the Cumberland in Chattanooga.

October 23 — Grant arrives in Chattanooga.

November 4 — Bragg sends Longstreet and 15,000 men to attack Knoxville, thus weakening his forces at Chattanooga.

November 19 — Lincoln, at Gettysburg, gives an immortal speech.

November 20 — Gen. William T. Sherman reaches Chattanooga with 17,000 men from the Army of the Tennessee. Hooker has already arrived on September 24 with 20,000 reinforcements from the Army of the Potomac. Bragg faces them with just over 64,000 troops.

November 24 — Hooker's men take Lookout Mountain at Chattanooga.

November 25 — Sherman's attacks on Bragg's right fail, but Thomas's Army of the Cumberland makes an incredible charge up Missionary Ridge and defeats the Confederates. Bragg, barely escaping capture, retreats into Georgia.

November 27 —   Gen. Morgan escapes from the Ohio State
                 Penitentiary.

November 29 —   Longstreet's attack on Knoxville fails, and he
                 soon retreats toward Virginia.

December 16 —   Gen. Joseph E. Johnston takes command of
                 the Army of Tennessee. Bragg is named an
                 adviser to President Davis.

1864

February 9 —   Col. Thomas Rose leads 109 Union prisoners
                 in a daring escape from Libby Prison in Rich-
                 mond. Rose and forty-seven others are recap-
                 tured.

February 14 —   Gen. Sherman occupies Meridian, Mississippi,
                 and his troops begin to dismantle the city.

February 17 —   The Confederate submarine *Huntley* sinks the
                 Housatonic in Charleston harbor, but goes
                 down with the Union sloop.

February 22 —   Gen. Nathan Bedford Forrest's cavalry defeat
                 Union cavalry under Gen. William Sooy Smith
                 at Okolona, Mississippi.

March 3 —   Gen. Judson Kilpatrick's cavalry raid on Rich-
                 mond ends in disaster with Col. Ulrich Dahl-
                 gren killed. Papers are found on Dahlgren's
                 body insinuating that his mission was to kill
                 Jefferson Davis.

March 17 —   Grant is named general in chief and promoted
                 to lieutenant general.

March 18 —   Sherman is named commander of Union
                 forces in the West.

April 8 —   Gen. Richard Taylor's Confederates stop Gen.
                 Banks's advance on Shreveport at Sabine
                 Crossroads to end the Union's Red River cam-
                 paign.

April 12 — Gen. Forrest captures Fort Pillow, Tennessee, where surrendering black soldiers are murdered by his troops.

April 17 — Grant halts the practice of exchanging prisoners.

May 4 — Grant advances across the Rapidan with 122,000 men. Lee faces him with under 70,000. Grant also orders troops under Gen. Benjamin Butler to move up the James River against Richmond. In Chattanooga, Sherman prepares to move south against Atlanta.

May 6 — Longstreet reinforces Lee, and Grant is defeated in the Wilderness. Longstreet is seriously wounded.

May 9 — Lee's forces entrench at Spotsylvania and repel Union assaults. Union Gen. John Sedgwick is killed.

May 9 — Grant sends Gen. Phil Sheridan's 10,000 cavalrymen on a raid against Richmond.

May 11 — Sheridan's cavalry defeat Stuart's horsemen at Yellow Tavern. Stuart, mortally wounded, dies the next day.

May 12 — Bitter fighting at the "Bloody Angle" at Spotsylvania does not break Lee's lines.

May 15 — In the Shenandoah, Gen. John Breckinridge's 5,000-man force, including V.M.I. cadets, defeats Gen. Franz Sigel's 6,500-man Union force at New Market.

May 16 — Gen. Butler is defeated at Drewry's Bluff, eight miles south of Richmond, by Gen. Beauregard.

May 20 — Grant abandons his Spotsylvania positions in an attempt to flank Lee.

May 24 — Lee takes up new positions on the North Anna River.

May 24 — Sheridan's victorious cavalrymen rejoin Grant.

May 25 — The Battle of New Hope Church, Georgia, begins between the forces of Sherman and Johnston.

May 31 — Sheridan's cavalry battles Rebel horsemen under Gen. Fitzhugh Lee and seizes the junction at Cold Harbor.

June 1 — Union forces, 109,000 strong, and Confederate forces, numbering 59,000, entrench for seven miles around Cold Harbor. In four weeks of constant fighting, the Federals have suffered 44,000 casualties and the Confederates 25,000.

June 3 — Grant launches futile frontal assaults against Lee's lines at Cold Harbor at a cost of 7,000 more casualties.

June 8 — Abraham Lincoln and Andrew Johnson are nominated for president and vice-president by the Republican (National Union) Convention in Baltimore.

June 12 — Wade Hampton's Rebel cavalry blocks Sheridan's cavalry at Trevilian Station from raiding westward to unite with Gen. David Hunter's forces in the Shenandoah. Both sides suffer 20-percent casualties in the bloodiest cavalry battle of the war.

June 14 — Grant begins to move his army across the James River to attack Petersburg.

June 18 — Grant's assaults on Petersburg fail and he begins a siege.

June 18 — Gen. Jubal Early defeats Gen. Hunter at Lynchburg. Hunter retreats into West Virginia, leaving the Shenandoah to Early.

June 19 — The *Kearsage* sinks the Rebel cruiser *Alabama* in a duel off Cherbourg, France.

June 27 — Johnston repulses Sherman's attacks at Kennesaw Mountain, Georgia.

July 6 — Early invades Maryland.

July 11 — Having swept aside Federal defenders at Monocacy River, Early reaches the defenses of Washington. The Sixth Corps, detached from Grant's forces, arrives on the same day.

July 12 — Early pulls back from Washington, heading for the Shenandoah.

July 17 — Gen. John Bell Hood replaces Johnston as commander of the Army of Tennessee.

July 20 — Hood attacks Thomas's forces at Peachtree Creek, Georgia, and is defeated.

July 22 — Hood attacks Gen. James B. McPherson's Army of the Tennessee and is again defeated. McPherson is killed in action.

July 28 — Hood again attacks the Army of the Tennessee, now commanded by Gen. Oliver Otis Howard, at Ezra Church and is again defeated.

July 30 — A 511-foot tunnel has been dug beneath the Rebel lines at Petersburg and four tons of gunpowder placed at the end. The explosion creates a 170-foot-long, 30-foot-deep crater, but the Federal assault that follows is disorganized and halfhearted. 4,000 casualties and a big hole in the ground is all Grant has by nightfall.

July 31 — Gen. George Stoneman, raiding south from Sherman's army to liberate the prisoners at Andersonville, is captured along with 500 of his men.

August 1 — Sheridan is given command of Union forces in the Shenandoah.

August 5 — Admiral Farragut defeats the defending Confederate ships in Mobile Bay. "Damn the torpedoes, full speed ahead," Farragut reportedly exclaims during the action.

August 22 — Gen. Judson Kilpatrick's cavalry raid against Hood's Atlanta supply lines fails.

August 23 — Fort Morgan, in Mobile Bay, falls to Union forces.

August 29 — George B. McClellan is nominated for president by the Democrats.

August 31 — Howard defeats Hood at Jonesboro while Gen. John Schofield's forces cut the last railroad line into Atlanta.

September 1 — Hood evacuates Atlanta.

September 2 — Sherman enters Atlanta.

September 4 — John Hunt Morgan is killed at Greeneville, Tennessee.

September 17 — John C. Frémont, nominated for president by Radical Republicans unhappy with Lincoln, announces that he will withdraw from the race for fear of splitting the Republican vote.

September 19 — Sheridan defeats Early at Winchester.

September 22 — Sheridan crushes Early's army at Fisher's Hill.

September 27 — Confederate guerrillas under Bloody Bill Anderson loot Centralia, Missouri, and murder twenty-two captured Union soldiers. They then slaughter over 100 pursuing Federals under Maj. A. V. E. Johnston. Young Jesse James kills Maj. Johnston.

September 28 — Sherman orders Gen. Thomas to Nashville to defend that city from Hood's army.

September 29 — In the fighting around Petersburg, Grant takes Fort Harrison but is repulsed from Fort Gilmore.

October 2 — A Federal raid into southwest Virginia is defeated near Saltville, and over 100 Union prisoners, mostly black soldiers, are murdered by their captors.

October 6 — Sheridan begins the systematic destruction of the Shenandoah Valley.

October 13 — Confederate partisans under Mosby capture a train near Kearneyville and escape with nearly $2 million from Union paymasters on board.

October 16 — Sheridan leaves his army for a meeting with Stanton and Halleck on the Valley Campaign.

October 19 — Lt. Bennett Young leads Rebel raiders across the Canadian border to St. Albans, Vermont. They rob three banks and escape back over the border.

October 19 — Sheridan's army is taken by surprise when Early's army strikes at dawn. The left flank of the Union army, under Gen. George Crook, is routed, but the sudden arrival of Sheridan on the field (he gallops in from Winchester) rallies the men. The Union counterattack destroys the Confederate army. The Battle of Cedar Creek ends the Rebel threat in the Shenandoah. The North is captivated by "Sheridan's Ride," soon immortalized in a popular poem.

October 23 — Gen. Curtis defeats Gen. Sterling Price at the Battle of Westport, ending the Confederate threat to Missouri.

October 26 —   Bloody Bill Anderson is killed in a Union ambush near Richmond, Missouri.

October 27 —   Lt. William P. Cushing destroys the Confederate ram *Albemarle* in the Roanoke River, North Carolina.

October 30 —   Sherman sends Schofield to reinforce Thomas at Nashville.

November 8 —   Lincoln is reelected.

November 16 —   Sherman's army, 62,000 strong, departs Atlanta to begin the March to the Sea to Savannah. Atlanta burns behind the Federals as they advance.

November 25 —   Confederate raiders fail in their attempt to burn New York City.

November 30 —   Schofield repulses Hood's assaults at Franklin and retreats under cover of darkness toward Nashville.

December 1 —   Schofield unites with Thomas at Nashville.

December 13 —   Fort McAllister, guarding Savannah, is captured by Sherman's troops.

December 15 —   Thomas attacks Hood before Nashville.

December 16 —   Hood's army is routed at Nashville.

December 21 —   Sherman's army enters Savannah.

1865

January 7 —   Gen. Benjamin Butler is relieved as commander of the Army of the James.

January 15 —   Gen. Alfred H. Terry captures Fort Fisher, closing the last major Confederate port at Wilmington, North Carolina.

January 23 —   Gen. Richard Taylor is given command of what is left of the Army of Tennessee.

January 31 — The Thirteenth Amendment to the Constitution, abolishing slavery, is passed by the House of Representatives and sent to the states for ratification.

February 6 — Lee is named commander of all Confederate forces.

February 17 — Sherman occupies the South Carolina capital, and that night the city burns. Sherman blames fleeing Rebels, but on the eighteenth his troops begin the destruction of what is left of Columbia.

February 17 — The Confederates abandon Charleston, and Fort Sumter again comes under Union control.

February 18 — Lee speaks out in favor of arming blacks for service in the Confederate army in exchange for their freedom.

February 22 — Schofield's Union troops occupy Wilmington.

March 2 — Sheridan's cavalry, under Gen. George A. Custer, destroys the last remnant of Early's army at the Battle of Waynesboro.

March 4 — Lincoln's second inaugural address calls for reconciliation: "With malice toward none; with charity for all; with firmness in the right as God gives us to see the right, let us strive on to finish the work we are in; to bind up the nation's wounds; to care for him who shall have borne the battle and for his widow, and his orphan—to do all which may achieve and cherish a just and lasting peace among ourselves, and with all nations."

March 13 — President Davis signs a bill, narrowly passed by the Confederate Congress after heated debate, that calls for the use of black slaves as soldiers. The question of emancipation in exchange for service is left to the individual states.

March 17 — Gen. Edward Canby opens the assault on Mobile, Alabama.

March 22 — Gen. James Wilson begins a cavalry raid through Alabama to capture Selma.

March 26 — Sheridan rejoins Grant before Petersburg.

April 1 — Sheridan defeats Gen. George Pickett at Five Forks, capturing that vital crossroads and large numbers of Rebel prisoners.

April 2 — Grant assaults Lee's weakened lines at Petersburg with great success. Gen A. P. Hill is killed in action. Lee retreats toward Amelia Courthouse.

April 3 — Petersburg is occupied. Richmond surrenders. Jefferson Davis and his cabinet flee to Danville, Virginia.

April 4 — President Lincoln tours Richmond.

April 5 — Sheridan blocks Lee's route southward, forcing the Confederates westward.

April 6 — 6,000 Confederates are captured at Sayler's Creek, including Gen. Richard Ewell, as Lee's retreat continues.

April 8 — Custer blocks Lee's retreat route at Appomattox Station.

April 9 — Lee surrenders the Army of Northern Virginia to Grant in the home of Wilmer McLean at Appomattox Courthouse.

April 12 — Wilson captures Montgomery, Alabama. Federal troops occupy Mobile.

April 12 — Grant accords to Gen. Joshua Chamberlain of Maine the honor of accepting the formal surrender of the flags and arms of the Army of Northern Virginia.

April 14 —   John Wilkes Booth mortally wounds President
                  Lincoln at Ford's Theater in Washington.

April 15 —   President Lincoln dies and Andrew Johnson
                  becomes president.

April 21 —   Mosby disbands his rangers.

April 26 —   Gen. Johnston surrenders his nearly 30,000
                  men to Gen. Sherman.

April 26 —   Booth is trapped by troops and killed.

May 4 —   Gen. Taylor surrenders to Gen. Canby in Al-
                  abama.

May 10 —   Confederate guerrilla chief William Quantrill
                  is mortally wounded near Taylorsville, Ken-
                  tucky.

May 10 —   Union cavalrymen capture Jefferson Davis and
                  his party in Georgia.

May 22 —   Davis is imprisoned at Fort Monroe, Virginia.
                  He will be released in May 1867.

May 23 —   Nearly 200,000 Union soldiers begin a two-
                  day grand review up Pennsylvania Avenue in
                  Washington, D.C.—once more the capital of
                  a united nation.